# Starting Right

# Starting Right

*How America Neglects Its
Youngest Children and What
We Can Do About It*

Sheila B. Kamerman

Alfred J. Kahn

*New York      Oxford*
OXFORD UNIVERSITY PRESS
1995

## Oxford University Press

Oxford   New York
Athens   Auckland   Bangkok   Bombay
Calcutta   Cape Town   Dar es Salaam   Delhi
Florence   Hong Kong   Istanbul   Karachi
Kuala Lumpur   Madras   Madrid   Melbourne
Mexico City   Nairobi   Paris   Singapore
Taipei   Tokyo   Toronto

and associated companies in
Berlin   Ibadan

## Copyright © 1995 by Oxford University Press, Inc.

Published by Oxford University Press, Inc.
198 Madison Avenue, New York, New York 10016

Oxford is a registered trademark of Oxford University Press

Library of Congress Cataloging-in-Publication Data
Kamerman, Sheila B.
Starting right : how America neglects its youngest children
and what we can do about it /
Sheila B. Kamerman, Alfred J. Kahn
p. cm.   Includes bibliographical references and index.
ISBN 0–19–509675–4
1. Child care—Government policy—United States.
2. Child care services—Government policy—United States.
3. Head Start programs—United States.
4. Child welfare—United States.
I. Kahn, Alfred J.   II. Title.
HQ778.63.K36   1995   362.7'12'0973—dc20
94–36552

1 3 5 7 9 8 6 4 2

Printed in the United States of America
on acid-free paper

# Preface

This book was in a late stage of production when the campaign for a social policy counter-revolution, symbolized by the Republican "Contract with America," took over the agenda of the U.S. Congress. Some of our assumptions about the givens and the issues, particularly those regarding welfare programs, federal–state relationships, and governmental treatment of our most disadvantaged and troubled citizens, have been seriously challenged. As we go to press, the full results of the campaign are not known, especially for Aid to Families with Dependent Children ("welfare") and for certain other "entitlements" (programs with assured funding for all those eligible).

None of this invalidates an effort to develop useful, realistic options for infant and toddler policies and programs, informed by European experience. Needs and knowledge are not invalidated by a shift in the political winds. But it does warn all concerned that it will now be far more difficult to get Congress to agree that the initiatives and expenditures proposed in our final chapter and considered as perhaps imminent remain no less sensible or urgent now than they were before November 1994. They may, however, take a little longer and require somewhat more effort.

We offer what follows with full conviction that informed American parents and the public at large want our youngest children to have the opportunity to get started well—for their own society's benefit. Furthermore, most of the time we are or want to be a humane society.

*New York*                                                     S. B. K., A. J. K.
*February 1995*

# Acknowledgments

We acknowledge the support of the Carnegie Corporation and the Spencer Foundation and our program officers, Michael Levine and Linda Fitzgerald, respectively. Their enthusiasm and commitment were an ongoing source of encouragement.

We also are in the debt of scholars and government officials in Denmark, Finland, France, Germany, Italy, and the United Kingdom, as well as officials in several international organizations, in particular, the European Community and Eurostat, the Organization for Economic Cooperation and Development, and the directors and staff of the Luxembourg Income Study. All in one way or another shared in this exploration and contributed to our ongoing education concerning child and family policies in other countries. Without their help, this study could not have been carried out, and this book would not have been written.

We acknowledge, too, the excellent suggestions from an anonymous reviewer; we think the story we have to tell is stronger as a result. We are grateful to Sydney Van Nort who handled the manuscript, at various stages, with expertise and good spirits.

With this our fifteenth jointly written policy study (there are also five coedited works), we acknowledge the good fortune of a research collaboration whose agenda remains vital. We continue to be fascinated by the social policy issues facing advanced industrialized countries and concerned with the consequences of policy choices for the well-being of children and their families. We remain convinced that research, writing, and debate are essential to wise politics, and that countries can learn from each other.

# Contents

# List of Tables

# Starting Right

# 1

## Starting Right: The First Three Years

America's children are in trouble, and Americans know it. There are disturbingly high rates of infant mortality as well as low birth weight, physical and functional developmental defects, childhood illnesses, accidental deaths, poor learning, school dropouts, delinquency, functional illiteracy, early alcohol and drug addiction, and children having children. And the proportion of children living in poor families is higher than it has been at any time in the last decade—almost as high as it was before the War on Poverty.

This means many suffering children, many unhappy and worried parents, and many unnecessary and expensive public burdens, as well as a terrible waste of human resources. It makes for neither an attractive civil society nor a productive and competitive work force. Looking at the situation of children elsewhere, we observe that some countries have found it important and possible to do better by children. The question is obvious: Can't we? Are there alternatives to the status quo? Can they win public support and lead to better outcomes for children? How should we begin?

While U.S. policy has largely ignored families with children of this age, some European countries have highlighted the youngest age group as a primary target for social policy attention. Over the last decade many western European countries have explored and experimented with alternative policy options supportive of families with children under age 3, focusing especially on economic resources, parental time, and child care; excellent health care has been available for a long time.

At the very least, the needs of very young children and their families deserve greater visibility on the national policy agenda, and the terms of the United States child and family policy discussion need to be broadened. This is our objective in this book. With new policy options visible and understood, it could become possible to mobilize more widespread support for policies benefiting the under-threes.

We begin this chapter by explaining why we focus on the youngest Americans, the under-threes. We discuss the importance of the early years and the serious consequences of inadequate attention to how children develop during this period. We then describe the current situation of very young children and their families and identify some problems that merit public concern. We highlight the limited progress the United States has made toward solving these problems. We point out the relative "invisibility" of critical issues in current child and family policy discussion and the major policy gaps requiring attention. Finally, we identify some important obstacles to improving policies toward young children and their families. We conclude the chapter with a challenge: Can the United States move ahead on a young-child policy agenda?

## Why Focus on the Under-Threes?

### *Starting Right Can Make a Difference*

No one stage of life is more important for shaping an individual's future development and life course than are the first three years. Although all stages of life have significant implications for development and none should be ignored, no other period is as important as these first years in setting the stage for an individual's ability to thrive physically, to learn, to love, to trust others, to develop the capacity for productive work, and to develop confidence and approach life in a positive way.[1] The importance of this life stage is that it does not differentiate between the rich and the poor. The latter face potentially costly deprivation and hazards, but the more prosperous are hardly immune.

David Hamburg,[2] nationally known physician and head of the Carnegie Corporation, a major U.S. foundation concerned with the well-being of children and their families, states:

> Early childhood is clearly one of the most crucial periods of development. It is characterized by rapid growth, specific environmental needs, maximal dependence on caretakers, great vulnerability, and long-term consequences of failures in development. It is a dramatic period, with great changes and striking contrasts. First, the nine months of pregnancy—from a single cell to a very complex organism. Next, the critical transition from living inside the mother's body to living in the world outside. Then

the period of forming the initial human attachments that shape so power-fully the possibilities for human relationship and social skills—and the infant's beginnings of discovery, the building blocks of learning skills. So this initial phase has a strong bearing on a child's entire life. Especially in poor communities, the risks of permanent—and largely preventable—damage are formidable.

Children under age 3 are more vulnerable to physical damage and social and emotional deprivation than they are at any other time in childhood; hence the importance of early nurturing, nutrition, protection, stimula-tion, immunization, and more—all while assured of a safe physical home environment.

Not every childhood problem can be prevented, but many certainly can. Child development and social science research confirm how some prob-lems can be exacerbated or alleviated, depending on what occurs during the first three years.

First and most important is what happens during pregnancy. Children develop a significant portion of their cognitive skills during the first years. Research indicates that an individual's capacity for learning is closely linked to brain development; and recent child development research indicates that the fetal period and the first year or year and a half of life is the time of the greatest growth of the brain itself. The brain's rapid growth during early life makes it highly sensitive to what occurs during the prenatal and postna-tal periods. Thus it is dramatically affected by what the mother does, eats, drinks, ingests in other ways during pregnancy, how she feeds, physically cares for, and relates to her baby during the first two years, and what else occurs in the baby's immediate environment. Prenatal substance abuse by the mother—use of alcohol and drugs, as well as smoking—can have last-ing and significant effects on a child's capacity to learn, as can any other condition (infection, nutritional deficiency, physical danger, absence of or inadequate medical care) that impinges on her health before or during birth.

Second, and equally important, is the family unit. Parents are the most critical element in the child's environment in the early years. Very young children are totally dependent on their parents and other caregivers. What happens in parents' lives has immediate consequences for the care they provide and how they respond to and meet the needs of their babies. Parents who are stressed or disturbed will have more difficulty in meeting their children's needs. Parents who have little support—from friends, rela-tives, neighbors, or the community—are more likely to be overburdened by the demands of their babies and to be unable to respond to them adequately. Parents who experience severe poverty or economic insecurity, who cannot satisfy their own basic needs, are likely to have difficulty in responding to their children's needs.

Third is adequate nutrition after birth, especially critical to how a child develops. Malnutrition can delay physical development (crawling, walking) and brain growth, which in turn may further delay development by restricting the baby's opportunities to explore the world and interact with the people in it.

Fourth is caregiving, whether by parents or others. Adequate and appropriate care and nurturing are critical in the early years and have consequences for the physical, social, and psychological development of the child. Picking up and holding a crying baby, comforting and soothing him, talking to the baby, playing, touching, and cuddling are all part of what a responsive parent and caregiver can provide that supports and enhances a child's development. Children differ in personality, in sensitivity to stimuli, and in responsiveness to caregivers. Understanding what the baby needs and how to respond appropriately is critical for parents or caregivers if they are to support the child's development; yet this may be very difficult for those who are stressed and overburdened—or too immature themselves to consider how to respond and to perform adequately.

Fifth is adequate and appropriate health care. For example, timely vaccinations are critical in preventing severe and possibly fatal infectious diseases. Preschool-aged children are particularly susceptible to life-threatening diseases such as whooping cough, diphtheria, polio, tetanus, measles, which these vaccinations prevent. The American Academy of Pediatrics recommends a series of vaccinations at about two, four, six, and fifteen months, with some booster shots later. An early start is critical, according to the U.S. Public Health Service, if the growing rates of serious infectious diseases among young children are to be reversed. Although President Clinton's efforts to ensure access to vaccine are important, improved access to appropriate medical care is equally so.

Sixth, experts stress that adequate, appropriate stimulation is as important for a child's development as is sufficient and appropriate food; indeed, adequate and appropriate stimulation is a form of social and psychological nourishment and as such it continues to be significant throughout the early and later childhood years. The responsibility begins with parents, extends to family and relative caretakers, and then to the formal systems that may have the child in charge.

Language skills are highly correlated with a child's social and cognitive development. The responsiveness of adult caregivers to infants' own language sounds—caregiver-infant verbal interaction—has great significance for later language and social development. Not talking to babies or talking infrequently may lead to retarded cognitive and related language development, and retarded learning ability generally. Mothers who are depressed, overburdened, stressed, or do not understand this, may be unable to interact responsively and effectively with their babies. In contrast, adequate stimulation in infancy provides the foundation for later language development. Building on such stimulation, the ability to use language increases dramatically during the toddler years, allowing the child to provide as well as receive new information, and to begin to ready herself for later more formal learning in school.

School failure has been a major concern in the United States for more than a decade. University of Michigan child development researcher Harold Stevenson, at the forefront of cross-national research on school achievements of children in the United States and other industrialized countries, has raised some critical questions regarding why U.S. children perform very poorly on standardized tests, in comparison to children in other countries. In a study of first- and fifth-grade children in five cities in the United States, Japan, China, and Taiwan, Stevenson found that only 2.2 percent of Beijing's first-grade students scored as low as the Chicago average in math.

The Carnegie Task Force on Meeting the Needs of Young Children recently reported that "only half (50 percent) of infants and toddlers are routinely read to by their parents and many parents do not engage in other activities to stimulate their young child's intellectual development. It is not surprising, then, that teachers report that 35 percent of American kindergarten children arrive at school unprepared to learn."[3]

School readiness is the first goal listed in the National Governor's Association's six goals designed to improve the U.S. educational system. President Bush incorporated these goals as "America 2000: An Education Strategy" in 1991, and President Clinton reaffirmed them when he signed into law the "Goals 2000: Educate America Act." The Committee on Economic Development emphasized even more strongly the importance of the development and education of all our children from the earliest stages of their lives. There clearly appears to be consensus: children must be better perpared for school.

Such school readiness—readiness to learn and to succeed in learning—encompasses physical, social, and emotional elements, not just cognitive aspects. It develops out of care, nurturing, and stimulation from the prenatal period through the early years. If a child receives the needed nurturing, care, and stimulation during the first three years, she is off to a good start. She may face all sorts of obstacles subsequently, but with the right start she will face those challenges equipped to learn, love, strive, trust, and succeed. Continuing and ongoing parental support and involvement are essential if the child's learning is to build on this foundation.

Although U.S. child development and medical research are unmatched and underscore the importance of the early years, we often—as a country— do not follow through on our scientific knowledge. The extra burdens faced by poor families and poor children are perhaps most visible, but the needs enumerated are universal and the gaps often affect services and supports relevant to most families. Yet we are struck by the fact that even when issues affecting the under-threes reach the national agenda, the options posed are clearly too constricted. In contrast, some European countries have been confronting infant/toddler policy issues for the past decade or more. In the later chapters we will be exploring what some other countries are doing and asking whether any of their policy and program initiatives might be suggestive for the United States. First, we turn to some specific problems experienced by the very young.

## Small Children, Big Problems

Examine the facts of life for America's approximately twelve million children under age 3, and the need for attention to their unmet needs, their less-than-optimal circumstances, and for some, their "plight," becomes apparent.

The living situation of very young children has changed dramatically over the last two decades. More than half (54 percent) the mothers of under-threes, including the mothers of infants, were in the labor force in 1993, up from 27 percent in 1970 and 42 percent in 1980. Under-threes in two-parent families are more likely to have working mothers (57 percent) than are those living in mother-only families (44 percent).

Almost one in three babies (30 percent) is born outside of marriage. About the same proportion of the under-threes live in single-parent families, overwhelmingly with their mothers, up from about 12 percent in 1970 and 20 percent in 1980. Almost one in five of the under-threes was receiving AFDC ("welfare") in 1991, overwhelmingly children in mother-only families.

In 1990, almost one-quarter of the under-threes, about half of the more than five million with working mothers that year, were in out-of-home, nonrelative care. About two-thirds of this group were cared for in family day care, largely informal and of poor or unknown quality,[4] and one-third in group care. Programs serving children under age 3 are in the shortest supply of all child care services, despite efforts in some states to recruit family day care providers. Some highly publicized cases of maltreatment and abuse in child care programs have also provoked extensive concern about the quality of available services. And the price of day care is a big worry for average working parents, who cannot easily afford the $4,800 average yearly bill for group care and certainly not the $8,800 price of high-quality-center care.[5] In some places, the cost of quality family day care reaches or exceeds that of center care.

The health condition of very young children also presents serious prob-

lems. Fifty-six percent of all pregnancies in the United States are unintended, one of the highest rates of unwanted pregnancy in the industrialized
world. According to an Institute of Medicine (IOM) report, unintended
pregnancies and pregnancies spaced too close together correlate with an
increased risk of low birth weight and of other maternal and infant health
problems.[6] Low birth weight is the single greatest cause of infant death
(two-thirds) and of major childhood disabilities. Over seven percent (7.3)
of all U.S. infants born in 1992 had a low birth weight, as did 13.4 percent
of black babies; this is the highest proportion since the mid-1970s.

The health condition of their mothers has serious consequences for
children. The same IOM report states that babies are much more likely to
be born healthy if their mothers receive early, regular, and comprehensive
prenatal care. However, about one-quarter of pregnant women fail to
receive the amount of prenatal care currently recommended; and, even
more shocking, more than 5 percent of pregnant women receive no, or
almost no, prenatal care at all.

The United States has disturbingly high rates of infant death; each year,
32,000 American babies die before their first birthday. In 1993 the United
States ranked nineteenth in the world with respect to infant mortality rates,
well below its rank in 1960 (ninth). Other countries have reduced their
infant mortality rates far more than the United States in the intervening
years. Among the advanced industrialized (OECD) countries, the United
States ranked below all except Greece, Portugal, and Turkey. Even among
white children, the U.S. infant mortality rates were higher than those of
any country with which we usually compare ourselves.

Two other childhood social indicators are at least as distressing. One-
third of all abused children are under age 1, and one-half of all deaths from
child abuse involve babies under age 1. Only 67 percent of children under
2 get the full series of immunizations recommended by the American
Academy of Pediatrics, as compared with 85 percent in Britain, for example, and a 90 percent rate announced by UNICEF in 1993 for twelve
developing countries! Indeed, the United States ranks seventieth world-
wide in preschool immunization rates! Yet preschool children are the most
susceptible to the serious infectious life-threatening diseases that these
vaccinations prevent.

Finally, despite all the official declarations on behalf of children, one fact
stands out above all: The U.S. child poverty rate was higher throughout
the 1980s than at any time since the middle 1960s, and consistently higher
the younger the child. In 1990 more than one-quarter of the under-threes
lived in families with incomes below the poverty threshold, the highest
poverty rate for any age group. During the 1980s, the number of poor
infants and toddlers increased by 26 percent, and in some cities and rural
areas over 45 percent of infants and toddlers live in poverty.[7] Twenty-five

percent of poor, very young children have a parent who works full-time, all year, and still has income under the poverty threshold. As might be expected, race, the mother's marital status, and whether or not she holds a job continue to have large effects on children's family circumstances. Black and Hispanic children are most likely to be living in families without their fathers, to have mothers at home rather than at work, and to be living in poverty whether or not their mothers work, although the rate is much higher among those with at-home mothers. About one in five white children under age 3 is poor, primarily those with at-home mothers.

Nor have children in nonpoor famlies been left untouched by economic pressures. The U.S. Bureau of the Census reports no increase in real median family income over the last two decades. In fact, "the median income of families headed by someone under age 30 fell 44 percent in real dollars from 1973 to 1990."[8] Real median income for one-earner husband/wife families also fell. Reflecting a somewhat more positive perspective, a Congressional Budget Office (CBO) report (1988) concluded that by adjusting family income to reflect the smaller size of families in the late 1980s as compared with the early 1970s, real family income has increased by about 20 percent since 1970. The main factors accounting for the more positive CBO conclusion were not related to improvement in earnings by workers, but rather to the smaller number of children in each family sharing family income, and the increased number of workers per family contributing to that income. Moreover, the additional workers in families also meant higher costs (child care, commuting, clothing) and thus a need for still more income—apart from the other intrafamily issues and pressures that are involved.

Indeed, despite the average smaller family size and the dramatic rise in women's labor force participation, the median adjusted family income for married couples with children rose only 13 percent between 1973 and 1986. Over a longer and more recent time span, and including single parents and the unmarried, the income of families with children fell between 1974 and 1991, while that of families without children rose.[9]

Young families and families with very young children have been especially hard hit. The median income of husband/wife families with young children in the late 1980s was 43 percent below that of comparable families in 1970. The attendant pressures are obvious, severe, and widespresd.

### The Invisible Under-Threes

The United States has made some progress in recent years in improving social policy toward children and their families. Politicians have stepped up their profamily rhetoric, but the progress has been modest.

The child and family policy gradually taking shape is narrow in scope and fragmentary; only the outlines are clear. Increasingly, the American public and its leaders assume that women with children aged 3 and older will be in the labor force, and that public subsidies will assist with child care for those in low-income families and deprived groups. Those who are better off will be helped with child care costs through tax credits. The Family Support Act (FSA) of 1988, our most recent major effort at welfare reform, is directed primarily at helping poor single mothers with children of this age to enter or reenter the labor force. Education, counseling, work training, and job search assistance are all part of the supportive effort.

There is growing consensus about child care and early childhood education, at least for children aged 3 to 5. Educators and other experts now generally view group experiences as conducive to the psychological and social development of children this age, as well as to their success in school and eventually at work. Significant federal child care legislation recently has been enacted for the first time. Head Start, a comprehensive, compensatory preschool program for poor children, has expanded, and, with new funding, will continue to expand. School districts are increasingly establishing prekindergarten programs, first for handicapped, deprived, and poor children, but ultimately to offer more universal coverage. Although part-day programs still predominate, in a growing number of school districts, prekindergartens and nursery schools are extending programs to a full school day to achieve child development objectives while meeting the care needs of working parents.

Medical care (Medicaid) has been extended specifically for poor young children, but the growth is modest and the implementation is very uneven. States must now provide prenatal and neonatal care to all poor pregnant mothers and their babies. An improved immmunization program that makes free vaccines available finally has been created for young children, but the legislation did nothing to improve the effectiveness of the delivery system. Whether, despite the failure of the 1993–94 effort, Congress will enact some form of national health legislation in the near future, and what its implications will be for very young children and their families, still are unclear.

More attention also has been paid recently to helping the working poor who have children. The Earned Income Tax Credit (EITC) was increased in 1990 and adjusted slightly for family size. A further expansion was enacted in 1993. As a result, some 17 percent of families with children were expected to benefit from this tax credit in 1994. If the minimum wage were also raised and indexed, as proposed, a family with at least one year-round, full-time wage-earner, even at minimum wage, would by 1996 be assured of income at or above the poverty threshold. Under such a policy, full-time work would pay off for low-wage earners, but child care, health care, and other supports—part of an interrelated cluster—also are essential if low-wage work is to become a truly viable option.

Finally, some modest funds have been appropriated for family support services, but targeted only on some high-risk families, not on most families with young children.

Despite these developments that, if modest, are a valuable beginning, there remain enormous holes in U.S. child and family policy. Research tells us that were all children "starting right," we would avoid many problems, even if this would not necessarily and automatically prevent or solve all future problems for all children. Currently, as we have seen, too much is not right for American children, and where there are international norms and comparative data, we do not compare well. Some problems are so overwhelming at the beginning of life that they immediately and severely impede later development. There is good evidence that many such conditions can be prevented. Other problems that emerge later in life are far more difficult and costly to deal with if there has not been a good beginning. Many of these, too, could be prevented or alleviated with a better start in life.

To the extent that there has been some movement toward better child policies, recent child-targeted initiatives, except for the Medicaid enhancements and the modest family support initiatives, have been largely concentrated on children aged 3 to 5 and school-aged children, and their families. No comparable consensus or change in social institutions has targeted national policy affecting children under age 3 and their families. Despite some recent stirrings, such as the Carnegie task force report and attendant publicity,[10] these children—and their families—remain largely invisible in the U.S. social and family policy debate.

Legislative initiatives on behalf of families and children have ignored the under-threes, have treated them as side-issues, or (when focused on them) have faltered. A brief history of three recent federal initiatives—welfare reform, parental leave, and child care—illustrates how invisible very young children are in U.S. policy.

*Welfare Reform.* The widely heralded 1988 FSA was itself a reflection of new expectations about the roles of women and the care of children. Aid to Families with Dependent Children (AFDC), the core of our welfare system, had its origins in mothers' pensions enacted early in this century on the premise that poor women should be supported at home to care for their children. But by the 1980s, with so many women in the labor force, it clearly no longer made sense to organize welfare on principles of domesticity that no longer applied to American women above the poverty level, not even married women.

The FSA introduced a new set of requirements for work and training, aimed at transforming AFDC from a program of income support for poor single mothers rearing children at home into a short-term program of labor market assistance to help the recipients gain economic independence. But the legislation distinguishes between welfare beneficiaries according to their children's age. On one hand, it requires recipients with children aged 3 and older to participate in job-training programs, if those opportunities are available and child care can be assured. On the other hand, the legislation exempts from work and training requirements the parents of children under age 3, unless the states choose to include the parents of one- and two-year-olds. Getting the parents of older children off welfare poses a considerable challenge, and the states have limited resources, so they are not likely to do much to expand job training and child care services for parents of infants and toddlers unless federal supports are increased.

Yet children under age 3 and their families constitute a very large part of welfare beneficiaries. Twenty-five percent of the 8.6 million children on AFDC in 1991 were under age 3. They constitute 18 percent of all children under age 3 in the U.S. and are the age group most likely to be recipients of AFDC. In approximately 42 percent of all families receiving AFDC, the youngest child is under age 3. More than half of all new AFDC cases involve a child under age 3, and more than 60 percent of all AFDC recipients at any given time are children under age 3. And, although women are especially likely to experience long-term poverty and to become long-term welfare dependents if they receive welfare for the first time when they have a child under age 3, the welfare reform legislation fails to provide any help to them, unless they are teenage mothers who have not finished high school.

Moreover, the inequities and inadequacies that have characterized AFDC since its beginning, fifty-five years ago, remain.There are still no uniform national eligibility criteria, no way of assuring that poor children in Alabama and Wisconsin, for example, will be treated the same. No minimum benefit has been established for AFDC recipients, and AFDC and Food Stamps together still do not bring the income of poor families with children to above the poverty level in almost all jurisdictions (a standard that is achieved for almost all elderly and disabled assistance recipients through Supplemental Security Income [SSI] and Food Stamps).

By failing to address the needs of mothers of infants and toddlers, the act fails to follow through on its own premises. The education, job, and training opportunites require enhancement and expansion. And if the new opportunities for training are of value to mothers of older children, they should also be designed to benefit mothers of children below age 3. There is now no adequate justification for not offering parents of small children on welfare adequate training and child care opportunities. It should be an option, however. Some will want and need to be at home with their infants. Some are poor training and education prospects. If the intent is to support some mothers in at-home care until the child is three years old, can we justify the enormous range in state AFDC grant levels and the failure to bring many of them even near the poverty line?

*Parental Leave.* Federal legislation (1978) shaped *parental leave policy* as a form of disability policy and as women's equality policy. Thus, short-term disability insurance coverage, where available, was required by law to apply to pregnant women and women at the time of maternity. It was not until 1993 that a federal parental leave policy was enacted outside of the disability framework.

The 1993 Family and Medical Leave Act (FMLA) mandates the right of employees to a family leave at the time of childbirth, adoption, or a serious health condition of a child or parent, and to temporary medical leave at the time of an employee's own serious health condition, with adequate protection of the employees' employment and benefit rights. To get the principle of family leave established, congressional sponsors of the legislation accepted a series of compromises. Moreover, it was to be only an unpaid leave. Thus, as important as a job-protected twelve-week leave might be, without some income protection, most working mothers, as much as they might want to take advantage of the policy, will have difficulty using it because they cannot afford the loss of income. And twelve weeks is not enough.

Despite the growth in female labor force participation and despite the enactment of the 1978 Pregnancy Disability Act, paid leaves have not increased significantly over the last decade, although as a result of the recent federal legislation, there undoubtedly has been some increase in "formal" policy protection for unpaid job- and benefit-protected leaves. Recent research has shown that the working women who are especially likely to be without the right to even unpaid leave include unmarried and part-time workers, low-wage workers, and young and/or less educated mothers; this pattern is likely to continue even with the 1993 legislation. Furthermore, women who do not have job-protected post-childbirth leave are more likely to experience additional unemployment solely attributable to lack of leave and/or to experience a disproportionate loss in earnings within the first two years after childbirth. No specific research has focused on the consequences of the lack of leaves for children—but the United States has more very young infants (under three months of age) in poor quality out-of-home child care arrangements than any of the other major industrialized countries. And child development theory gives grounds for concern.

Thus, the national policy for parental leave, central to under-three policy, even after a hard-fought campaign for the limited 1993 legislation, constitutes a major family policy gap. In one sense, parental leave ought to be the easiest issue for liberals and conservatives to settle, for it encourages a parent—nearly always the mother—to remain at home with her baby after childbirth. And this, after all, is what conservatives, too, approve. But parental leave, as a form of government regulation of business, raises another set of issues for conservatives committed to deregulation or to minimizing what they regard as "nonwage" labor costs.

The compromise leave legislation ignored three basic premises: that a baby's overall well-being depends on the availability of adequate care and nurturing for more than two or three months; that it is essential for parents, especially new parents, to have time to be with a new baby; and that a new baby's economic situation often depends on the earnings of both fathers and mothers.

Although a valuable first step, the current, unpaid parental leave policy leaves millions of Americans, particularly low-income and single-parent families, without much protection. It provides important new protection for individual workers, when ill, and for the care of all ill parent or spouse; but it is clearly inadequate in providing economic security to families with new babies, and adequate time for parents to get to know and to be known by their new baby.

*Child Care.* Although some advocates recognize the interrelationship between child care service policies and parental leave policies, the public debate has been carried out as if these are separate issues. One wonders whether opponents of parental leave legislation have considered the situations of infants under three or six months of age in inadequate care in the United States in numbers unknown elsewhere in the industrialized west.

The United States never has had a national program for child care as such. Rather, the federal government finances child care through a variety of avenues, direct and indirect, including a miscellany of programs with child care provisions, such as AFDC, the child care food program, child welfare services, and various tax benefits. Among all these programs, four stand out as especially important: the Dependent Care Tax Credit, Head Start, Title XX of the Social Security Act, and the Child Care and Development Block Grant. There are no precise figures on the numbers of children benefiting from federally funded child care; however, several recent studies do offer firm data on the numbers of children of different ages in out-of-home child care of different types.

For the past decade, the largest single federal source of child care funding has been a demand subsidy (a subsidy provided to some parents to help them purchase child care), the Dependent Care Tax Credit. The credit was estimated to be worth $3 billion in 1992, but it provides no benefit to many of the families who need it most—those with incomes below the tax threshold. The credit is also of limited value to low- and moderate-income families who use informal family day care. These deficiencies could be partially alleviated if the credit were made "refundable"—that is, if the value of the credit were paid out as reimbursement for part of the child care expenditures, even to people whose incomes are too low for them to owe taxes.

Head Start, budgeted at $3.3 billion in 1994, has become the largest source of child care assistance, albeit mostly part-day. It is the single biggest subsidy on the "supply" side (i.e., going directly to programs providing services) and provides a compensatory education program that in the early 1990s served about forty percent of the nation's poor three and four year olds (overwhelmingly, the four-year-olds). During the Clinton Administration, Head Start became even more important, emerging as the pillar of early childhood education among the poor. Currently Head Start does nothing much to fill the infant/toddler child care gap, but an advisory group has urged that part of this problem be remedied. The 1994 reauthorization of Head Start included, for the first time, some modest funding for launching an under-three Head Start initiative and for more all-day programs.

Third, a 1990 budget agreement gave $2.5 billion over three years to the Child Care and Development Block Grant and allows the states discretion in subsidizing child care for the working poor without as strict income limitations as under previous programs. This was a major improvement in the federal commitment. It will largely serve three- to five-year-olds, but some funds are reserved for infants and toddlers. Under yet another 1990 program, Entitlement Funding for Child Care Services (also referred to as the "At-Risk Child Care Program"), states receive $1.5 billion for families who are at risk of a return to the welfare rolls because of their difficulty in affording child care.

Fourth in importance is the Social Services Block Grant program, which, under Title XX of the Social Security Act, provides grants to states for subsidizing, purchasing, or operating a variety of social services including child care. In recent years, about one-quarter of the total value of the grants, or $700 million in 1990, has gone to child care for low- and modest-income working families and children.

A miscellany of other programs that provide smaller amounts of child care funds include AFDC (the exclusion of child care expenses under a specified level from earnings when calculating financial eligibility, the JOBS child care provisions, and the transitional child care services), the child care food program, child welfare services, and other tax benefits. Extensive additional support is provided by some states as well for child care and for compensatory education programs for four year olds.

In short, for the first time in twenty years, after several abortive efforts and major compromises between committees in the House and between House and Senate on the financing of child care and the program focus, federal child care legislation passed both houses of Congress in 1990. The specifics are summarized above. This was a landmark development, the first major federal child care legislation enacted after several failures to pass such legislation in the 1970s. Nonetheless, as should be expected, most of the existing and projected supply of child care services is for three- and four-year-olds. Infant/toddler care requires a special effort. Despite some initiatives for recruitment of family day care providers in some states, and some beginning attention to the under-threes in Head Start, there still is a major shortage of child care places for infants and toddlers.

There also is extensive concern about the quality of the care available to children of all ages, the costs of good-quality care, and the extent to which average working parents not eligible for public direct subsidies can afford such care. As noted, President Clinton's emphasis on Head Start, as his current major initiative in this field, however laudable, makes it extremely unlikely that there also will be an adequate supply of affordable, good-quality infant and toddler care within the near future. Even if access to all-day Head Start programs for three- and four-year-olds were expanded further and there were some beginning development of Head Start programs for the under-threes, and if full-day public-school kindergartens and prekindergartens became the national norm—an understandable priority for many—the problem of inadequate infant and toddler care would remain unresolved. However, labor force data show that parents of infants and toddlers are nonetheless at work, away from home, in record numbers.

In conclusion, in neither welfare reform, family leave, nor the 1990 child care initiatives was concern with the well-being—or even the situations—of very young children an issue. Yet, as we have seen, these early years comprise an especially important life-cycle stage, and these children are experiencing serious problems.

If the country wishes to help children "start" right, the great challenges we now face concern families with children below age 3. Leading child development and social science experts stress the importance of the first few years of life. Most Americans are convinced that the experts are right. Yet many very young children in the United States are living in increasingly hazardous situations, and there is little attention to what could, indeed should, be done. Moreover, when new policy initiatives are proposed, they still fail to target the youngest children and their families.

Thus, for example, although millions of mothers of under-threes are at work, many Americans—and that includes many policymakers—continue to expect them to be at home full-time. Federal parental leave legislation, finally enacted in 1993, provides only a brief *unpaid* job-protected leave, clearly important if only symbolically, but of limited real value to families increasingly dependent on mothers' wages. Infant/toddler care continues to be in scarce supply, and few resources are directed specifically toward these programs. Head Start now serves about 40 percent of the eligible three- and four-year-olds, overwhelmingly the four year olds, but almost no children under age 3. Most of the promising proposals for actions designed to reduce infant mortality to levels achieved in other industrialized countries have been ignored or deferred.

## Inhibitors and Imperatives

The United States has never seriously taken on the problems of adequate income and support for families with children, nor has it even considered the problem of adequate time for parenting as a policy issue. We have dealt with income for the poorest—but most inadequately. We have been much preoccupied with personal social services, but not with some of the most essential services (medical care and child care on a broad basis) and often not with the quality, adequancy, or accountabilitiy of others. Moreover, in the history of American social policy, services (especially counseling) often have become a substitute for money, where such substitution becomes a different and questionable policy.

It will not be easy to focus policy attention on very young children in the United States. Policymakers disagree about the substantive issues, and many Americans suspect or say they suspect that child policy proposals will disproportionately benefit black and other minority children and will encourage more out-of-wedlock, minority births. The debated substantive issues call for analysis and data. The anxieties and emotional or racist sources of opposition, often latent and unacknowledged, should be confronted openly and answered directly. We are unlikely to make much progress unless we can show that effective family polices are consistent with widely shared values and provide broad benefits across racial and class lines.

Even if we overcome prejudice and racism, and analyze options rationally, we face great obstacles to consensus because of the deeply conflicting moral values and cultural practices in America. The United States is truly a large and heterogeneous country whose population holds pluralistic value systems. We include almost as much variability among the states as among the European countries. Our federalism tradition will insist that for some purposes, at least, states should continue to carry the program and policy leads and thus reflect our diversity. However, this does not mean that we do not require national leadership and participation and core guarantees for all children.

Then there is the U.S. tradition of church/state separation, a doctrine protected in part by carefully avoiding complicated issues of family policy. The abortion fight has shown how difficult things may become if we forget or cannot avoid challenging the tradition of respect for family privacy.

Furthermore, in the current era, there is a preference for market solutions to problems where they are available or can be encouraged. Whether real or not, proposals along such lines do serve to block public action.

Nor do we in this country have the powerful labor movement that in come countries have actively moved family benefit proposals. Organized labor has not nearly the influence in the United States that it has in some other countries. U.S. unions have been neither at the forefront of the child and family policy debate nor have these issues been high on the policy agenda of the labor movement.

Moreover, the United States has no history or tradition of concern with declining fertility, a factor driving child and family policies in some other countries. The U.S. birth rate (just about at the "replacement" level) is high by OECD standards, and our immigration rate has more than compensated for any decline in the birth rate. We will not lack a future labor force or taxpayers to meet social security financing needs (the concern elsewhere). However, the education, preparation, and socialization of that labor force could be a problem.

Nor is it easy to overcome diverse values in designing social legislation. Certainly, child care proposals were stalled, blocked, and compromised almost beyond recognition, as value clashes within and between parties took over, and until compromises were negotiated in a broader (deficit reduction) context in 1990. Family leave legislation was similarly cut back before final passage in 1993.

Some conservatives would support family policy initiatives, but only if they were limited to traditional families. Some feminists are concerned that policies designed to improve conditions for children may have harmful consequences for women. While some conservatives object to providing paid leaves for working mothers, some feminists fear the consequences (lower wages, constricted career paths) for women who take extended leaves.

All these issues are debated in a context in which government has traditionally avoided family issues because of the racial, ethnic, religious, and cultural diversity within the country, and the concomitant difficulty in reaching consensus.

Inevitably, in the present national budget environment, questions of cost will influence the debate over child and family policies. Clearly, we must make choices rather than pretend that the society can do everything at once. Yet we also should remember that countries not as wealthy as ours do many of the things that opponents label as too costly for the United States. Although there is growing evidence that universal programs—

programs available regardless of the user's income—are the best and most supportive, one can acknowledge nonetheless the need for some targeting, initially, where it can work.

Whatever the targeting, the phasing, and the modest starts, the youngest cannot and should not be forgotten; indeed, attention to the under-threes should be a priority. In the terms of the economist, they are an investment good, not merely a consumption frill. They are our society's future. If it is necessary to start slowly with the under-threes, then the poor, the deprived, and the handicapped are logically the groups to target first. But, as we shall see, the European experience offers other, more universal possibilities. Their example provides neither fixed formulas nor final answers, but suggests broad lines for thinking about the path we ought to take. At this point the United States has not assured its very youngest childern of adequate care outside their homes or adequate nourishment and care within them. However, recent congressional achievements and new commitments to children should encourage us to reach for bolder alternatives.

Given these obstacles, what can be done? How can the United States move on a policy agenda?

## Conclusion

Despite all that we know as a society and believe about the earliest years of a child's life, we have left unaddressed crucial problems of income, parental time, parental competence and information (among the most deprived and stressed), child care services, medical care, and much else. There have been some policy improvements for three- to five-year-olds in recent years, but far fewer for the under-threes. Despite some modest beginnings, we have no policies at all in many areas, or they are grossly deficient. The lag is serious and merits urgent attention.

Is this "invisibility" of the under-threes in the national policy debate characteristic of all the industrialized countries in the same way as the demographic and social changes (changes in family structure and gender roles) are? Or are there differences between the United States and the other countries with regard to this issue?

In the next chapter we explore whether other countries have followed a different approach, whether we can learn from their experiences, and what help and insight other research offers in developing a policy strategy.

# 2

## Developing a Strategy

How might the United States develop an expanded policy agenda and strategy addressing issues of special importance to very young children and their families? First, we discuss learning across countries, and why the experience of other countries is relevant to the United States. We point to a policy strategy suggested by the European experience. Second, we explore the way in which gender is an integral part of child and family policies and, therefore, the need to remain sensitive to issues having to do with women while promoting the well-being of children. We show how research on this issue can help shape our strategy. We then propose a three-pronged policy strategy that we believe is essential if comprehensive child policy reform is to be carried out.

### Can We Learn from Other Countries?

The experiences of the northern and western European countries offer a particularly rich array of child and family policy options that have consequences for the well-being of very young children and their families. Information about these developments could contribute to U.S. policy explorations concerned with infants and toddlers.

We will refer specifically to six countries (Britain, Denmark, Finland, France, Germany, and Italy), subjects of a two-year study of "social policy and the under-threes." Where relevant, we will refer as well to several of our earlier studies, which will enable us to add to the picture from developments in Austria, Norway, Sweden, and elsewhere. The increasingly rich reporting within the European Community (now the European Union), Council of Europe, and Organization for Economic Cooperation and Development (OECD) facilitates updating and supplementation, as does work by scholars in a number of countries.

Before turning to substance, however, we explain briefly why "borrowing" or attempting to learn from other countries, particularly in social policy, makes sense.

First, social-program learning from Europe is a long and successful American tradition. We refer to the settlement houses and charity organization societies of the nineteenth and early twentieth centuries (English models provided the inspiration), the kindergartens that followed soon thereafter (with much German influence), and the Social Security Act of 1935 (with several European precedents). We might cite influences on university education and medical training, but this would take us too far afield, as would reference to the interest in the past two decades in Japanese modes of workplace organization. Canada and Germany were much studied as the options were conceptualized for the 1993–1994 health policy debate. And, of course, Europe has learned much from the United States in social service programming, as in much else, with little American effort to discourage the process.

The point is that this world—for this purpose, the industrialized, urbanized, democratic world—is in one sense a vast arena in which different strategies are tested and adopted for coping with problems and social change. Formal laboratory experiments are rarely possible in broad social policy for lack of time and because the necessary experimental manipulations are not possible. But policy and program planners are neglecting their responsibilities if they ignore completely the "experiments in nature" that take place as various countries innovate, explore, and attempt to cope (and sometimes even assemble data relevant to evaluation).

None of this is to propose direct "copying" and duplication. Social policy in such domains as income support, child care, and family support services may touch on deeply held values and cultural traditions about work incentives, parental roles, family privacy, and much more. The models found elsewhere serve to enrich the options, and to suggest new possibilities; but a country developing policy obviously considers its own objectives and value contexts and adapts to its circumstances those models found helpful.

Cross-national borrowing is thus attractive and potentially enriching and not a major threat to those characteristics unique to the American scene or to a desire to protect state and regional differences. To generate our agenda of possibilities, the six countries we chose include several that explicitly or implicitly had decided to give special attention to children under age 3 and their families. We added several as exemplifying what we expected to be good child and family policy, with no special attention to the under-threes. Yet in some sense, in today's Europe all countries give special attention to the under-threes, although some have gone further than others. Thus, we also included Britain, without an under-three policy, and where some services, especially child care, are even less developed than in the United States, but which has a stronger infrastructure than we in the form of child benefits (child allowances) and a national system of health care. Italy although it does not have exemplary national child and family policy (except for universal preschools for the three- to five-year-olds), was included because of some extraordinarily interesting developments, in the north and north-central regions, with regard to infant/toddler care and family support services. For several topics we draw on our earlier studies in other countries that have significant child policy developments that are relevant.

What do the explorations disclose? Propelled by different priorities but responding to similar demographic and social trends, many European countries are beginning to target special policies on very young children and their families. Among the similar demographic and social changes affecting these families are the increase in the proportion of mothers in the labor force, the decrease in fertility rates, the increase in the use of out-of-home child care, the high and rising costs of good-quality care, the increase in mother-only families, and the continued economic vulnerability of families with young children.

In contrast to the United States, the European countries long ago established an extensive social infrastructure for families with children, which includes national health insurance or services, cash benefits given families based on the presence and number of children (child or family allowances), guaranteed minimum child-support payments, and often housing allowances for low- and middle-income families as well.

Child care for children aged 2½ or 3 until primary school entry, is close to universal in much of Europe. It is provided in preschool programs, usually under educational auspices, and is voluntary and in most countries free to children whose parents want them to attend—regardless of their mother's employment status. Child care for the under-threes involves almost as diversified a delivery system as in the United States, includes both family day care and center care, and serves wide-ranging proportions of children.

The takeoff points for developing new child and family policies in Europe vary depending on the country, as do the specifics. But all seem to share a common goal: support for very young children and their parents, at home and in the community, during the earliest years. And all involve provision of financial resources, leaves from employment, and a variety of services to make this possible.

These policies merit attention because they are associated with good child outcomes. Infant mortality rates are consistently lower than those in the United States, fewer babies have low birth weights, childhood immunization rates are higher, and therefore certain disease rates are lower than in the United States. School learning is more successful, and disruptive school problems are fewer in some—but not all—comparison countries. And, later, fewer European adolescents have babies or abortions than in the United States. Later in this chapter we document the significantly lower child poverty rates in Europe.

The countries we are discussing have built their interventions for high-risk, vulnerable, and seriously troubled children and their families on a firm and universal social infrastructure, moving from what the society owes to all children to what it must provide for those in need and those at risk of various harms. Here is perhaps the largest difference from the United States. Reluctant as we in this country have been to "interfere" with families and privacy, we have limited much of what is done in social welfare to children with problems, in poverty, or from deprived groups. Thus, U.S. policy offers mostly safety-net income and remedial services, not the basic preventive and developmental services that can enhance socialization and development and prevent problems.

But observers ask whether European relative homogeneity and U.S. ethnic and racial heterogeneity do not constitute a difference so great as to invalidate any effort at learning. We believe that the question has two aspects: Will American heterogeneity create opposition to child policy by those who hold prejudices against racial minority children or children of new immigrants and refugees? Does the heterogeneity create programming barriers that affect the adaptability of models? On the first, there is little question that some aspects of the lag in child policy here are attributable to racism; for example, the belief in some that child allowances would motivate black single women to have more children out-of-wedlock (even as earlier, some opposition to child allowances stemmed from anti-Catholicism). All of this speaks to political obstacles to child and family policy in the United States—not to the need for such policy or the urgency of enriching the options by considering developments in countries in the lead.

On the question of programming barriers, the issue is empirical. In countries that have been relatively homogeneous, any move toward diversity creates anxiety and generates concern. We have sought to determine how the countries studied deal with immigrants, refugees, and members of minority groups in their service programs—and shall report on this in the appropriate context. It is useful to recall that although most of the western and northern European countries truly are relatively homogeneous in contrast to the United States, a country of immigrants, there are some significant regionalisms and, since World War II, an important movement of people of color or of different religions, from the poor "South" to the more affluent "North," even if not on the U.S. immigration scale. Since the collapse of Eastern European communism and the disappearance of the "wall," as well as the wars in what was Yugoslavia, western Europe has experienced an immigration and a refugee influx on a scale that has stretched both tolerance and resources. This process was under way during our research field work, so we can affirm that increasing heterogeneity complicates programming and very much challenges the social solidarity on which family and child policy rests, but does not cause countries to lose confidence in their systems or invalidate our efforts to enrich the discussion with experience from other countries.

Furthermore, although individual countries may be relatively homogeneous in American terms, there is great heterogeneity within the group of countries observed. Thus, the European initiatives are driven by a variety of diverse motivations and priorities. All care about child and maternal well-being. Beyond this, and on other levels, the French want not only to protect the economic well-being of children in vulnerable families but also to ensure that women continue to have children even while entering the labor force in ever-increasing numbers. The Germans and Austrians (to whom, incidentally, federalism is no less significant than it is for us) want to acknowledge and affirm the value of children and of "family work." The Finns shaped their policies out of a concern with the consequences for children of shortages in infant and toddler care while the demand for women in the labor force was increasing, and they see their policies as supporting the values of parental choice and family work. The British have been focused on child poverty and "special needs" children. The Italians stress maternal protection and support for child well-being. The Swedes, and to a lesser extent the Danes, have sought to promote gender equity, child well-being, responsiveness to labor market demands, and support for a strong work ethic. The Danes are especially aware of the quality of life of young children.

Contrary to American impressions, the European countries with comprehensive child and family policies fit no political stereotype. Some of the governments have been conservative, some social democratic, and some coalition-oriented. Some have changed in the course of our research. Their child and family policies have continued to advance despite shifts in the political pendulum. Some of these countries are heavily Catholic, others Protestant, and some highly secular in their political patterns in recent years. The countries that have embarked on innovative policy and program experiments include those with high labor-force participation rates for mothers of very young children and some with low rates. Currently, unemployment rates are high in most of these countries, and conservative governments are dominant in most, but the core policies are not being dismantled even where fiscal pressures dictate some adjustments at the margin. Among the policy leaders are some countries with very low fertility rates and some with not-so-low rates. And these include some with high rates of mother-only families and some with lower rates. Moreover, in European terms, these are both large and small countries.

Clearly, diverse political and economic environments have not prevented the Europeans from achieving a common recognition of the problems facing families with small children. Obviously, something worthy of attention is going on. Can the United States learn from these developments?

## Gender and Family Policy

In recent years, scholarship in comparative social policy has begun to be joined by feminist scholarship, with the announced purpose of introducing gender-related issues into mainstream comparative social policy research.[1] However, in some sense, despite a primary focus on children, comparative family policy scholarship (scholarship on social policy toward children and their families) has always included a gender component, if only because family policy, by definition, must pay attention to family changes as well as to the situation of children.[2]

Family policy includes attention not only to childbirth, child care, parenting, and child rearing, but also to the relationship between men and women in the family and in the workplace, and to the relationship between family responsibilities and employment. If the traditional family assumes two parents, i.e., the man earning wages in the labor market and the woman bearing, caring for, and rearing children, then nontraditional families include two-earner couples and single-parent, female-headed families in which the woman has never been married or is divorced, not just the widowed—all with the same child-related responsibilities. These changes in family structure, composition, and gender roles have immediate implications for policy.

Although two-parent, husband/wife families remain the dominant child-rearing group in all the advanced industrialized countries, many of these families are reconstituted (merged, melded), formed by one or two adults who had been married previously and had children by a former partner. Out-of-wedlock childbirths have increased dramatically, too, now ranging in these countries from about 7 percent in Italy to almost 50 percent in Denmark and Sweden. Single-parent families also have increased, as a consequence both of divorce and of out-of-wedlock births, and now constitute between 7 (Italy) and 30 percent (United States) of families with children, depending on the country. The issue of how financial support for children is to be assured when there is only one parent, a woman, or when both parents are alive but only one is the custodial parent (usually the woman), has emerged as a much-debated family policy issue in the late twentieth century.

How family economic security is assured has been a central component of family policy for almost a century. Policies concerned with this goal have changed dramatically since World War II as well, from an earlier emphasis on a family wage, whereby a minimum wage, earned traditionally by a male wage earner, was sufficient to support a man, his wife and two children, to acceptance of a market wage and to the growing concern with the gap between wages and family needs, the inadequacy of one wage as support for a family, the still greater inadequacy if that wage is a woman's, and the growing need for one and a half or two wages to provide adequate financial support for a family. These developments, too, have policy implications that relate to women.

Of all family policies, those focused on very young children are by far the most likely to involve women in their family roles. Maternity policies provide protection for women at the time of childbirth. Parenting policies assure time for working mothers and fathers to spend with new babies. There are policies to help working parents in their child-rearing roles and policies that facilitate parental employment while assuring good care for children. All these policies address child well-being while also maintaining sensitivity to women's needs, both women in their family roles and women in their individual employment roles.

The women's movement in the continental European countries, in contrast to that in the United States, for example, has always stressed the value of maternity. There are now U.S. feminist scholars as well who remind us that maternity (and parenting) should not be viewed as women's "special burden or curse" but rather as a special gift that encouraged women in the past (and could encourage them again in the future) to gain a greater measure of personal and political autonomy.[3] In effect, women constitute an important interest group in support of child and family policies. At certain points—as Skocpol has shown with regard to the late nineteenth and early twentieth centuries in this country—women and women's clubs have in fact been in the leadership in successful social reform (mother's pensions, maternal and child health, workplace protections).[4]

The challenge for contemporary family policy is to protect and enhance the well-being of children while being sensitive to women's needs and aspirations. Orloff points out that if good social policy is expected to respond to the claims of workers/citizens to compensate for failures in the labor market, "women make claims as workers but also as members of families, and they need programs especially to compensate for marriage failures and/or the need to raise children alone."[5] We would add, they also need programs to support their parenting roles as well as to facilitate their access to employment and labor market roles.

Our focus here, however, is on parenting roles and on how society can help parents fulfill these optimally. The extent to which the state recognizes the caring work of women as being valuable, necessary, and worth supporting, whether in the family or in the larger society, and whether paid or unpaid, is an important indicator of the effectiveness of its family policies, as is the extent to which the state acknowledges the dual roles of women and men, in the family and in the workplace, and the need to recognize these in promoting the well-being of children.

Any responsible (and responsive) family policy strategy for very young children and their families must be premised on this new reality. Balancing adult family and work roles without shortchanging children is most important and most difficult when children are very young. A policy model may support one option as reflective of the country's preferences or deliberately support parental choice across the options. We clearly endorse the latter. Our objective here is to point out how to do better by children within this context, whatever the preferences and choices: children as the parental (usually maternal) priority for the early years; family and work as a simultaneous and dual priority for both parents (or a single parent); and family and work as sequential priorities for a parent even in the early years.

## Money, Time, and Services: A Comprehensive Strategy

We have described the need for public policy to pay attention to very young children and their families, both to their economic well-being and their social-physical-psychological well-being. Although it is not clear what proportion of child and family problems is due to inadequate income and what proportion is caused by failures in child socialization, inadequate parenting skills, and antisocial and inappropriate parental behavior, it seems clear that these are intertwined and interdependent. Economic pressures have negative consequences for children and their families, as do intrafamilial stress, inadequate parenting and care, and disadvantaged neighborhoods. No one factor alone can account for the problems experienced by very young children in the United States. As a result, no one intervention will solve these problems.

We arrived at the concept of a three-pronged policy strategy by generalizing from observed European experience. Several decades ago, we began our studies of what some countries were doing for very young children and their families by focusing first on child care and other social services, then on income transfer policies, and then on innovative parental leave policies.[6] We have since concluded that the countries that have been most successful in improving the condition of children are those that have stressed income *and* services *and* time, not one or the other.

Because of the significance and pervasiveness of the poverty problem, we begin by describing why reducing poverty is critical for the well-being of very young children. We discuss, subsequently, the importance of time and service strategies.

## *An Income Strategy to Assure the Essentials*

The general child poverty picture is by now familiar. More than one in five children and four in ten minority children were poor throughout most of the 1980s, rates that were higher than at any time since 1965. These rates are higher than those in any other major industrialized country, including Canada, our neighbor to the north. Moveover, child poverty rates in the United States rose during the 1980s, while they declined elsewhere.

For young children, the problem is even more severe. The under-threes are the poorest of all. Our own special analysis of census findings for 1990 showed that while one in five older children was in poverty, one in four children under three lived in families with incomes below the poverty threshold.[7] The extraordinarily high poverty rates among very young minority children are especially shocking.

Children under three also constitute a disproportionately large group among poor children. In 1990, more than 20 percent of all poor children were under three, as compared with 18 percent of those just a little older (aged 3 to 5), and 60 percent aged 6 and older. Taking account of the differences by race, ethnicity, and family structure, children under three remain consistently worse off than older children. And, of course, black and Hispanic children in this age group are much worse off than white children (Table 2.1).

Nor does parental work always eliminate the problem of poverty among children, although it does improve their chances considerably. Sixty percent of poor children under age 3 have at least one full-time or part-time working parent. This includes 70 percent of poor white children, 60 percent of poor Hispanic children, and 50 percent of poor black children. More than 40 percent of the poor under-threes living in lone-mother families have full-time or part-time working mothers. But these jobs (Tables 2.2 and 2.3) do not protect them from poverty. Nor would one

**Table 2.1.** Children in Poverty in 1990, by Age and Race/Ethnicity (Percentages)

| Age | All Children | White | Black | Hispanic |
|------|------|------|------|------|
| 0–2 | 24.3 | 14.6 | 52.4 | 41.6 |
| 3–5 | 21.5 | 13.7 | 46.3 | 38.5 |
| 0–5 | 23.0 | 14.2 | 49.5 | 40.1 |
| 0–18 | 20.6 | 15.1 | 44.8 | 38.4 |

*Source:* Special analysis prepared by Susan Einbinder for the six-country study of "Social Policies and the Under Threes" from 1990 Census data and the data base used for the National Center for Children in Poverty Report.

necessarily want to recommend full-time work for all lone mothers of very young children.

The economic situation of very young children is far worse in the United States than in at least six other major industrialized countries (Canada, France, Germany, the Netherlands, Sweden, and the United Kingdom) for which we have comparable data.[8] Using 40 percent of median income as

**Table 2.2.** Distribution of Children Aged 0 to 2, by Poverty Status, Parental Employment Status, and Race/Ethnicity, 1990

| Age, Employment Status, and Race/Ethnicity | Poor Children | Poverty Rate (%) |
|------|------|------|
| Children 0–2 | 2,858,930 | 24.3 |
| Full-time or more | | |
| All | 716,458 | 8.5 |
| White | 348,013 | 5.0 |
| Black | 135,899 | 18.0 |
| Hispanic | 213,351 | 23.0 |
| Less than full-time | | |
| All | 1,003,990 | 53.9 |
| White | 465,986 | 47.0 |
| Black | 342,885 | 66.0 |
| Hispanic | 157,286 | 61.0 |
| Not employed | | |
| All | 1,138,481 | 77.3 |
| White | 342,129 | 69.0 |
| Black | 506,588 | 81.0 |
| Hispanic | 248,608 | 85.0 |

**Table 2.3.** Distribution of Children Aged 0 to 2 in Single-Mother Families, by Poverty Status, Parental Employment Status, and Race/Ethnicity, 1990

| Age, Employment Status, and Race/Ethnicity | Poor Children | Poverty Rate (%) |
|---|---|---|
| Full-time or more | | |
| All | 77,085 | 18.7 |
| White | 16,220 | 8.2 |
| Black | 39,891 | 26.4 |
| Hispanic[a] | * | * |
| Less than full-time | | |
| All | 609,178 | 59.8 |
| White | 234,549 | 52.3 |
| Black | 304,222 | 69.0 |
| Hispanic[a] | * | * |
| Not employed | | |
| All | 945,823 | 77.4 |
| White | 258,675 | 67.4 |
| Black | 476,339 | 81.3 |
| Hispanic[a] | * | * |

[a] The estimates for Hispanics and 'other' race/ethnicity are too small to report reliably.

the poverty threshold, we found that families with children under age 3 are poorer in the United States than in any of the other countries (See Table 2.4). Indeed, the U.S. poverty rate of 21 percent, shown in the analysis for the latest year for which comparable data are available, is almost 50 percent higher than the next-highest rates in Britain and Canada (15 and 14 percent, respectively), about three times as high as in Germany (7 percent), more than four times as high as in France (5 percent) and Sweden (4 percent), and almost eleven times as high as in the Netherlands (2 percent). This pattern holds true regardless of family structure, i.e., two-parent or one-parent families. Of particular interest, our special analysis using Luxembourg Income Study data showed that the difference in poverty rates of families with children in the United States as compared with Europe is far greater for families with children under three than for those with older children. More specifically, the ratio of U.S. child poverty rates to those of the four countries with the lowest rates is about 5:1 for children under three as compared with 3:1 for families with older children. The United States has a unique under-three poverty problem.[9]

Given the high rate of poverty, U.S. families with children of this age are the most likely to be recipients of public assistance, Aid to Families with

**Table 2.4.** Percentages of Families in Six Countries with Young Children, Younger and Older than Age 3, with Incomes Below 40 Percent of the Median, 1984-1987

| Country | All Families with Children | Families with Children Under 3 | Families with Children Over 3 |
|---|---|---|---|
| Canada | 0.12 | 0.14 | 0.12 |
| France | 0.06 | 0.05 | 0.06 |
| Germany | 0.05 | 0.07 | 0.05 |
| Netherlands | 0.02 | 0.02 | 0.02 |
| Sweden | 0.04 | 0.04 | 0.04 |
| United Kingdom | 0.12 | 0.15 | 0.10 |
| United States | 0.16 | 0.21 | 0.15 |

*Source:* Special analysis prepared by Beth Jean Heller from the Luxembourg Income Study data base, for the six-country study of "Social Policies and the Under Threes."

Dependent Children (AFDC) and to be caught in the welfare and poverty traps. It is poor families with very young children who have the fewest alternatives. Moreover, although there was a slight decline during the 1980s in the proportion of AFDC families with very young children, from 42 percent in 1979 to 35 to 38 percent in most of the 1980s, the rate is now approaching 42 percent again. Of perhaps greater concern, the number of children under age 3 as a percentage of all children receiving AFDC has increased steadily, from 15 percent in 1969, to 19 percent in 1979, and 25 percent in 1991 (Tables 2.5 and 2.6). Children who begin on AFDC at a very early age have a high risk of spending long periods of time on AFDC, as well, according to available research.

Moreover, as already noted, although AFDC offers some economic support, it does so at a very inadequate level. At best, the package of AFDC benefits and Food Stamps in high-benefit jurisdictions brought family income up to about 90 percent of the poverty threshold for a mother and two children in 1992. In the median state, the package was worth only 72 percent of the poverty threshold, and less than 50 percent in Alabama and Mississippi. Nor has this pattern varied significantly over the past decade. In fact, the real value of AFDC benefits was eroded by 40 percent from the mid-1970s to the late 1980s as states failed to adjust benefit levels to inflation.

Poverty has especially serious consequences for infants and toddlers. Children born into poor families are more likely to be premature, to have low birth weight, to die within the first year of life, and to experience more illnesses and health-related problems. They are more likely that others to be physically "stunted" (low height-for-age) or "wasted" (low-weight-for-height) and to suffer related learning and other school performance difficulties.[10] Their mothers are more likely to be depressed, and child develop-

**Table 2.5.** Families with a Child Under Age 3 as a Percentage of the AFDC Caseload in Selected Years

| Year | Percentage |
|------|-----------|
| 1979 | 42.2 |
| 1982 | 35.3 |
| 1983 | 38.3 |
| 1986 | 38.4 |
| 1987 | 38.9 |
| 1990 | 41.2 |

*Source:* U.S. House of Representatives, *Background Material on Programs Under the Jurisdiction of the Committee on Ways and Means* [later entitled: *The Green Book*], Washington, DC: Government Printing Office, 1982–1992.

**Table 2.6.** Children Under Age 3 as a Percentage of AFDC Recipient Children in Selected Years

| Year | Percentage |
|------|-----------|
| 1969 | 14.9 |
| 1975 | 16.5 |
| 1979 | 18.9 |
| 1986 | 21.9 |
| 1988 | 21.1 |
| 1990 | 24.2 |

*Source:* U.S. House of Representatives, *Background Material on Programs Under the Jurisdiction of the Committee on Ways and Means* [later entitled: *The Green Book*], Washington, DC: Government Printing Office, 1982–1992.

ment experts have found that maternal depression is closely linked to negative outcomes for children. Poor, young children are more likely to have higher rates of developmental delays and learning disabilities, to have inadequate home environments, to experience violence, and to live in disadvantaged neighborhoods, which then further exacerbate their other problems.

A University of Michigan study found that children who experience persistent poverty during the first five years of life have IQs that are 9.1 points lower (at age 5) than those of children who suffer no poverty during

that period.[11] Nor are the problems these children face the direct consequence of *welfare* dependency per se. Children of the *working* poor have
similar levels of health and behavior problems and nearly as many learning
problems as do children in AFDC families. The issue is *poverty*. Nor are
their problems the consequence of living in a mother-only family; more
than 40 percent of poor very young children live in husband/wife families.

Sandra and Sheldon Danziger, University of Michigan scholars, in citing
a number of studies reporting the negative consequences of poverty for
child well-being, note that child poverty would remain high even if there
had not been as great an increase in lone-mother families as occurred over
the last two decades, because child poverty rates also have increased for
children living in two-parent families. Indeed, the poverty rate for children
living in two-parent families in 1990 was higher than in 1968; and the
same is true for children living in lone-mother families. Child poverty rates
for the working poor have risen also.[12]

Donald Hernandez, Chief of the Marriage and Family Statistics Branch
in the Census Bureau, offers further insight with a report that notes that
although there has been much discussion about the impact of the increase
in one-parent, mother-only families on rising child poverty rates, there is
more to the story. Poverty also significantly increases the chances that two-
parent families will break up.[13]

As a result of stresses arising from low income and poverty, poor two-
parent families are about twice as likely to break up as nonpoor two-parent
families. Moreover, the probability of breakup as a result of poverty is even
more dramatic among black two-parent families than among whites. Poor
black families are about twice as likely to break up as nonpoor black families (21 percent versus 11 percent).

The Danzigers elaborate: Apart from the direct and indirect impact of
poverty on children, they note that poverty exacerbates the other problems
poor parents may have. Thus, for example, many poor parents live in
stressful situations characterized by marital conflict and/or social isolation.
According to the Danzigers, "Their lack of time, inability to pay attention
and address the child's needs, absorption with other family crises, etc., may
compromise their children's development."[14]

Some analysts note how difficult it is to be completely sure about how
the causal chain operates. For example, Isabel Sawhill, long-time Urban
Institute economist and now an official in the Clinton Administration,
finds that low income is associated with family instability, school and job-
market failure, and other problems. Increased income may improve school
success and raise birth weights. Nonetheless, she would argue that the
specific causal mechanisms are unclear; income may be a marker for other
things.[15] We conclude that whether as marker or as prime cause, poverty is
clearly implicated in a major way in children's problems and cannot be

ignored as solutions are explored (and perhaps as more precise causal patterns are slowly unraveled).

Mary Jo Bane, also a high-level official in the Clinton Administration, concurs on the basis of careful review of a group of studies using data from the Panel Study of Income Dynamics (PSID), a twenty-five-year longitudinal study of five thousand American families, and from the National Longitudinal Survey of Youth (NLSY), that looked at the effects of family background on children. She states ". . . in most of the good studies an income effect remains even after controlling most of the things that might be affected by services. Thus . . . children's lives are likely to be improved if children's families have more money."[16]

Finally, even if not poor, families with very young children are likely to be under severe economic pressures. The median income for families with very young children is about 20 percent lower than that of families with no children or with older children, either because there is only one wage-earner or because wages for young heads of households are low. These families, too, need help—something well understood throughout the rest of the industrialized world.

## Services For Care, Help, and Support

It is difficult to imagine how children might be assured a good start in the absence of good medical services for them and their mothers; or how working families with children could manage without child care; or where families who are isolated, deprived—or simply inexperienced and without information—would find needed advice or help in the absence of some family support resources. Here the debate, if any, is about the need for public provision or support, as compared with market or voluntary measures. The case also needs to be made, perhaps, that a money and market strategy alone—allowing people to purchase services—will not meet the need.

Something more should be said about the special problems, disabilities, risks, and individualized treatment and rehabilitative service needs of children facing particularly deprived and dangerous environments. Often their circumstances include poverty or low income, but not always. To explore the service question is to go across social classes and beyond "basic" services like medical care and child care.

For example, a growing number of children suffer from prenatal exposure to substance abuse and/or AIDS. The immediate consequences of substance abuse during a mother's pregnancy include infant mortality, low birth weight, persistent and severe developmental disturbances, and poor social development. The annual U.S. rate of drug-affected newborns more than quadrupled between 1979 and 1987 (from seven per ten thousand to thirty two per ten thousand). Although 17 percent of all children are under age 3, 20 percent of the children of mothers who used drugs in the past year and past month, as reported in surveys, are of that age. There is little debate as to the need for treatment-oriented services and other initiatives to reduce the use or abuse of substances that negatively affect or seriously endanger the fetus and newborn—or the daily lives of infants and toddlers.

Very young children also have a high risk of child abuse or severe neglect as a result of parental misbehavior (e.g., drug addiction) or inadequate parenting (by immature or uninformed parents). About five hundred thousand babies are born to teenage mothers (under age 20) each year, and the children are especially vulnerable to all sorts of problems. Sustained efforts at pregnancy prevention are especially critical here, as are educational and employment-training services and services to improve the parenting skills of the adolescents having babies.

With the increase in rates of reported child abuse and neglect (and despite relatively stable rates of postinvestigation substantiation), it should be no surprise that foster care placement rates for very young children have increased. What is astonishing, however, is that the dramatic rise in foster care placement in the late 1980s is accounted for *largely* by the increased placement rates for the very young.

Infant placements (children under one year of age) more than doubled between 1986 and 1991. Although infants constitute only a little more than 3 percent of all children in foster care, they constitute a far greater share of first admissions. Of particular concern, these babies are likely to be medically fragile—suffering from low birth weight, born addicted, or born HIV-infected—and to need extensive and expensive care.[17]

Wulczyn points out that the data make it very clear that the time between the onset of pregnancy and a child's first birthday is especially risky. Infants placed for protective reasons are in care largely because of maternal substance abuse, poor nutrition, and/or inadequate prenatal care. Once placed, infants tend to remain in foster care longer than older children.

Many families with very young children from all social groups experience stress just in trying to cope with everyday life. Some mothers are socially isolated, some are involved in marital conflict, and many are depressed. Others are desperately trying to balance job, home, family, and children, and often are distraught about inadequate child care or unaffordable care of decent quality. Services would not cure all their problems but might help.

In her 1992 review of the situation of young children and their families, Sawhill summarizes three approaches to improving children's lives: first is providing additional income to families with children; second is expanding service programs for children; and third is encouraging parental responsibility. She rejects the third strategy on the grounds that "no one knows how to fix the family." She recommends the first strategy, in a targeted form, and recommends the second strategy in the form of expanding a few carefully selected, proven, service programs.

The Danzigers also point out that if poor families had "greater access to high-quality services needed by all families in the health, education, and employment areas, the cycle of risk might be attenuated . . . Parents with severe economic stress might not as frequently pass on their distress if their children received better and earlier health care, were placed in quality child-care programs, and had access to school-enrichment and comprehensive employment and training opportunities."[18]

Lizbeth Schorr would add to all the above the importance of establishing supportive services for children and their parents as a strategy for reducing child abuse, neglect, and some family crises.[19] Important attributes of effective family support service programs, in her view, are that they be community-based, comprehensive, coordinated, culturally sensitive, and child-centered within a family context; that they be publicly subsidized; and that they sustain a balance between personal and societal responsibility. Others would argue as well the need for safe and secure housing, neighborhoods, and environments for child rearing.

Thus, the need for money *and* services.

## Time For Parenting

Many parents, especially working single mothers, are both money-poor and *time-poor*. Time is the third component of a strategy concerned with the under-threes.

The problem begins as soon as a child is born. Census Bureau expert Martin O'Connell points out that even more dramatic than the growth in the labor force participation of women during pregnancy has been their increasingly rapid return to work after childbirth.[20]

Europe provides a dramatic contrast. All new mothers appear to remain in the labor force, technically, because they are home on paid and job-protected leaves. Vacation time, sick leave, time to care for an ill child at home, and time for parenting a newborn are policies that are taken for granted throughout Europe, and in Canada as well, but not in the United States.

Close to 60 percent of U.S. married women with children under age 3 are in the labor force, as compared with 27 percent in 1970. Although only about 40 percent work full-time all year, 3 percent are looking for work at a given time, and the remainder work part-time. In the United States, more than half the mothers of infants are back at work before their children are one year old. One-third of children in the zero-to-three age group are in center care or family day care. One does not see nearly as many infants under six months of age in out-of-home care in Europe as one sees in U.S. child care facilities.

Clearly, women have less time for child care at home than previously; and single mothers have even less time. In 1975, this meant that working mothers spent about half as much time with their preschool-aged children as did their at-home sisters. Later studies found that there was no differ-ence in the amount of time working mothers spent with their school-aged children, but there was a difference with regard to preschool-aged children. Gershuny, in his research on changing patterns of time use, found that the primary child care activity of women declined by about one-third between 1965 and 1985, largely since 1975, as a result of increased labor force participation.[21]

These statistics reflect a complex situation. As Suzanne Bianchi notes, most mothers and fathers work more hours today to provide the same standard of living for their families than they did two decades ago.[22] As a result, they have less time for the care and nurturing of their children. Some of those working full-time would prefer to work part-time, but they either cannot afford the reduction in income or do not have the option. In contrast, others would like to work full-time but cannot find such a job. In any case, many parents have less time available for their families than earlier. Some—at a cost—give priority to protecting time with young children—with little societal support.

For families without adequate leave after childbirth, this is too little time for a parent to get started with a new baby. Then, in the toddler period, the effect of all this is that significant numbers of parents lack the time to manage household chores and to respond to their children's routine and special needs. The combination of balancing home-job-parenting, some-times with no partner and other times with a not-very-helpful partner, while at the same time managing with a tight budget, can be overwhelm-ing. For the single mother or father, parenting alone, without another set of hands, a sounding board, or a helpmate, can exacerbate an already stressful situation, increasing the pressure placed on children, or leading to inappropriate and insensitive parental behavior. Many households do not have relatives nearby who can assume caregiving responsibilities; few have family members or relatives living within the household, let alone a domes-tic servant.

Parental time thus becomes a problem for society, too, as does the question of services to help one manage and balance.

## Conclusion

We have pursued the question of whether countries can learn from the experiences of other countries and how this can be done. We also have noted the need to be sensitive to gender-related issues when developing a young-child policy strategy and agenda. In the next five chapters we explore what such an agenda might look like.

In Chapter 3 we turn to the components of an income strategy for families with very young children. In the subsequent chapters we look at a time strategy and at service strategies—health care, child care, and family support services. In the final chapter we present a young-child and family policy agenda for the United States.

In each of the following chapters, even as we elaborate on the inadequacies of the present U.S. policy response to critical aspects of young children's lives, we both highlight promising U.S. developments and draw upon European experience and exemplars. We identify, as well, the alternative strategies of focusing on high-risk, vulnerable children and their families, or on a more universal strategy, supplementing this with special attention to the more needy. We conclude with some estimates of the cost of what we propose. All of this is directed at the question: how can this society assure children a better start?

# 3

# Toward Economic Security

We begin with the family's economic underpinnings. Beyond—or perhaps, more accurately, before—parental leave, health care, and child care, families need money if they are to manage well with young children. Food, clothing, rent, transportation, as well as access to and use of services depend on having money. Some families do have adequate funds, earned at a job, or received from their own families (far less often), or provided as public "insurance" or "assistance" for a variety of reasons. Some families lack the usual sources, or the public supports received are inadequate. Their children may live in poverty.

We have already noted that in the United States the child poverty rates are higher for younger children. They are highest (24.3 percent in 1990) for the under-threes. Our own special tabulations also show that the U. S. under-three poverty rate is significantly higher than that in any of the six European countries with which we can make comparisons. We also have found that children under age 3 have comprised increasingly large proportions of our AFDC (public assistance) child caseloads over recent decades, constituting about a quarter of the load in 1991. And almost all AFDC clients live in poverty, given the low benefit levels.

It should be understood in reading these poverty rates that they are measurements taken after the workings of a country's tax and transfer (benefit) systems. Indeed, the pretax and pretransfer poverty rates, the rates generated by the market alone, do not at all show the United States' poverty to be out of line or in the lead. It is the U.S. government's failure to deal with poverty created in the marketplace that distinguishes us from the better-ranking European countries.

41

There is another relevant finding about these comparative data: the United States leads these countries in persistent child poverty as contrasted with brief spells. It takes little imagination to understand how much more important this is for the environment in which a child is to get its "start," its launching and send off. In the previous chapter we reported statistical evidence of some of the worst consequences. Family poverty is the best predictor of low birth weight, infant mortality, nutritional deficiencies with effects on physical growth and brain development, and also (with a less clear causal process) poor cognitive development and clusters of social problems such as child abuse/neglect and emotional difficulties. These factors in turn are associated with exposure to drugs, crime, and poor housing, and lead to lives that are neither happy for the individual nor productive from the society's point of view.

Despite the high poverty rates, most families, of course, are not living in poverty. But even families with incomes above the inevitably arbitrary and quite low "poverty" line often find it difficult to provide or acquire what children need to develop well and to fully participate in and become successful members of their societies. And it is the families with very young children that are far more likely to have limited resources than those with older children. In such families, diets may not meet the needs of growing infants and toddlers. Parents may lack or be constrained in use of medical care. Their child care choices may be unsatisfactory. Their incomes may not provide for comfort, for some needs, or for emergencies. Their children may live under deprivation or tension. And there are research indicators that infants and toddlers under tension show lasting effects. Therefore, some believe that since wages are not based on family size and structure, families with limited earnings—whether or not technically "poor"—also may need supplementary income based on the presence of a child or children. Perhaps all families with children need or should have such supplementation because children are an important cost for almost any family and a valued resource for a society. Perhaps all societies should see such investment as essential.

In this chapter we examine the question of publicly provided income in support of child rearing. We say relatively little about the current situation in the United States because this has already been discussed in earlier chapters. Our overview is offered in the context of international experience with child or family allowances, and child tax benefit systems. We subsequently discuss other forms of income supplementation, where it is conditioned by the presence of a child, not necessarily a child under age 3.

First, however, some comments about employment are in order. Earnings remain the primary source of income in industrial societies and are likely to continue in this role. Ours are market economies and the market-earned wage is essential to most citizens, either as the immediate source of money or as the basis of savings, investments, and social insurance entitlement. Therefore, any systematic consideration of incomes of families with young children perforce must concern itself with jobs, education, work training, and the related apparatus for recruitment and access. We already have mentioned the turning of U.S. welfare policy for single parents with children toward a work strategy. Beyond this, for the most part, we bypass the subject of employment as extraordinarily important but as requiring and receiving extensive attention by others, at a time of uncertain job futures for many in the context of a little-understood restructuring global economy. We focus here on specific benefits and concessions that assist families and children with their economic needs. For, as we have seen, there are many such families with insufficient funds or (short of public aid) no resources at all for their child rearing responsibilities.

## Child or Family Allowances and Tax Benefits

Although the details, including the financial significance to families, vary, all major industrial societies except the United States, and even many less-developed countries, supplement family incomes to take account of the costs of rearing children. Some eighty-two countries have such legislation. The historical roots of these measures have been diverse. They have included the employer or governmental desire to acknowledge the employee burden in support of large families, without accepting a general wage increase or enacting salaries that reflect family obligations, rather than the work done.

Some family allowances have been instruments of governmental population policy, aimed at encouraging births that otherwise might be avoided or postponed for financial reasons. The success of pronatalist efforts has been questionable, or certainly debatable (it seems possible to affect short-term fertility and *when* to have children, but not ultimate family size), yet family or child allowance (in usage, these are interchangeable terms) also persists for other than natalist purposes.

Countries have given up the ideologically attractive notion of relating wages to family needs, a policy that proved very complicated in the several countries that tried and the others that played with the idea. A family wage often was defined as one adequate for the employee-husband, an at-home wife, and two children. However, such a wage system creates many problems in a modern industrial economy in which wages must be related to productivity on one hand, and union priorities on the other. On a factory floor, a family wage may seem quite unfair. Nonetheless, several traditions that grew out of this history persist: family or child allowances may require workforce attachment (but far less frequently than they once did) and often are part of the social insurance system.[1]

The core child and family allowance philosophy and modern rationale, shared by many of the countries offering family allowances—many having begun after World War II—is this: Children are a societal good, a societal investment, rather a than only a private "consumption" pleasure for the individual family. The family economic situation is a major factor in how children fare and develop. Therefore, society should share some of the costs of child rearing as a matter of justice, solidarity, and societal self-interest.

Many countries study the "costs" of a child, although few in fact attempt to pick up much of the bill. Parents who have children continue to undertake a considerable, uncompensated expense everywhere. Child allowances supplement other income sources, they do not substitute for them. There is a range in generosity. In most countries, child allowances may bring the per-child equivalent of 5 to 10 percent of an average salary in a one-child family, more where there are several children. Some countries provide for more generous benefits. The allowance is almost always tax-free. Depending on the country and the particular policy, the grants can be very modest "token" amounts or, for low-income families with several children, very significant sums. A few countries have departed from the usual universalism philosophy connected with these allowances to target larger allowances on families with modest incomes or to limit benefits to the poor alone. The allowance is indexed according to the cost of living in a few countries, subject to annual review in most. Table 3.1 summarizes the allowance amounts at the end of 1992, translated by us into dollars.

The allowance paid in most countries consists of a uniform amount for every eligible child, regardless of the number of children in a family. However, some countries raise or lower the payment amount, depending on the ordinal position of the child, while others increase the allowance with a child's age. France, which is conducting a national campaign to encourage a "third" child, gives no allowance to the first and more to the third than to the second. Some countries supplement the basic allowance in some types of situations (single-parent families, handicapped children, the poor); some interpose a means or disability test for this purpose. Some countries, we will note, provide a supplement to families with a child under three. Special family allowances to assist with housing costs exist in some countries.

Eighteen is the most common cutoff age for the family allowance in Europe, but some countries continue only until the age that compulsory school ends, or, occasionally to age 25 or 27 if the "child" is in school (thus converting it into an educational stipend).

**Table 3.1.** Family Allowances, Selected Industrial Countries, 1991–1992[a] (Monthly Amounts in Dollars)[b]

| Country | Child's Ordinal Position | | | | Age and Other Supplements |
|---|---|---|---|---|---|
| | 1st | 2d | 3d | 4th | |
| Belgium (1992) (employer) | 71.40 | 140.10 | 208.99 | 208.99 | 6–2, 25.96 12–16, 40.24 over 16, 42.84 over 16, 49.33 (others) |
| Denmark (1992) | Flat rate, per child under 6, 102.55 7–17, 77.89 | | | | |
| Germany (1992) | 44.14 | 83.08[c] | 140.20 | 154.00 | |
| Finland (1992) | 81.62 | 92.10 | 114.18 | 143.84 | |
| France (1991) | —[d] | 114.62 | 277.71 | 433.69 | 10–15, 35.05 Over 15, 61.66 |
| Ireland (1992) | 27.26 | 27.26 | 27.26 | 27.26 | |
| Luxembourg[e] (1991) | 61.46 | 126.02 | 225.03 | 184.64 | 6–12, 15.00 Over 12, 45.25 |
| Netherlands[e] (1992) | 54.52 | 64.90 | 67.50 | 67.50 | |
| Norway (1992) | 136.95 | 143.55 | 162.53 | 170.90 | |
| Portugal (1992) | 16.30 | 16.30 | 24.45 | 24.45 | |
| United Kingdom (1992) | 77.89 | 61.01 | 61.01 | 61.01 | |

*Sources:* European Observatory on (of) National Family Policies, *National Family Policies in EC Countries, 1991* and *Trends and Developments in 1992* (W. Dumon and T. Nrielant) (Brussels: Commission of the European Communities, DGV, 1992 and 1994); Erika Neubauer et al., *Twelve Routes to Family Policy in the European Community* (in German) (Bonn: Ministry for Families and Seniors, 1993), 1: 274–6; Jonathan Bradshaw et al., *Support for Children: A Comparison of Arrangements in Fifteen Countries,* Department of Social Security, Research Report No. 21 (London: Her Majesty's Stationery Office, 1993), Appendix; Alfred J. Kahn and Sheila B. Kamerman, *Social Policy and the Under-3s: Six Case Studies* (New York: Columbia University School of Social Work, 1994).

[a]We include all EU countries plus Norway and Finland. Spain abolished its child allowance in March 1991. The Greek scheme is too complex to summarize in this type of table. Italy has a means-tested system with variations by occupational sectors.

*(Table 3.1 notes cont'd.)*

   [b] For standardization we relied mostly on EU analyses translated into European Currency Units, which we converted into dollars. In several instances we made direct conversion from country currency. There are variations among sources, depending on the month of reporting or the month for conversion rates, therefore all numbers should be regarded as ± 1 to 10 percent. Nor do these numbers signify the relative purchasing power of these currencies in their countries. For such considerations, see our Appendixes for 1991 and 1992 exchange rates and purchasing-power parities.

   [c] Germany has a two-tier family allowance system. Those above a relatively high threshold receive lower per-child benefits for second and subsequent children.

   [d] A "first" child in a French family receives no allowance. We show results for families with two, three, and four children.

   [e] In Luxembourg and the Netherlands, a child's allowance is affected by age, ordinal position, and number of children in a family. Herein we present a simplified schema.

A few countries still finance child allowances by employer contributions. Most, having by now separated eligibility from parental labor force status, finance the allowances out of general revenue.

Taxes offer an alternative or additional way to help with family income. For people above the tax threshold, a child-conditioned tax exemption is another way of transferring public resources. Some countries reduce taxes modestly in the presence of children, while others make significant tax deductions for children. In many countries (as in the United States) the exemption is worth more to the higher-income families with higher marginal tax rates. Bradshaw, in a recent fifteen-country, study identifies three significant patterns: countries that do not use the tax system at all to redistribute income in favor of couples with children (United Kingdom); countries that use the tax system to redistribute in favor of families with low income (Germany, Italy); and countries that use the tax system to redistribute in favor of higher-income families with children (Belgium, France, Germany, United States). Beyond this, in some countries—but by no means all—there are additional personal allowances for lone parents.[2]

A few countries use a refundable tax credit as a child allowance in lieu of a direct cash benefit (Israel). This can be an efficient mechanism that relies on the tax system rather than on a special social welfare agency. The Earned Income Tax Credit (EITC) in the United States, to be discussed subsequently, may be regarded as a modest example of this, applicable only to the working poor.

The country illustrations that follow specify the income supports that are cornerstones of child policy in some places and necessary—if more modest—foundations in some others. The United States lacks child or family allowances or refundable tax credits, except for EITC. Our Aid to Families with Dependent Children (AFDC), classified by Bradshaw as an income-related family allowance, compares per se not badly with similar

European Union grants, if one uses a relatively high-benefit state (New York), but here the "allowance" is not supplemented with the other income resources added in Europe, does not ensure adequate funds for housing rental,[3] and is limited to people in absolute poverty who usually remain in poverty despite the grant. The key point is that the European family allowance supplements income from other sources; AFDC is a subsitute source for what becomes the family's entire income for almost all recipients.

*France.* France's child policy reflects not only pro-natalism but also an ideology of compensation of families for the economic costs of child rearing, redistribution in favor of low-income families with children, protection of equality between families in which parents choose to work outside the home or to remain at home to rear children, and also a general determination to protect the well-being of children. While the political "right" has stressed pronatalism and the "left" social justice, all adopt the notion of "solidarity," and there is little interest on either side in wiping out the system of supports to which the various political blocs have contributed as they have been positioned to do so over the years.

As a result, family allowances are a major policy instrument in France, among the most generous in comparative perspective, and constitute a complex categorical system not readily grasped by the outsider. The most important part of the benefit, at the core, is the traditional basic and universal family allowance, but there also are a variety of income-tested categorical (usually taxable) supplements for orphans, children with handicaps, children under age 3, and single-parent families. Apart from the benefits to be mentioned in subsequent chapters (paid and job-protected maternity leaves for working women, allowances for pregnant mothers that are linked to prenatal care), the French family allowance system has given special attention to the under-threes, the age group in focus here, and to families with three or more children.

An allowance for young children (APJE), extending from the fourth month of pregnancy until three months after birth is provided to all families. A longer APJE, lasting until the child is three years old, is income-tested but carries an income ceiling that permits 80 percent of all families with a child under 3 to qualify, and was worth 11.5 percent of median wages (13 percent of median female wages) in 1989.

The APE, a child-rearing benefit, worth 40 percent of an average female wage in 1989, is available regardless of income, for up to three years, to working families with at least three children—one must be under age 3—if a working parent's work hours are reduced by half or more after the maternity leave.

A sense of the general importance and specific monetary worth of these cash family benefits in France is suggested by the following, referring to two-child families (children aged 9 months and 4 years, as of 1990, and including the effects of income tax credits as well:

Husband/wife family, with the mother at home: 28.5 percent added to median-wage income

Husband/wife family, mother in the labor force: 22.4 percent added to median-wage income

Single mother at home: receives 64 percent of a median wage

Single mother in the labor force: 35.5 percent added to median-wage income.

Also part of the family allowance system is the housing allowance scheme. Some 30 percent of all family allowance recipients receive this allowance, which significantly supplements family income, especially for low earners, large families, and single-parent families (see below).

France also has a family-oriented income tax system that provides for a kind of income-splitting among family members.

*Germany.* Germany offers families with children a universal child allowance, with payments increasing according to the ordinal position and involving somewhat more limited payments to a small group in the upper-income brackets. It is "middling" in the European Union in relative generosity. Thus, early in 1992, a monthly child allowance payment of DM 420, for a three-child family, roughly the equivalent of more than $250, represented a supplement of 9.4 percent of the average production worker's wage. For an average one-salary, one-child family, the supplement was worth only 1.6 percent.

Germany has a push-pull history, juxtaposing child tax benefits and child allowances, with the conservatives, when in office, favoring the former and the social democrats the latter, but neither attempting a clean sweep. Recent analyses show that if one adds tax benefits for children to the picture, the level of subsidy to parents below the tax threshold by means of child allowances and a small low-income supplement has been about equal to that provided middle- and upper-income families through the combination of tax benefits and child allowances. The tax benefit repertoire includes income-splitting, especially valuable to one-earner families, a deduction for those who employ in-home care for children under age 10, so that the second adult in the family may hold a job; and a home-building and renovation allowance for families with children.

Although Germany is not comparable to Sweden or France in child allowance generosity, and clearly biases its policies in favor of the traditional husband/wife family with a breadwinning father and a mother at home, recently it has begun to develop a constitutional doctrine about income support, which is of some interest. In 1990 the Federal Constitutional Court, ruling on a class-action petition from taxpayers who claimed deductions for child dependents were too low, supported the petitioners. The Court ruled, in effect, that if the social assistance grant is seen as a minimal maintenance standard for a child, parents not receiving social assistance have the right to similar basic help through tax benefits or child allowances. The government in 1991 raised child allowances and child-conditioned tax concessions to meet the Court's standard. Although one may probe and dispute the choice of the social assistance grant for a child as the support minimum, the principle apparently has been accepted, and the courts analyze consumption surveys in making their judgments. Other cases are waiting in the wings. A basic income guarantee for children may be developing and apparently would be consistent with constitutional philosophies.

*Finland.* Discussed under the European rubric of "equalization of burdens," Finland's child allowances are explicitly intended to ease the pressures that come with the added costs of raising children. Earlier, pronatalist concerns predominated, and they remain important for some. However, Finland's social welfare minister told a European ministerial meeting in 1987: "We have no population policy program. . . ."[4]

After some benefit declines in the 1950s to 1970s, interest revived and motivation shifted from the desire to head off a "family-needs" wage increase (as occurred much earlier in France) to a broader concern for enhanced child development through equalization of burdens. Most recently increased in 1991, child allowances are universal, tax-free, and increase in value with the child's ordinal position.

Also, unlike the situation in other European countries where conservatives tend to favor the tax-exemption route, while the center-left, left, and unions favor child allowances, Finland's conservative parties are advocates for child allowances. This perhaps derives from the important role of agrarian smallholder parties with a low-income constituency. Finland also includes child-conditioned tax benefits in its income tax system.

Finland gets the family started financially with its new child with a cash benefit of FiM 640 (or a package of child necessities)—worth $158 by exchange-rate calculation. Thus, the child allowance and the maternity-paternity-parental allowance, which are followed by the home caring allowance (Chapter 4) for a period in more than 80 percent of families, represent a considerable infusion of cash as part of the child's "good" start. These benefits represent about 17 percent of an average wage, to which can be added a supplement if there are siblings in the family. For low-income families, there also is a supplement, equal to almost 14 percent of an average wage—so that the combination of basic amount, sibling addition, and low-income supplement add up to about 30 percent of an average wage. Even this should not be exaggerated, however. Most child benefits are modest. According to one Finnish study, because of increased total consumption costs as a child grows, government cash benefits, tax deductions, and free services decline steadily as a proportion of the total cost of a child in an average family. When a child is age one and a half years old (according to this study), parents themselves cover 36 percent of the total costs of rearing a child. This increases to 70 percent by age 12 and to 84 percent by age 13. For our purposes, the 36 percent when a child is being given a "start" is of interest.[5] Recently a conservative government doubled the home care grant and dropped the income testing of the supplement—representing a cash addition for stay-at-home parents. Some cities also supplement this cash—as an alternative to building more child care centers.

*Britain.* Britain's child allowances have developed as part of an anti-poverty strategy. The core relevant benefit in Britain is what is called the child benefit, the current term for the child or family allowance. This is a universal, tax-free cash grant, paid until a child is aged 16 (or 19 if still in school). It is financed out of general revenue and (since 1992) is indexed according to wages. In United Kingdom, the benefit is paid to the mother and is thus discussed as a kind of mother's wage. Since 1991 the benefit has been higher for a first child (more than $900 annually, by current exchange rates) and has continued at a flat rate (more than $700) for all other children. It is also unique in its system of weekly payments (with a monthly option). In 1992 this benefit for a two-child, two-parent family was worth 6.5 percent of average male earnings. In European context, it compares well for one- or two-child families but not for larger ones (since a number of countries raise the benefit levels for subsequent children).

The British also pay a significant benefit supplement (more than $500 annually) for support of the first child in a single-parent family.

Low-income working families with children also may receive Family Credit, a modest wage supplement when the family head works full-time (defined as at least 24 hours for a man, and 16 hours for a woman in a lone-parent family). In some ways Family Credit reflects the United States' EITC but is more generous. In 1992 it was set at £41 weekly (about $70 by currency exchange rates) for a couple (or a sole adult head), £10.4 per child under age 11, and somewhat higher for older children. For a lone mother and two children, this benefit is equal to 33 percent of an average female wage. For a family headed by a couple, it totals 10 percent of an average male wage. As do all countries discussed herein, Britain offers additions to social insurance payments (pensions, unemployment assistance, disability pensions) on behalf of dependent children. However, because the child benefit was conceived as an integration of taxes and direct benefits, there are no longer tax exemptions for children in Britain.

Britain also has a means-tested safety-net program, Income Support, covering approximately the same territory occupied in the United States by AFDC, Supplemental Security Income (SSI) and General Assistance. However, Income Support is more generous than the American counterparts because it offers uniform national coverage and is seen as defining the poverty line. The benefit provided a two-parent family is equal to one-third of an average male wage.

It must be noted that child and family allowances and tax concessions do not solve the income problem for families without wage income or other public transfers (social insurance or public assistance). But they do add useful supplements for children to low wages and low transfers. Alone, they would not protect under-threes or older children, but along with other child-conditioned aid, they may make the difference between deprivation (or marginal getting by) and sustainable family economies for those with very young children. They also may make part-time work viable, thus protecting parenting time, especially for single mothers.

Next, we turn to other parts of a potential income package. As are most child allowances and most tax benefits, they should be understood by Americans as *nonwelfare* child and family policies.

## Advance Maintenance or Child Support Assurance

Separation or divorce of parents or birth by an unmarried mother who is not cohabiting with or supported by the father creates a very high risk of poverty. In a recent book[6] we are reminded that in the United States "over half of the next generation is likely to spend part of its childhood in single-mother families" and that "as many as half of these families will live in poverty. . . ." In 1993 approximately one in four children under age 18 lived in a single-parent home, and in many such homes there was either no support or inadequate support from a living nonresident parent. The regular Census Bureau survey of child support tells a good deal about mothers who do or do not collect support from absent fathers—but data about the children and their ages are not collected. However, it is obvious that many are under-threes because many of the mothers involved are young and unmarried.

In a series of reforms that began in the mid-1970s and aimed largely at increasing support payments by nonresident parents (usually fathers), the United States has been attempting to ensure that (1) each child's paternity is established, (2) absent parents are located, (3) courts order regular support contributions by the nonresident parent, (4) the support level be made adequate, when feasible, by creating a presumption that a state-established payment rate (percentage of wages or salary) be followed, and (5) collection rates are improved by virtue of better collection mechanisms, interstate cooperation, wage and other income withholding, and related measures.

Although Congressional interest in these matters derived initially from concern with "welfare" rolls, meaning AFDC, many nonwelfare mothers including middle-class and educated mothers called for help in collecting support. As a result, the improved mechanisms are available to all single parents. Indeed, the results—not surprisingly—are best for those who are not AFDC recipients. Over 70 percent of the collections in 1992 were not on behalf of AFDC recipients. Nonetheless, child support discussions and research in the United States are usually associated with "welfare reform" initiatives. To the extent that public welfare authorities or others have been able to achieve support payments by nonresident parents in these cases, the payments become reimbursement for AFDC grants. In 1991, 11.4 percent of AFDC payments were thus recovered.

Current support levels by nonresident parents leave many children destitute. More specifically (in 1990), approximately ten million mothers aged 15 and over were living with sixteen million children in households with absentee fathers. Of these ten million mothers, 58 percent (5.7 million) had been awarded child support payments by a court or through voluntary agreement. In part their poverty relates to nonpayment, inadequate payment, and perhaps lack of capacity to pay adequate—or even minimal—court-ordered child support. Only half the 5.7 million women who had been awarded child support collected it all. Of the other half, equal numbers received partial payment or nothing. The rate of court-support awards was 72 percent for women who had been married and 24 percent for the never-married. The average (mean) child support payment was $2,995. Of the 4.2 million women not awarded child support payments, only 22 percent did not want the award; the others could not obtain it for various reasons (64 percent) or were awaiting agreements or had made other arrangements (14 percent).[7] The awards and payments were significantly higher for nonpoor than for poor women, and for the white and college-educated than for members of minority groups and those with less education. The average payment for the divorced and separated was $3,268; for the never-married it was $1,888. The above-poverty women are more likely to receive awarded support than are the below-poverty women.[8]

A $2,000 or $3,000 annual per-child support payment is not insignificant in the budget of a low-income household. Indeed, it compares favorably with some of the child allowance values cited for several countries in the earlier section. However, $3,000 will not rear a child for a year and is far less than what an employed resident parent contributes to the support of a child each year. (It is less than 10 percent of what an average full-time male worker would earn.) And it is less than can be afforded by most nonresident spouses with employment. Therefore, it is sound social policy, as well as morally and socially desirable, to do all that can be done to assure that child support orders are written by courts whenever there are not adequate voluntary arrangements, and that such orders are adequate.

The federal policies have evolved in this direction. Important legislative requirements were added in 1988. States are developing strong guidelines as to the percentages of income that should be paid in support of one or more children, another federal requirement. (The Wisconsin standard, recommended by Garfinkel after considerable analysis, is 17 percent for one child and "25, 29, 31, and 34 percent, respectively, for two, three, four, and five or more children."[9]) Unfortunately, many states write the computed monetary value of the award (not the percentage) into the court order at the time it is issued, creating the problem of award erosion over time, through inflation. This is an important, but easily remedied, practice.

Federal law now provides for automatic withholding of the award from the salary of the absent spouse, and there is also the right to garnishment, liens, and seizures, as needed. All of this is backed by state support registers, new mandates and mechanisms (not yet fully effective) for interstate cooperation, and a variety of improved collection devices—none of which needs to be elaborated on herein, but included is a powerful Federal Parent Locator Service that has access to social security, tax, and other federal data bases.

We must focus on the big gap in all of this: what if the nonresident parent is unknown, unlocatable, or unable to provide any or adequate child support payments (even when wage withholding is instituted)? Here there are useful European precedents in what the Europeans call "advance maintenance"[10] and what Garfinkel and his colleagues have named "child support assurance" for the United States.[11] The central concept of advance maintenance is this: if for one of the reasons cited above, a nonresident parent does not pay ordered or agreed child support, a government agency pays a specified sum regularly. This is child support "insurance" or a guarantee, conceptually similar to other social security components. Society recognizes a "risk," in this instance the risk of growing up with one parent while the nonresident parent does not contribute to support. Government responds by providing a payment and attempting to recover the funds from the nonresident parent.

Beyond this core principle, there are many variations among the countries that have instituted such plans.[12] In some countries the agency involved is a court; in others it is an administrative body. In some countries government acts for all single-parent families; in others it is concerned only with low-income women. Other variations deal with whether a court order is required for the process to begin, whether the award considers only the children or the custodial parent as well, and whether the preoccupation is with public expenditures or with adequacy of support. Thus, some country guarantees are generous, some are minimal. Some provide payments whatever the family income; others are the equivalent of a public assistance payment, requiring a means test.

Our own concerns suggest the need for a focus on payment adequacy, consistency or regularity of payment, and elimination of any stigma. The objective of all proposed measures should be a "good start" for a child.

From among the countries that illustrate advance maintenance, we turn to Sweden and Denmark. Germany might be mentioned for a "low guarantee" plan at the level of welfare assistance.

*Sweden.* We begin with the most generous plan. Sweden's long-standing system, established in 1964, involves payments from the social insurance office following an application by the custodial parent (the mother in 85 to 90 percent of cases). The grant is not income-tested, is tax-free, and is equal to a set percentage of a reference wage (a hypothetical sum used in social insurance benefit-setting and designed in this instance to protect a child against the nonresident parent's nonpayment, low payment, or irregular payment). The benefit level is viewed as the equivalent of what one parent would contribute to support a child, or a little more. The full designated sum is paid by the government if there is no payment at all from the absent parent; the difference between the guarantee and what is paid is provided to all others.

Prior to the award of the payment, the mother must cooperate in the establishment of paternity. A social service unit in the hospital initiates the process, and paternity is established in 90 percent of cases, including the large number of unmarried but "permanent" cohabiting couples. The country's debt collection agency takes responsibility for collection of the advance from the nonresident parent. Payments are made voluntarily or through wage withholding. Child support is tax deductible to the payor (as is alimony to a spouse but *not* child support in the United States). The collection agency has been recovering about one-third of what is paid out in advance maintenance, but this is about 83 percent of the potentially collectible debt that the court has ordered. The rest is attributed to the fact that the public guarantee is far higher than typical court orders or voluntary agreements.

Payments continue if the custodial parent remarries or cohabits. According to the last available report, such payments were being made for 14 percent of Swedish children (a rate almost identical to that in Denmark). In a several-country comparison, our earlier research showed that single parents in Sweden were receiving advance-maintenance payments equal to 27 to 29 percent of an average production worker's wage (APWW). For a single mother with two children, not employed, the addition of the child allowance (12.4 percent of APWW), an income-tested housing allowance (21 percent of APWW), and a generous income tax policy brought her close to a net APWW without public assistance. If she worked to earn half an APWW, her after-tax income was about 125 percent of the net APWW.[13]

From the point of view of the child rearing-environment, Swedes and others find this type of income supplementation which keeps single-parent families out of poverty, free of means-tested public assistance, and living on a good standard, as most desirable. There is a problem currently recognized and due for correction, however. Because the public guarantee is high, and assured, the custodial parent is too-frequently willing to make a low voluntary support agreement with the nonresident parent if she (or he) does not foresee or want to demand a possible court award above the guarantee. In effect, if the agreement amount cannot be above the guarantee amount, the custodial parent has no incentive to keep the nonresident parent's payment high.

Courts on their own have tended to make modest awards in any case. The government guarantee picks up the rest, and the collection agency collects at a too-low ceiling. The public expenditure burden is considered too heavy. A number of correctives are under consideration, but none involves dropping the core advance-maintenance concept. One could conceive of solutions that could lower the guarantee to what people with adequate incomes can normally be expected to pay, as well as preclude deposit of voluntary support agreements without investigation of the means of the nonresident parent.

*Denmark.* Denmark, we have noted, pays advance maintenance to about the same proportion of its child population as does Sweden (15 percent). In Denmark's highly decentralized system, it is the local social welfare office that advances the standard child maintenance allowance and attempts to collect subsequently from the parent who owes support. This practice has a long history in Denmark, with eighteenth century roots, and is part of a successful Danish effort to protect children in lone-parent families economically, regardless of parental marital status. As in Sweden, these payments are integrated into the family allowance system and are not considered as income if there is application for social assistance or a means-tested rent subsidy. The benefits are taxable to the child, but few child incomes are above the tax threshold.

A series of paternity-establishment procedures begins with the physician and midwife, moves to the local social welfare authorities, continues with the office of the country governor, and moves to the courts as necessary. In practice, paternity is established in well over 80 percent of cases and with few court trials. Despite high out-of-wedlock birth totals, most children of unwed parents reside with their cohabiting biological parents. Parental child support obligations in marital and consensual unions are identical. If a consensual union breaks up, the support obligations are similar to those in divorce. Child maintenance must be paid until a child is eighteen, or twenty four if the child is still in school.

Parallel to the paternity establishment process, there are voluntary or administratively ordered arrangements for child support. If the mother does not request the support, the local social welfare authorities will. Most of the procedures are within the social welfare and county administration systems. Payment norms are set by the social welfare ministry and vary according to parental income and number of children. The point of departure is "the costs of having a child taken care of in a private home." Although in the twice-annual adjustments of this normative payment base over the years the connection to the actual cost has ended, the concept remains, as does the important notion that parents share the costs equally (since most women work) or almost equally (men earn somewhat more). The public guarantee protects the possible gap between the amount ensured and what is deemed payable at the given salary level.

The Danish guarantee is slightly below the Swedish, and as in Sweden, its full significance is seen only in the context of the sum total of child allowances, housing allowances, and other benefits. It, alone, would not support a child. Here, too, however, it is part of a solid package that protects the economic well-being of all children and keeps child poverty low.

The payment of child support in Denmark takes place once every six months—in advance—usually via deposit to the entitled parent's bank account. This fits a general Danish practice; most wages, salaries, family allowances, and social benefits are paid directly to bank accounts.

As the United States reforms child support, increased attention also is being paid to the issue of the establishment of paternity, part of the process everywhere, and vital to the under-threes. The 1988 federal legislation in the United States inaugurated a series of requirements and incentives to the states to establish paternity: financial penalties if high percentages of out-of-wedlock cases receiving AFDC or child support services are left with paternity not established; incentives to encourage genetic testing in contested cases at the request of either party; federal payment of 90 percent of laboratory costs in such cases; and a requirement that states obtain the social security numbers of both parents when the mother is in the hospital for childbirth. Paternity was established for 515,000 children in 1992 according to U.S. federal child support enforcement authorities, a considerable increase over earlier years.

While there are those who object to such measures, believing they constitute an invasion of privacy, we tend to see the lack of paternity establishment as trivializing a child's rights and as carrying undesirable financial and psychological consequences. It is highly questionable whether any society should permit depriving any child of paternity information throughout life if there is any possible way to avoid it. The Scandinavians, who have established the strongest paternity measures, are known, as well, as the most preoccupied with and recognized for leadership in children's rights.

We make one final comment about European exemplars in this section. The general question of learning from other countries has already been discussed. We should note here, as well, that the series of enacted U.S. child support reforms begun in 1975 and climaxed in 1988 were in fact planned with close attention to European (especially Swedish) precedents. There was direct and useful borrowing within the Congressional process. What has been left out of the borrowing thus far is something now actively discussed in the United States, almost tested in Wisconsin, and the subject of a small New York State experiment: child support assurance. It is an important gap.

## Cash Sickness Benefits

We defer for the next chapter the very important cash maternity and parenting benefits that characterize many countries. Here we turn to another closely related system, underdeveloped in this country.

The issue of insured basic medical coverage and its relationship to primary medical coverage for pregnant women and infants/toddlers is, as we write, on the national agenda (Chapter 5). Here we wish to call attention to a gap in social provision, which proposed health reforms will not address, and which can create income crises for families with young children. We refer to cash sickness benefits.

There are both European and American exemplars. Five U.S. states (Rhode Island, California, New Jersey, New York, and Hawaii) and Puerto Rico have temporary disability laws as part of their insurance systems. These laws, involving practically universal coverage of the workforce and a small per-worker payroll contribution (usually by the employee), provide a cash benefit for a disability period resulting from illness or other nonjob-connected disability, and usually at the level of unemployment insurance (about half the average wage). This cash benefit is essential for those whose illness or injury leaves them unable to meet the requirements for unemployment insurance, e.g., availability for work. Moreover, as discussed further in the next chapter, antidiscrimination amendments in 1978 made it illegal to preclude maternity-disability as a form of disability. These became the only American states with statutorily guaranteed income replacement in connection with maternity, usually eight to ten weeks.

Other workers are protected in the private sector by employer-provided sickness or disability coverage or by union-negotiated benefits that ensure a flow of income despite illness or injury. Most public employees have some city- or state-provided protection. A significant portion of the workforce, one-third is a good estimate,[14] lack any protection. Others have limited coverage. These are families in which the illness or injury of a working parent can lead to economic stress or crisis, which affects children too. After six months, in instances of prolonged problems, there is potential eligibility for long-term disability insurance under social security.

Foregoing detail, we note that *Italy* covers all employed workers in commerce and industry with cash sickness (and maternity) benefits, financed out of a small employee and larger employer payroll contribution. The sickness benefit covers 50 percent of earnings for the first twenty days, and two-thirds thereafter, with a reduction during hospitalization, but only if there are no dependents. This payment may extend for 180 days (and longer under special circumstances).

*Denmark's* cash sickness benefits are financed by the general pension contribution. The benefit is equal to 60 percent of average weekly earnings during the previous thirteen weeks and is payable for up to twenty-six weeks.

The *United Kingdom* provides for a sickness benefit and statutory sick pay in its national health service and social security legislation. The payroll deductions for pensions cover these benefits as well. The sickness benefit, available to those with adequate contributions, provides a modest flat-rate benefit for the insured plus a somewhat smaller sum for a dependent wife, husband, or other adult who looks after a dependent child or children. Statutory sick pay is paid by the employer to the employee, is geared to the earnings level, and is somewhat higher than the sickness benefit, but does not cover dependents.

*Finland's* cash sickness benefit program includes students among the employed and self-employed who are covered. The insured pay their share through a municipal tax, and employers through a payroll tax. Government finances the rest. The benefit involves an assured minimum—about 80 percent salary replacement for the average-wage earner, and lower replacement for high earners. After a seven-day waiting period, the sickness benefit is payable for up to three hundred workdays. There is also a child supplement.

*Sweden's* cash sickness allowance covers not only the gainfully employed but also, on a minimal level, most housewives and dependent husbands who join the system and pay a small, regular contribution. Costs for most of the system are met by an employer payroll contribution, supplemented by government. The employees do not contribute. The sickness benefit is expensive and was recently "reformed" to require a two-day wait because it was believed that people took frequent "sick" days with immediate benefit claims that could be avoided; the benefit is expensive. Perhaps the income loss on the first day or two would be a disincentive. The benefit now begins at 60 percent of earned income to a specified maximum for the first few days, rises to 80 percent of earnings through the ninetieth day, and then to 90 percent (which is what it was before the recent modest cutbacks). It is taxable. (This creates a coverage period for social security.) The payment continues for the duration of the illness.

*Germany's* sickness benefit system covers wage-earners, some self-employed (up to an annual earnings ceiling), apprentices, and unemployment beneficiaries. It is financed by employer and employee payroll contributions, excluding the lowest earners. All members of sickness funds (part of the mandated medical insurance administrative system) are covered for a benefit. The employer pays the full wage or salary for the first six weeks of illness (or after childbirth), and the sickness fund then pays 80 percent of covered earnings for as much as seventy-eight weeks in the course of three years, up to a modest weekly maximum.

*France's* sickness benefit involves membership in one of the special employee categorical or general social insurance systems and a payroll contribution. Pensioners, the unemployed, and trainees also pay set percentages of their regular allowances. Employers pay at a significantly higher percentage rate, in relation to the total payroll. A specified period of employment and coverage by insurance are also required. After a three-day waiting period, there is eligibility for up to twelve months of sickness benefit, involving replacement of one half to two-thirds of covered earnings, as the illness extends beyond thirty days. The higher rate is paid at once for families with three or more children. In cases of chronic or prolonged illness and related special qualifying conditions, the sickness benefit may be extended to three years.

Thus we return to that third of the U.S. workforce without cash income during sickness or temporary disability. We do not know precisely how many children are affected, but the numbers are certainly significant. Young workers, including the parents of young children, are less likely to be protected by existing benefit systems than are more established workers—again, an important infrastructure problem. It probably must remain off the agenda in the United States at this time, as the country debates and then reforms its medical care system. The recently enacted family leave legislation, discussed further in Chapter 5, is a potentially helpful beginning.

## Housing

Can one imagine a satisfactory life for a newborn, an infant, or a toddler if the family lacks a decent place to live?

The appearance in recent years within the United States homeless population of homeless *families*, usually involving mothers and young children, has shocked the American public. Such people usually lose housing because of difficulties in managing low AFDC grants, because of fires or problems in their housing, or because of a split with the relatives or parents with whom they shared space. They are not readily rehoused, in part because of supply problems at their low-income levels.

A parallel problem is more widespread. The nationwide housing cost inflation in the 1980s has pressed families with children who try to manage on limited incomes as decent housing consumes as much as half or more of their funds. Something gives—whether food, clothing, medical care—or the housing itself. They move "down" to what is affordable, even if it is inadequate or even dangerous for children.

In our modern urban economies, the economics of real estate or construction do not necessarily produce housing at costs all population elements can manage. In fact, in the United States in the 1980s, low-average earners could not afford housing being built in large cities. They depended—where available—on rent control, rent stabilization programs, or sharing—or they simply did not manage. One group of big-city residents also had public financial help, but far from all those who needed it.

The United States helps citizens meet their housing costs in two ways. Since World War II, and very much behind the growth of our suburbs, tax concessions in the form of deduction of mortgage interest and local property taxes have been of major assistance to middle-class and upper-income families. The interest deductions were protected even in 1986, when all other deductions for personal indebtedness were disallowed. These housing-related provisions accounted for $59.2 billion in tax expenditures (potential tax collections foregone), 23 percent of the total in 1994.

The second type of housing cost assistance that aids renters and homeowners is buttressed by another $5.8 billion in tax expenditures but depends in a more basic sense on federal, state, and local appropriations, usually intertwined, but heavily dependent on a federal base and often launched with relatively smaller but important voluntary-sector (again, tax-aided) contributions. Federal cash subsidies for these purposes (current dollars) were in the $20 to $30 billion range in the 1970s, between $8 and $14 billion annually between 1982 and 1990, and are now again at the $20 billion level.

The full repertoire in this second category has included rental assistance for very low income renters, whether through aid for project construction (including low-cost mortgage guarantees) or rehabilitation or household-based subsidies, and encompasses various programs, including public housing and help to low-income homeowners by long-term commitments to reduce their payments.

These programs involve many different statutes and a complex array of initiatives traceable to the New Deal, enriched by the Great Society, and cut back in the Reagan-Bush years. Inevitably, objectives, priorities, and preferred vehicles have changed. What has not changed is this: *housing assistance to low-income households "has never been provided as an entitlement to all households that qualify for aid."*[15] Coverage therefore depends on Congressional appropriations.

The sum total of coverage has been and remains modest. In 1993 some 5.7 million American households were subsidized either as renters (4.9 million households) or as homeowners (0.8 million). Although this does not include the large homeowner groups helped by the tax deductions, nobody believes that this is enough. Advocates are told that more cannot be afforded at this time, and there are some debates as to means. Legislation in 1990 created new block grants to states and localities to assist homeownership by lower-income families through a variety of flexible mechanisms, including assistance to nonprofit groups, cooperatives, and others. Some of the programs may address the special needs of the elderly, the mentally ill, or the homeless.[16]

Estimates of the numbers of homeless children in America have ranged from 35,000 to 40,000 using shelters on a given night, to 100,000 to 220,000 (Department of Education), to 500,000 (advocates). The children are disproportionately from single-parent and minority families. Millions of others are poorly or inadequately housed, whether in rural slums or urban ghettos.

While space considerations preclude country-specific detail, European housing allowance experience deserves attention. Among the countries discussed herein, France, Finland, Sweden, Germany, and the United Kingdom offer good illustrations. Denmark tends to rely more on the market and has a means-tested rent subsidy. Italy offers quite modest means-tested housing benefits to families with children.

The core idea of the housing allowance is simple: if families make a reasonable contribution to meeting their housing costs out of their own incomes from all sources, and if they rent or own standard housing, government will meet a share of the excess costs. The contribution from government is usually based on family size, income, housing costs, a concept of a fair share of income to be assigned to housing, and some requirements as to housing quality and amenities. All this is separate from what government may do to augment the housing supply through monetary and fiscal measures, construction of public housing, or the easing of the costs of mortgages.

Although some countries, one of which is Britain, also developed housing shortages and homelessness affecting single-parent families with children in the 1980s, the problem was not widespread. The countries with large numbers of impoverished refugees and illegal immigrants also experienced housing problems no less serious than those in the United States. However, in general, housing was not, by far, the large problem for families in the "housing allowance" countries that it is in the United States. Secured housing is by all evidence and calculation an important part of the infrastructure on which the social situations of families with young children rest. A recently completed multicountry study confirms the centrality of housing allowances and subsidies in helping differentiate countries that do well by families and children from those that do not.[17] Our own calculations in an earlier study demonstrate dramatically how, for families with very low incomes or families with several children, the housing allowance adds a significant component to income.[18]

For example, looking at the two lead countries that we studied earlier, depending on family types (single-parent or two-parent, few or many children, one or two earners or no earners), in Sweden in the 1980s housing allowances added between 17 and 30 percent of the APWW to family income, and combined with family allowances to constitute a total addition of between 30 and 56 percent of the APWW. In France, the housing allowance—for similar family types—ranged from 6.5 to 17.6 percent of the APWW, and combined with somewhat higher family allowances than in Sweden to constitute a total addition to family income of between 27 and 63 percent of the APWW. The specific numbers may have changed over the years, not (as the recent Bradshaw study showed) the principles and impacts.

Housing allowances are major policy tools in a strategy that supplements either earned income or social insurance benefits. Such allowances often make public assistance unnecessary. They are critical to the well-being of children.

The United States has such legislation on the books, but allowances are not an entitlement and appropriations are small. We record their value as a policy instrument, while not expecting them to be accorded short-term priority—at least on a significant scale—in the United States.

## Conclusion

Children cannot start right in life without some protection against the risk of being born into poverty or into families with grossly inadequate incomes. Their life chances would be enhanced further if the underpinnings could be somewhat above our very meager poverty line. Therefore, our recommendations must begin with the income question. (We have referred to the jobs issue as critical but beyond our immediate scope.)

World experience suggests that a child or family allowance, a monthly check by entitlement, is the proven method for societal sharing of a modest part of the cost of child rearing. Most recently, a number of U.S. policy analysts and a nonpartisan National Commission have proposed creation of a $1,000 refundable tax credit for all children through age 18, to be partially paid for by elimination of the personal exemption for dependent children in the income tax code.[19] The tax credit or a taxable family/child allowance are both sound mechanisms. The issue for the United States may be political attractiveness.

The argument against a universal child/family allowance is that it is an "inefficient" device: for people above the median income it adds little, yet for the society, costs can be high. However, this is an easily solved problem. The allowance can be taxable, and a portion will be recouped, at the family's marginal tax rate. For administrative economy, recipients might have the option of receiving monthly or quarterly checks and having direct bank deposits made, similar to the social security procedure. The advantage of the universal family allowance is that it is administratively simple and inexpensive and that the universality removes stigma, emphasizes the entitlement, and keeps child policy visible on the national agenda.

The refundable, indexed, tax credit mentioned from time to time over more than a decade by experts as a form of child allowance compatible with American cultural patterns was endorsed by the very visible statutory National Commission on Children in 1991, picked up by a number of political leaders (some of whom suggested benefits of less than $1,000 per child), and then dropped from public view as the Congress began to wrestle with the problem of a slow-growth economy and a large budget deficit. A $1,000 per-child tax credit would cost about $65 billion, only $21 billion of which would be recouped by eliminating the current dependent exemption for children in the income tax code. Nonetheless, the proposal has considerable merit, and it was offered with rich analytic detail and specificity.[20] It can and should be revived quickly, as soon as circumstances support new initiatives.

A strong argument can be made to the effect that the present costly dependent exemptions for children in the income tax system are of greatest benefit to high-income families (at the highest marginal tax rates), who need the resources least. Low earners, or "no" earners, have low or no tax eligibility, and the dependent exemption is "wasted." The 1992 personal exemption of $2,300 was in fact worth $713 to a family in the 31-percent tax bracket and $345 in the 15-percent bracket. A tax credit, in contrast, benefits people with tax liabilities; the low earners gain proportionately most. A refundable credit ensures payment to families below the tax threshold; the credit is *not* "wasted." As put by the Commission:

> It would substantially benefit hard-pressed single and married parents raising children. It could also help middle-income employed parents struggling to afford high-quality child care. Moreover, because it is neutral toward family structure and mother's employment, it would not

discourage the formation of two-parent or single-earner families in which
one parent chooses to stay at home and care for the children."[21]

Of course $1,000—or whatever the likely allowance or credit—does not
constitute a family income. Like family allowances in Europe, it could be
an important supplement to wages or other income assistance entitlements
for families with children.

Thus, it would still be important for current and potential AFDC recipients that the Family Support Act of 1988 be implemented well and improved. More funds are needed for the JOBS program, the work-training,
education, and referral activities designed to help a maximum number of
eligible parents become self-supporting. Federal budgets have been too
low and state take-up constrained by their "matching" costs. The effort was
further depressed by a job-recession environment, but prospects are improving.

Moreover, more effort must be made to open these job preparation and
placement activities as they are upgraded, to mothers of the under-threes
who do not want to mark time before training or returning to work. They
should have both the "at-home" and the work options of nonwelfare parents while their children are infants—and perhaps toddlers.

As we write, the Congress is at work on a welfare reform measure
initiated by the President, but its passage does not appear imminent. If
financing obstacles can be overcome, the JOBS program in fact will be
expanded and improved, as will child care services, and there will be stricter
requirements for recipient participation. An effort will be made to enforce
a two-year cutoff of these revised "welfare" supports. However, we assume
that Administration and Congressional leadership—even those with apparent punitive impulses— will not enforce cutoffs when there simply are no
jobs for "good faith" applicants—or for those not able to enter the
workforce because of personal unsuitability or because they have babies so
young that Europeans finance their care by at-home parents on parental
leave and regard this as sound child development (see Chapter 5). To allow
some states on waivers of federal regulatons to refuse food budgets for
second or subsequent out-of-wedlock children—as the most punitive of
advocates urge—is completly immoral. If the parents are deemed incapable
of rearing children, neglect proceedings are in order. If such actions are not
taken because parents are not neglectful, children should remain in a home
with sufficient funds to feed them.

No serious analyst of the welfare caseloads believes that all recipient
mothers or fathers are potential students, or job trainees, or placement
candidates, even when children are over two or three. Some AFDC caretakers are truly unemployable or beyond employment, or earn too low
wages, yet merit public assistance if deemed competent to raise their children. For such mothers/fathers, with no option but AFDC, it is uncon-

scionable to continue with AFDC grant levels as low and as inequitable as they currently are. In Janurary 1993 the combined AFDC and food stamp monthly benefit levels for a mother and two children were:

$456 in Alabama (49 percent of the poverty threshold)

$412 in Mississippi (44 percent of the poverty threshold)

$477 in Tennessee (51 percent of the poverty threshold)

$476 in Texas (51 percent of the poverty threshold)

$496 in Arkansas (53 percent of the poverty threshold)

The high totals at the same time were:

$1,191 in Alaska (102 percent of the poverty threshold)

$826 in California (89 percent of the poverty threshold)

$866 in Connecticut (93 percent of the poverty threshold)

$1,104 in Hawaii (103 percent of the poverty threshold)

$762 in Minnesota (82 percent of the poverty threshold)

$809 in New York City (87 percent of the poverty threshold)

The national state median combined AFDC/food stamp grant was $652 for such families, or 70 percent of the poverty threshold.

Thus, even as we move to create tax credits or child allowances, we need to federalize AFDC (as we did Supplementary Security Income [SSI] for the aged, blind, and disabled in 1974) and to establish a national minimum grant, combining AFDC and food stamps, at least at the poverty line. Thus, the combination of tax credit and child allowance would help make either low-pay jobs or AFDC living almost financially viable for families with under-threes. More will be needed, however, particularly medical care, access to child care, and probably housing assistance. Unfortunately, as we write, despite much talk of "welfare reform," there is no widely backed proposal for upgraded benefits.

Also important to the living standards of pregnant mothers and their infants/toddlers is the WIC (Women, Infants and Children) special supplementary food program. Available to those deemed to have inadequate income and to be at nutritional risk, the program offers a valuable food "package" whose impacts have been validated in a series of studies. (It was worth $31.63 per month in 1991.) Eligibility is at 185 percent of the poverty line (with some state variations permitted). With coverage at about 67 percent and 1994 costs of $3.2 billion, there is every evidence that a modest addition could hold important benefits for infants, toddlers, and pregnant women. Full funding would add one million women and children to the current 5.9 million receipients. Urban Institute researchers estimate this would include one-fourth of all children under age 4.

For low earners, those who are the lucky escapees from AFDC via its JOBS program, and for the unskilled or irregular workers in general, even minimum-wage work must pay or offer access to enough cash and services to exceed the public assistance level. This means medical coverage, an improved minimum wage, and the recently improved EITC. The latter program, begun very modestly in 1975, recently has been upgraded somewhat and already (1994) reaches 17 percent of families with children. It offers a refundable tax credit to low earners in a selective (indexed) income band, with a taper below and above that band. When 1993 changes are fully implemented in 1996, the band (expressed in 1994 dollars) will cover the earnings range between $8,425 and $11,000, and the credit will then equal $3,370 for a family with two or more children. Earners will have a credit equal to 40 percent of their earnings, with the rate declining after the $11,000 threshold. (It would be as though one's hourly pay rate increases from $4.25 to almost $6.00.) However, there will be some credit until the $27,000 level. This is a significant income aid for the working poor. In fact, if the minimum wage also were to be raised and indexed, a proposal by the Administration, minimum-wage earners would remain above the poverty line.

A child tax credit or child allowance, the EITC, and an improved minimum wage—all of which would be added to basic earnings—fit the Clinton Administration objective of "making work pay" and, thus, making it more attractive than long-term dependence on public assistance. We see these nonwelfare income supplementation devices as having broader implications than cutting welfare, however. They will buttress family earnings or low public benefits so as to change the economic and moral context into which children are born. Of this list, only the *child tax credit* or *child allowance* derives inspiration, if not its specifics, from Europe. Two other programs, both with European precedents already mentioned, should be added to round out the picture.

First, progress has been made recently in child support enforcement (see above). Here our gap—which affects many children in single-parent families—is a government guarantee. The Europeans have demonstrated the value, *not* as a welfare measure, of an advance-maintenance payment. This government guarantee becomes available if court-ordered support is not paid, or is paid irregularly or at an inadequate level. Proposals for a U.S. equivalent, here called "child support assurance," are convincing and urgent.

Another measure in the *nonwelfare* class of benefits is the *housing allowance*, as described earlier in this chapter. This country studied the idea in a well-controlled evaluation, which produced positive but modest results.[22] Conservative and progressive public officials have endorsed it. The Reagan administration implemented it, but only on a small scale. Appropriations were and are very modest for what should be an entitlement, when it can be afforded. The European record shows that it can be a targeted and effective instrument with major impact. It is essential entitlement in a world in which the building construction and real estate markets do not produce standard affordable housing for moderate- and low-income families.

These are the urgent underpinnings that could convert many families currently under economic stress into good environments prepared to greet new children:

A child tax credit or a child/family allowance

An improved EITC

Child support assurance

A federalized AFDC program with a higher, indexed minimum benefit

Greater access to the JOBS program for parents of toddlers

An increased WIC appropriation

A housing allowance

We sum up and suggest immediate priorities in the final chapter.

# 4

## Time For Parenting

Successful child rearing requires time; especially for infants and toddlers, time is an important component of nourishment. The parent and child need the time to start together. Child development is an interpersonal process, and at the very beginning the mother and child gradually learn to relate to one another; the process involves time and patience. The ongoing caretaker, mother or father, needs time for feeding, for physical care, to learn to understand signals, to respond, and to talk. A newborn is best protected physically and developmentally if its early months are at home with a parent or other consistent caregiver. A mother needs time for physical recovery after pregnancy and childbirth. Later, there is the joint experience in relating to others, in taking "trips" out of the home, in the transition to new foods, and in "visits" with the nurse and doctor.

We have argued that starting right requires money and basic supports. It also is premised on time—yet American children are spending less time with their parents. In 1965 the average child spent about 30 hours per week interacting with a parent; by the late 1980s this figure had dropped to about 17 hours. According to economists Haveman and Wolfe, this constitutes a decline in one type of investment that parents make in their children.[1] It is largely a result of increased labor force participation by the parents—in particular, their mothers—who previously were at home, caring for and interacting with them. A second major factor is the growth in single-parent households: the working single parent juggles a complex schedule and is inevitably time-poor.

On the other hand, real family income has been sustained over the same period largely through the increased labor force participation of mothers, especially married mothers. Haveman and Wolfe also remind us that policies designed to raise family income by increasing parental employment also are important instruments for investing in children, providing economic resources, increased self-esteem, and the independence associated with employment. In effect there is a trade-off for parents and children between adequate income and adequate time, with each having consequences for child well-being.[2]

To repeat a figure mentioned earlier, labor force participation rates in the United States for women with a child under age 3 rose from 27 percent in 1970 (26 percent for married women, and 44 percent for single mothers) to 54 percent in 1993 (almost 58 percent for wives, but still 44 percent for single mothers). More than 70 percent of all American women aged 20 to 54 now work outside the home, and almost three-quarters of all husband/wife families include two wage-earners, both husband and wife. Divorced women have the highest labor force participation rates, young never-married mothers have the lowest rates; but overall, the rates for single mothers have increased only slightly over the last few decades, while those for married mothers rose dramatically. Of particular importance, median family incomes in 1991 of families with working wives were about 60 percent higher than those of families with at-home wives.

Given, on one hand, the importance of family income and parents' earnings for child well-being and, on the other, the concomitant negative consequences for the availability of parental time for children when parents work in the paid labor force, how is society to resolve the apparent conflict? Clearly, one strategy is to protect parents' time with their children at critical points, and to protect family income at such times as well.

The first and most critical point when children need access to parents' time, yet need to be protected against the family's loss of income, is at the time of childbirth (or adoption). What happens now at the time of pregnancy and childbirth? Women's work patterns during pregnancy and after childbirth have changed dramatically since the early 1960s.[3] The proportion of women working during their first pregnancy increased from 44 percent in the early 1960s to 65 percent in the early 1980s. Women continuing to work during the last trimester of their pregnancy increased from 52 percent to 78 percent during the same period, and almost 90 percent of the women who worked during their pregnancy in the 1980s worked full-time.

Employment before pregnancy is the strongest predictor of work during pregnancy, and as we have seen, the vast majority of women today are working before becoming pregnant. (Only teenage mothers are not following that pattern.) Employment during pregnancy is the strongest predictor of working soon after childbirth. About three-quarters of the women who gave birth during the 1980s and worked during their pregnancies were back at work before their child was six months old, in contrast to about 17 percent who gave birth in the 1960s.

The availability of a job-protected leave—in particular if it is a paid leave—is still another very strong predictor of rapid return to work after childbirth. About two-thirds of working women were entitled to a job-protected leave following childbirth in the 1980s (47 percent as a matter of formal policy, and 20 percent by informal agreement); about half of these were fully paid. Close to 75 percent of these women were back at work within six months after childbirth.

Given this changed pattern of working during pregnancy and shortly after childbirth, it is the availability of a job-protected and paid leave following childbirth that is most essential if mothers are to have the opportunity to recover physically from the childbirth experience and if parents are to have time to provide care and nurture to an infant, to have the family's economic security protected, and to be assured of employment continuity. And it is the availability of good-quality, affordable child care when the leave ends that is also essential if employment is to continue to be an option for women with very young children (see Chapter 6).

Yet if most Americans seem in favor of child care for four and five-year-olds, and accepting of out-of-home care for three-year-olds when parents work, the debate takes on a different cast for the very youngest children, particularly infants under one year of age. Experts continue to debate the developmental effects on infants of out-of-home care. Some researchers find that some infants in full-time care display behavioral characteristics in interactions with their mothers (anxious-avoidant attachment) that could be a cause for concern. Other equally reputable researchers do not find negative effects or interpret the infant behavior as constructively adaptive. Reviewing the research, a 1990 National Academy of Sciences report concludes there are "unresolved questions concerning full-time care (more than twenty hours a week) in the first year of life."[4] While all concerned urge further research, the consensus is that, in any case, mothers should have a "financed" opportunity to remain at home for at least six months or a year. Beyond that, culture, personality, family preferences—and family economic considerations—will take over.

Some parents are guided by scientific findings, others by traditions, instinct, or family plans. Whatever the decision mode, the case for another component of child caring policy is strengthened: the option of a paid and job-protected parental leave.

Indeed, given the deep moral differences among Americans in their views of proper modes of infant and toddler care, as well as the cost of launching new family policies, it probably will not be possible or desirable to arrive at a single uniform policy about child rearing. In the United

States, child policy will have to provide choices. But real choices are precisely what many American parents currently do not have, particularly with respect to infants and toddlers.

## Maternity And Parental Leaves

The concept of a job-protected maternity leave is not new, nor does it date from the increase in female labor force participation over the last two to three decades in the western industrialized countries. Bismark first established a paid maternity leave for working women more than a century ago, along with old-age pensions and paid sickness benefits. Soon after the close of World War I, an International Labour Office (ILO) convention was adopted, recommending a minimum standard of twelve weeks' maternity leave, six weeks before birth and six weeks after; later this recommendation was extended to fourteen weeks, including eight weeks after birth. By 1919, the year of the ILO convention, Britain, France, and Italy in addition to Germany had already established similar policies, and other countries followed soon after. By World War II almost all the western industrialized countries had such policies in place, and by the late 1980s more than 100 countries, including many less-developed ones, did so as well. Among the major countries, only the United States remained without such a policy.

The European policies began with a focus on protecting the health of working women (in a sense defining "maternity disability" as a social risk, beyond the control of a working woman). Only after about half a century, with the dramatic rise in female employment, were these maternity policies gradually transformed into policies concerned as well with parenting, child rearing, and child development.

Clearly, with rapidly increasing rates of employment among women with very young children, either subsidized infant and toddler care or subsidized leaves from work would have to be put in place. In several countries, recognition of the high costs of decent infant care coupled with concerns about the consequences of out-of-home care for infants, led to a move toward longer "parental" leaves (available to mothers or fathers). Several eastern and central European countries established a policy following a Hungarian innovation—an extended leave after the basic maternity leave, paid for at a low, flat rate, for working women who remained at home to care for their young child well beyond the period of maternity "disability." Sweden initiated an alternative, a gender-neutral "parent insurance" benefit, paid as a wage-related social insurance benefit, replacing all or most of the parent's wage and available either to cover a period of full-time leave from work or to make an extended period of part-time work viable without financial loss. In the course of the 1970s, all the Nordic countries followed the Swedish pattern, at least in part. In the 1980s, Germany and Austria followed the Central European model, now, however, a gender-neutral parental policy as well. Balancing work and family life became a major family policy theme in the 1980s, and more extensive and varied parental leave policies were the result.

Historically, in the United States, the most common maternity policy was for employers to discharge their pregnant female employees; indeed, only in the 1950s were such employees likely to be rehired some time after birth. While other nations moved quickly to develop maternity protection policies, the United States remained without any federal statutory provision until the limited enactments of 1978 and 1993; and only modest provisions existed in some states. Most maternity benefits in the United States were either the product of collective bargaining, or were voluntarily provided by employers, or derived from statutory short-term (temporary) disability benefits (TDI) provided in the five states with such laws (New York, New Jersey, Rhode Island, Hawaii, and California).

Like the European countries, the United States focused first on the period of maternity "disability"—the period during pregnancy and after childbirth when women were physically "disabled." However, unlike the European developments, U.S. policy focused on the prohibition of discrimination in the provision of employment-related fringe benefits rather than on protecting the health of mothers and babies. The first U.S. law establishing a maternity-related policy was the Pregnancy Disability Act of 1978 (Title VII of the 1964 Civil Rights Act as amended in 1978). Defining pregnancy as a disability, this law required employers to treat pregnancy in the same way as any other temporary disability for all employment purposes. While employers were not required to provide maternity-disability benefits to their employees, any employer who did provide disability benefits had to cover pregnancy and childbirth as well; this provision thus established coverage for all employed women in the five TDI states. In effect, the law established an employment standard regarding equitable access to benefits. Almost inevitably, the next step was to move toward making this standard apply to most women workers and not to limit it to women.

The first law covering parental leave as well as family leave and medical (sickness) leave was introduced into Congress in 1985, referred to firms with at least fifteen employees (the same standard as the 1964 Civil Rights legislation), and provided for a twenty-six-week leave. Failing to pass, the law was reintroduced in 1987 and then modified so that it applied only to larger firms and to a shorter leave. It was reintroduced in 1989 and finally passed in both houses of Congress in 1990, only to be vetoed by President George Bush. In 1992 it was reintroduced again, passed again, and again vetoed. With a new President and a new administration, finally, in 1993, it was passed and signed into law by President Bill Clinton, an important if largely symbolic act of the new administration. It is worth noting that by that time, affected by the debate and public attention, about half the states had already passed similar bills.

Why was it so difficult to enact a bill that some considered largely symbolic and many were convinced was inadequate without a cash benefit replacing at least some of the wages foregone? The main argument of opponents was ideological. Some employers objected to any form of "government interference," despite the various forms of regulations on business (including unemployment insurance) that already existed, and despite the prevalence of such policies in the rest of the world. Some argued that labor costs would rise—at a time when the United States was finding it increasingly difficult to compete with developing countries because of their lower labor costs. Small businesses were especially impassioned in their objections. Others argued that, without wage replacement, it was a "yuppie" bill, designed to help middle-class and professional women but not low-wage working women.

The advocates, of course, took a different stance. They argued, first, that given current social and demographic trends—and the international developments—a job-protected leave at the time of childbirth, adoption, or individual illness, was the least that could be provided. Some researchers pointed to findings that showed that working women bore the heaviest costs of the current policy in job and income loss; indeed, their costs were far heavier than the costs to employers of the proposed policy.[5] Other researchers found that most employers in the states that already had parental- or family-leave policies had experienced neither significant financial costs nor any other problems as a result. The Government Accounting Office (GAO) estimated that the costs to employers would be far less than employers' organizations were projecting, only about $7.00 an employee, per year, a mere 2 percent of the Chamber of Commerce's estimate.[6] Finally, in response to those who accused the proposed bill of "yuppie" attributes, researchers showed that, in fact, workers without job-protected leaves were the most likely to experience unemployment; and low-wage, low-skilled, part-time, and young workers were the most likely to benefit from a statutory policy.[7]

The U.S. Family and Medical Leave Act (FMLA), enacted in 1993, requires private-sector employers of fifty or more employees, and public agencies, to provide up to twelve weeks of unpaid, job-protected leave to eligible employees for certain family and medical reasons. The leave includes protection of seniority and fringe benefits in addition to job protection. Employees are "eligible" if they have worked for a covered employer for at least one year, and for 1,250 hours during the previous twelve months, and if there are at least fifty employees working for the company within seventy five miles. An employer must grant such a leave to an eligible employee for one or more of the following reasons: for the care of the employee's child (birth, adoption, or foster care); for the care of the employee's spouse, child, or parent, who has a serious health condition; or, for a serious health condition that makes the employee unable to perform his/her job.

It is the first reason, and part of the second (leave to care for an ill child), that are in focus here. The "package" of other components grew out of political coalition building.

The major limitation of the new U.S. policy, of course, is the absence of a cash benefit while on leave. Another limitation is the exclusion of employees of "small" employers, and the definition of "small" in this context would exclude about half of all employed American women. According to estimates of the GAO, the small business exemptions incorporated into the FMLA eliminate significant percentages of employers and employees from the FMLA. Thus, for example, the GAO analyses found that the various thresholds have different impacts (Table 4.1).[8]

At the end of the 1980s, it was estimated that, as a result of existing policies, agreements, and mandates, about 44 to 47 percent of working women were covered by a paid and job-protected maternity-disability leave, involving about eight to ten weeks from the time of childbirth.[9] Many leading child development scholars have recommended the establishment of a statutory (unpaid) parental leave policy covering six months. The 1991 National Commission on Children could not even agree on this minimum standard. A 1990 National Academy of Science panel of experts recommended one year, half of which should be partly paid. The more recent report from the Carnegie Task Force on Meeting the Needs of Young Children urged that the FMLA act be broadened to cover smaller firms, be extended to four or six months, and that there be wage replacement for at least part of the time.[10]

How do the U.S. policy and the above recommendations compare with the European reality?

**Table 4.1** Relationships of Firm Size to Employee Coverage

| Firm-Size Threshold (No. of Employees) | Percentage of Employees Covered | Percentage of Employers Exempt |
|---|---|---|
| 15 | 71 | 82 |
| 20 | 47 | 88 |
| 35 | 43 | 92 |
| 50 | 39 | 95 |

## Parenting Policies Internationally

The parameters are set by the European Union (EU) to the east, and Canada to the north. A 1990 EU (then EC) directive sets a minimum standard and requires that women workers be entitled to at least sixteen weeks' job-protected leave at the time of childbirth (with seniority and benefits protected), including up to two weeks before anticipated birth; that the leave be an "entitlement" (a right) but not an "obligation" (the decision to take the leave is up to the woman, it is not a required leave); that women qualify if they have been employed, or were registered as unemployed, since the beginning of their pregnancy; and that while on leave they receive a benefit equal to at least 80 percent of their wage.

Canada, our neighbor to the north, has a maternity (birth), parental (birth or adoption), and medical leave benefit paid for through its unemployment insurance system. The job-protected maternity leave covers up to seventeen weeks at the time of childbirth, beginning as early as eight weeks before birth and ending no later than seventeen weeks after birth. A cash benefit equal to 60 percent of wages (up to a ceiling) can be paid for fifteen weeks to qualified working women. Eligibility criteria include having worked for at least twenty weeks at the time of taking the leave (or having been on unemployment insurance). Parental leave extends the maternity leave by an additional ten weeks. Parental benefits (also at 60 percent of wages) can be collected by both natural and adoptive parents while they are home caring for a newborn or adopted child. The maximum of ten weeks' benefits can be received by one parent or divided between the two if both parents are eligible. For handicapped children or those with special needs, the leave and the benefits may be extended by another five weeks. In effect, biological parents are entitled to a twenty-seven-week job-protected leave following childbirth, and twenty-five weeks are paid; adoptive parents are entitled to a paid and job-protected leave of ten weeks. (Sickness benefits are provided on the same basis, for a maximum of fifteen weeks.)

The modal European policy is even more generous. The takeoff points for new parenting policies in Europe vary depending on the country, as do the specifics, but all seem to share a common goal: support for parental care for very young children at home for some time following childbirth.[11] This involves provision of financial support to make a period of parental care possible. The Europeans seem to be moving toward a policy package that defines infant care as care by a parent who is home on a paid and job-protected leave from his or her job for all or most of the first year following childbirth, and a menu of policy options for toddler care (care of one to two year olds) (see Chapter 6). The components of the policy package vary significantly in detail but include, to some degree, the following core elements:

*A basic benefit:* a paid, job-protected leave lasting six months (average) but ranging from a three- to four-month maternity (disability) leave to a one-year parental leave, depending on the country

*An extended or supplementary job-protected parental leave* for an additional six months or for a period up to the child's third birthday, paid as either an earnings-related cash benefit or a modest flat-rate benefit, designed either to acknowledge the value of family work and child rearing or to compensate for an inadequate supply of infant/toddler care services, or both

*The right to work part time* for some time after the postchildbirth leave ends, or perhaps also during the extended parental leave

In addition, all the countries provide full health service or insurance to cover prenatal care, maternity hospital and medical care, postnatal care for the mother, and sick and well-baby care for the child (see Chapter 5). All the countries provide, in varying amounts, subsidized child care services (Chapter 6). And in almost all the countries, the postchildbirth leave applies in cases of adoption as well (See Table 4.2).

A few country-specific illustrations of the leave policies and the related cash benefits follow.

A *German* working mother is entitled to a fourteen-week, fully paid, job-protected leave at the time of childbirth, six weeks before birth and eight weeks after. A German parent (overwhelmingly a mother), regardless of prior employment status, also may stay at home for up to three years after childbirth. The mother/parent may work up to half time (up to 20 hours a week) while on leave (for the original employer or, with that employer's agreement, for another employer). If previously employed, she is assured of a comparable job on return to work. Also while on leave, she/he receives some modest financial support for the first two years ("child rearing money"). This financial benefit, equal to about one-fifth of the average female wage, is helpful for married-couple families primarily as a supplement to family income; it is not adequate to support a single mother at home unless child support, social assistance, or other income also is available.

Working mothers in *Austria* are entitled to a sixteen-week mandated maternity leave, paid at 100 percent of prior wage. In addition, an employed parent can take a job-protected leave from work and stay at home for up to three years after childbirth, or work part-time during the second and third year after birth. Part of the time the benefit is wage-related, and the rest of the time it is provided at a flat rate; and it is financed out of some combination of sickness funds, unemployment insurance funds, and family

**Table 4.2.** Basic and Extended Job-Protected Maternity/Parental and

| Country | Maternity/Paternity Leave as Indicated | | |
| | Duration in Weeks | Benefit as Percentage of Wage | Other |
| --- | --- | --- | --- |
| Australia | — | — | |
| Austria | 16 | 100 | |
| Belgium | 14 | 75–79.5 | |
| Canada | 15[a] | 60 | |
| Denmark | 28 | 100 | Paternity, 2 wk. |
| Finland | 18 | 80 | Paternity, 2 wk. |
| France | 16[b] | 84 | |
| Germany | 14 | 100 | |
| Greece | 14 | 50 + dependent benefit | |
| Iceland | 6 mo. | Flat rate + dependent benefit | All parental |
| Ireland | 14 | 70 | |
| Italy | 5 mo. | 80 | |
| Japan | 14 | 60 | |
| Luxembourg | 16 | 100 | |
| Netherlands | 16 | 100 | |
| New Zealand | 6 mo. | Flat rate | Income-tested |
| Norway | 18[c] | 80–100 | 18 wk. including 12 parental |
| Portugal | 3 mo. | 100 | |
| Spain | 16 | 75 | |
| Sweden | 12 mo. | 80 | All Parental |
| Switzerland | 10 | Varies | |
| Turkey | 12 | $66^2/_3$ | |
| United Kingdom | 14[d] | 90[d] | |
| United States | — | — | |

[a] Plus two unpaid weeks.

[b] Six months for third or subsequent children.

[c] In 1993, the Norwegian policy was extended to 52 weeks with replacement of 80 percent of salary, or 42 weeks with 100 percent replacement (each to an income maximum).

Extended Parental Leaves, OECD Countries, 1991–1992

| Extended Parental Leave | | Maximum Total Maternity and Parental Leave |
| --- | --- | --- |
| Duration | Benefit as Percentage of Wage | |
| 3 yr. | Varies | 3 yr. |
| 10 wk. | 60 | 25 wk.[a] |
| 52 wk. | 80 of unemployment insurance benefits | 1.5 yr. |
| 28 wk. | 80 | 3 yr. |
| 2 + yr. | Flat rate | |
| 2 yr. | Flat rate | 3 yr. |
| 2 yr. | Flat rate | 2 yr. + 1 yr. unpaid |
| 6 mo. | 30 | |
| 1 yr. | — | |
| 6 mo./part-time | | |
| 27 wk. | 80–100 | 42 wk. |
| 6 mo. | Flat rate | 1.5 yr; right to part-time work guaranteed until a child is 8 |

[a] As of late 1994, the United Kingdom leave became available to the full work force, covering 14 weeks, while those who previously had more generous benefits were protected.

allowance funds. In general, the benefit is worth about half the average female wage for a single mother and one-third for a married woman.

A *French* working mother is entitled to a fully paid, sixteen-week maternity leave, six weeks before birth and ten after. If there are multiple births or complications, or if it is a third or subsequent birth, the leave may be extended by two to fourteen weeks longer. French working parents also are entitled to a two-year job-protected leave at the end of the maternity "disability" leave; and if the child is a third or subsequent one, they also are entitled to a modest cash benefit paid through the family allowance funds, until the child is three years old. At the beginning of the 1990s, the benefit was equal to the minimum wage.

A *Danish* working mother is entitled to a twenty-eight-week, job-protected maternity leave, including up to four weeks before childbirth, paid at full wage up to the social insurance ceiling. The last ten weeks of the leave are a parental benefit and can be shared by the parents or used completely by either parent. Fathers have the right to a two-week, post-childbirth "paternity" leave as well. In addition, a working parent can take an additional six-month leave (until the child is one year old) paid for through the unemployment insurance system.

An *Italian* working mother is given a mandatory five-month, job-protected maternity leave, two months before expected birth and three months after. A cash benefit replacing 80 percent of wages is provided through the social insurance system. Civil servants, and all workers covered by national labor contracts (in effect almost all nonagricultural and non-domestic workers) receive a benefit equal to their full wage. In the event of death or the disability of the mother, working fathers are entitled to the leave and the benefit as well. In addition, working mothers have the right to a supplementary six-month leave, also job-protected, and paid at the level of 30 percent of their wages. Some workers receive a higher level benefit. Parents (natural or adoptive) of a handicapped child may extend this supplementary leave and benefit until a child's third birthday.

A *Swedish* working parent (mostly mothers, but about 40 percent of fathers take some part of the leave) can remain at home on a job-protected leave for up to eighteen months after childbirth and receive his or her full pay for the first year, and a modest flat rate benefit for the next three months; but the final three months are unpaid. Fathers also have the right to a two-week, postchildbirth, paid "paternity" leave. Working parents are guaranteed the right to work part-time (a six-hour day) until their youngest child is eight years old, and they may use part of their paid parental leave to cover part of their wages foregone while working part-time.

A *Finnish* working parent (overwhelmingly mothers) can remain at home until the child is three years old, with her job (or a comparable job) saved for her, and receive almost her full wage for one year and a modest cash benefit (available at a higher level for low-income families) for the other two years. She can use the benefit to supplement family income or to purchase private child care. (Or, she can avail her child of a guaranteed right to a good-quality subsidized place in municipal toddler care.)

Several other European countries, such as Norway, have similar policies. In several countries with federal systems, such as Germany and Austria, there are also state add-ons to the packages; in Finland the municipalities offer supplements. There are also add-ons provided through collective bargaining agreements, or voluntarily by some large firms, in some countries. And several of the eastern and central European countries, such as Hungary and the Czech and Slovak republics have similar policies.

### Eligibility Criteria, Coverage, and Take-Up

In all the countries but Germany, eligibility is contingent on a prior history of employment. Sweden and Finland offer "housewives" a minimum level benefit; however, there are very few such women in these countries. Even in Germany, the basic, fully paid maternity leave requires a prior work history. The postmaternity-leave child-rearing grant is available to mothers who do not work outside the home.

For the most part, countries have a work-history requirement similar to that posed in the EU directive: working at least since the beginning of the pregnancy. In some countries, one year is the requirement, or one year out of the last two (Austria). Britain, after long resistance, recently enacted a maternity leave policy following the EU directive: fourteen weeks after childbirth (and two before), with a wage-related cash benefit. This is supplemented by an additional leave, paid at a much lower level, for the women who qualify according to earlier, more stringent criteria.

A smaller proportion of mothers qualify for the extended leaves in the countries that have work requirements. For example, in Austria, despite full take-up of the basic sixteen-week maternity leave, and a strong incentive for women to take the extended leave when they have a second child, only 60 percent of mothers qualify for the extended benefit. Of those who qualify, however, 95 percent use it.

In Germany, 97 percent of the parents of newborns claim the child-rearing grant (the extended parental leave), and more than 95 percent of these are women. Although not a "work-tested" benefit, it is income-tested after the first six months. However, the income ceiling is set so high that approximately 80 percent of the beneficiaries continue to receive some portion of the benefit for the remainder of the paid leave (eighteen months in 1990, but two years in 1993).

The unpaid extended leave in France is mandated on employers only for those working in firms with one hundred or more employees, whereas the paid extended leave is limited to those having a third or subsequent child.

Just about all parents qualify for the six-month leave in Denmark, but the extended leave is too recent for take-up data to be available. Finally, in Sweden, all parents use the one-year, fully paid parental leave, either to cover full-time work or to permit part-time but fully paid work. By the time children are one year old, about 80 percent of their mothers are back at work, albeit largely part-time.

### *Financing*

Health insurance and sickness funds, family allowance funds, and unemployment insurance funds are the major strategies for financing these benefits, in some cases further supplemented by employer payments. More specifically, in Denmark and Finland, the basic leave is paid for through the health care and sickness benefit funds, and the extended leave is paid for through unemployment insurance in Denmark and through general revenue in Finland. In Austria, the basic leave is paid for equally through health insurance and family allowance funds. The extended leave is paid for on the same basis, through unemployment insurance and family allowance funds. In Germany, the basic benefit is paid for through sickness funds topped off (if the woman's salary is higher) by the employer. The benefit covering the extended leave is paid for out of general revenue. In France, the basic benefit comes from health insurance, and the others are paid for by the family allowance fund. In Sweden, parent insurance is a special social insurance benefit.

### *Benefit Level and Costs*

The basic benefit replaces between 80 percent (Sweden, Denmark, Finland, Italy) and 100 percent (Austria, Germany, France) of wages up to a specified ceiling, usually the maximum wage covered under social insurance.

Benefits are included in taxable income in all the countries except Germany.

The extended benefit is always provided at a lower rate, and usually is not wage-related. In Austria, the extended benefit is provided at a flat rate, and at a higher level to single mothers. As a result, the benefit is worth about 50 percent of the average female wage to a single mother and about

30 percent to a married mother. In Italy, the benefit is worth 30 percent of prior wage. In Finland and Germany, the flat-rate benefits are equal to about 19 percent of the average female wage; in France, the benefit is valued at about half the minimum wage.

These benefits may only be a modest component in family and social protection benefits generally, but they are important to the individual family, nonetheless; and they are not cheap. Investment in these benefits does vary across countries, however. France, Denmark, and Luxembourg spend a far greater proportion of the gross domestic product (GDP) on maternity benefits than the EU average, as do Finland and Sweden, now EU members. In Austria, where family benefits constitute about one-fifth of federal government expenditures, parenting benefits account for less than 10 percent of family benefit expenditures. In France, young-child cash benefits equal more than 13 percent of public social expenditures and 3 percent of the GDP. About half of these are universal benefits, and the remainder are income-tested. (We do not have cost estimates for the leaves.) In Sweden, expenditures on parent insurance are almost as large as child allowance expenditures.

Finally, despite little in the way of evaluation or child impact studies of these policies, we note some interesting outcomes. In Germany, it is already quite clear that the extended leave opens up some jobs, and most important, raises the incomes of husband/wife one-earner families and adds to the amount of parental time available to children in husband/wife two-earner families. Because of the low level of the benefit, it has no significant impact on the situation of single mothers. In contrast, in Austria, where the original extended leave policy was designed for single mothers, it adds to family income in both one- and two-parent families, as well as adding to time in both two-earner and sole-parent/earner families. In Sweden, it adds dramatically to family income, especially in lone-parent families; and it adds to parental time availability in all families. Indeed, it adds especially to a father's availability to his children. Time-use studies show that Swedish fathers spend significantly more time with their children than do the fathers in other countries.

Most view the policy developed in Sweden as the exemplary parenting benefit. The Swedish parent insurance benefit provides for an eighteen-month job-protected leave following childbirth or adoption, paid now at 80 percent of wages for one year and at a modest flat rate for an additional three months. It can be used to cover part-time work by either parent, and the right to work part-time while children are young is guaranteed by law. The policy provides for a paid and job-protected leave to care for an ill child and also to visit a child's school, and it continued to have strong support after the election of a conservative government.

## Other Paid Leaves for Parents

The arrival of a child is certainly an occasion when employed parents have particular need for some protected time off. But there are other critical times as well. When a child is ill, when a child begins school, and when there are special critical events at school, parents need parenting time. It should be possible for a parent to take occasional, moderate amounts of time off from work for such occasions without losing a job, and without being unduly penalized financially. Some such benefits are described below.

### *Caring for an Ill Child at Home*

In Italy, working parents whose child becomes ill, or whose child is handicapped, are entitled to a job-protected leave, similar to the extended maternity leave, until their child is three years old. The benefit attached to the leave is worth about 30 percent of the average wage and varies depending on the category of worker and industry.

More limited time but more generous income protection is provided in Sweden. Swedish working parents are entitled to up to sixty days of paid leave each year (the same as their personal sick-leave entitlement) to take care of an ill child under age 12. As in all other countries that provide a long leave, this would be contingent only on a doctor certifying the severity of the child's illness.

In Germany, working parents are each entitled to up to ten paid days off a year to care for an ill child. A lone mother would be permitted to take both parents' entitlement, and thus would qualify for up to twenty days a year, if needed.

In Finland, working parents with a child under 10 are each entitled to a maximum of four days' paid leave a year to care for an ill child at home. They receive a cash benefit for part of their wage, equal to what they would have received if they were out ill themselves. However, about 75 percent of Finnish working parents are covered by collective bargaining agreements that assure them of full pay at that time.

Finally, in Denmark, working parents are entitled to only one paid day off in the case of routine child illnesses, but up to one year in the case of a serious illness. All would be paid at the same rate as for their own personal sick days.

### *Vacation and Other Personal Time*

No discussion of time for parenting would be complete without noting the far-more-extensive vacation and holiday time all workers have in the conti-

**Table 4.3.** Working Hours, Vacation Days, and Holidays for Industrial Workers with Union Contracts, 1992; and Absenteeism as a Percentage of Total Scheduled Hours (Selected Countries)

| Country | Hours | Vacation Days | Holidays | Absenteeism |
|---|---|---|---|---|
| Germany (West) | 37.5 | 30 | 10 | 9.0 |
| Britain | 38.8 | 27 | 8 | 6.8 |
| France | 39.0 | 25 | 10 | 8.2 |
| Sweden | 40.0 | 27 | 11 | 12.1 |
| United States | 40.0 | 12 | 11 | 3.0 |
| Japan | 42.0 | 11 | 14 | 1.7 |
| Italy | 40.0 | 40 days (total) | | 6.0 |

*Source:* Compiled by *The New York Times* (Feb. 12, 1994) (Aug. 9, 1993) from Institute of German Industry, OECD, U.S. Bureau of Labor Statistics, German Federal Labor Office.

nental European countries as compared with the United States (one to two weeks for most people, four weeks for the privileged) (see Table 4.3). Depending on the country, four, five, or six weeks is the standard for paid vacations, in addition to a significant number of paid holidays. Of some interest, German workers have the most extensive paid time off (thirty vacation days plus twelve public holidays), with the Scandinavians following. The French have twenty-five vacation days and ten public holidays, and the British have twenty-seven vacation days and eight public holidays—also, all paid. In the context of current high unemployment rates, there is also much discussion of shorter work weeks and days.

In addition, in Finland and Sweden, as already noted, working parents are now guaranteed the right to work a shorter day while their children are young, if they wish (by drawing on the extended-leave time; some of this may be partly compensated).

Finally, we note that in Sweden, working parents are also entitled to take two days a year to cover child-related needs such as bringing a young child to a new child care center for the first time, bringing a child to school on the first day, or meeting with a child's teachers at school.

Clearly, these constitute very different policies than those that prevail in the United States. What would be a viable U.S. policy? What would we recommend?

## Conclusion

Time flexibility is essential for smooth meshing of family responsibilities of both parents with their work responsibilities (or single parents with jobs).

It also makes extended periods of dedication to "family work" possible for mothers who also have work-career interests and for fathers who are similarly inclined. Not long ago, the *New York Times* (May 29, 1994) headlined a page-one story as follows "Childless Workers Demand Equity in Corporate World." Some of the colleagues who fill in for parents making use of leaves or other job flexibility are said to complain because their own "different" needs as childless workers or as parents of grown children are ignored. FMLA also applies to elder care, but all employees need "time" at some point for a variety of contingencies of living, underscoring the need for workplace flexibility even for those without young children. Employers in the lead have developed balanced policies.

There is another point to which one needs to return in considering expenditures and time for young children: this new generation constitutes our future civil society—voters, workers, contributors to the social security trust fund—whether or not they are our own children. We have a major stake in the quality of their rearing. Europe offers some useful leads.

European parents, despite similar or higher proportions of women and mothers in the labor force, have far more opportunities to spend time with their children than do American parents. Maternity leaves, paternity leaves, parental leaves, child-rearing leaves, leaves to take care of an ill child at home, and leaves to help a child adjust to a new school are all built into the regular work year and, indeed, are mandated by government legislation. At every critical period in a child's life, there is opportunity for working parents to take some time off from work or to work shorter hours. Moreover, family income is protected while parents are on leave. Often, social benefits replace a parent's full wage; at other times the benefit covers only a part. Family time is considered to be very important and a significant component of nonwage labor costs. Nonetheless, even when the economic situation is difficult, the right to take time off at critical transitions remains an entitlement. Social and fringe benefits are protected during all such leaves. The duration may vary from country to country, but every country other than the United States provides them in some form, to some extent. They are paid for in a variety of ways, all involving some cost sharing by the larger society; and none of these policies is targeted only on the poor. Children's need for parents' time is a universal need and is recognized and supported as such.

Ultimately, we would urge exploration in the United States as to how this country could move toward the European pattern of *support for family time for working parents*. At the very least, Congress should enact a one-year paid leave, something that would permit U.S. babies to be cared for at home just as their European siblings are; but for now, that does not seem like a realistic option. What might be possible interim steps? Here we present some suggestions for essential reform of the FMLA.[12]

First, apply the FMLA to firms with fewer than fifty employees. This firm-size criterion now excludes more than 60 percent of the labor force. Moreover, while the provision was initially included to protect small business, research by Bond and others on the implementation and impact of state parental leave laws found that the small-employer exemption threshold could be lowered to twenty-one to twenty-five without creating hardships.[13]

Second, reduce the number of months and hours per week that employees are required to work in order to qualify for the benefit. The present criterion requires women to have worked at least three-fifths of a full-time job, for at least twelve months prior to going on leave. The provision excludes large numbers of women with young children who now work fewer hours. At the very least, half-time work (twenty hours or more) for ten months (one month before the pregnancy began) should be sufficient.

Third, include some provision for leave to care for a child with a normal childhood illness. At present, the FMLA does not address the needs of employed parents to provide care for their children at such times. As a consequence, many employees misuse their own paid sick days to provide care at such times, or just miss work. At the very least, give working parents the right to take up to one week off, when the parental care is certified by a doctor as being needed.

Fourth, eliminate another current FMLA provision that permits employers to deny the leave to a "key" employee, one of the highest paid 10 percent of their employees, if that employee's presence is defined as necessary for the firm to function. Parental leave should not be limited to less-valued or lower-paid workers.

Fifth, and most important, develop a mechanism for paying for the leave, either through statutory temporary disability insurance (TDI), as in many other countries and as now exists in the U.S. five states that have such a program; through a special new "parent" (social) insurance benefit; or, as the Canadians do, through unemployment insurance. The evidence is that costs are moderate. Any one of these mechanisms would "pool" costs and protect individual employers. This country has had good experience with TDI.

TDI as it now exists in five states provides a cash benefit to workers temporarily away from work because of nonjob-related disabilities, for up to twenty-six weeks. A federal TDI benefit was considered following passage of the 1935 Social Security Act but not enacted. All but one of the state TDI plans were enacted in the 1940s.

Typically, a normal pregnancy and childbirth involves between eight and twelve weeks (two to four weeks before childbirth and six to eight weeks after); complicated pregnancies and births as well as multiple births may require more time for convalescence. The benefit is provided at about the same level as unemployment insurance, although many large employers supplement what the state pays and cover the employee's full salary. Some collective bargaining agreements do this also. The benefit is financed either by employees only (in Rhode Island and California) or employees and employers (in New Jersey, New York, and Hawaii). It is an inexpensive benefit. There has been little growth in its use since the legislation extending it to pregnancy and maternity was enacted in 1978. About 22 percent of the workforce is now covered under the existing TDI plans. Galinsky and Bond report that about 40 percent of employees in firms with one hundred or more employees have access to TDI benefits either by statutory right or through voluntary employer coverage, and about 25 percent in smaller firms.[14] Congress could mandate employer provision or establish a national TDI program, financed as a contributory benefit by employees alone, or by a combination of employee and employer contributions, or through the same model followed in unemployment insurance. Whatever strategy is followed could apply as well to all the provisions of the FMLA, including the recommended new provision of a one-week leave to care for young children with routine illnesses.

If the United States is to demonstrate its concern with the well-being of young children, a national TDI could be an essential beginning.

There is plenty of research suggesting that in the absence of financial protection during the period of parental leave, most parents of newborn and newly adopted children are not able to afford to take advantage of such a leave. Galinsky and Bond note that "If as a nation we really believe that working parents should not only have access to, but actually take parental leaves to care for newborn, adopted, foster, and seriously ill children, then we should consider ways of providing at least partial wage replacement during parental leaves."[15]

If income replacement were added to the FMLA, perhaps along the TDI pattern and covering eight to twelve weeks, it also would be good to add another twelve weeks of job protection, to a total of twenty-four. Most European countries do more. Six months is probably the earliest for parents to be fully comfortable with any out-of-home child care arrangements if we judge by the practice of those with options in the United States and abroad. And some parents *can* stretch for another twelve weeks without income replacement.

In the long run, one sees more generous "solutions" on the horizon, in the context of a society that will be "time-rich". The United States led the way from the sixty-hour week and showed that it could be more than paid for by improved productivity. Currently, European countries are cutting the work week to share work at a time of high unemployment. The French base is thirty-nine hours, the German is thirty-seven; there is talk of a four-day week in many places; it has arrived in some. In some places the workers on the shorter schedules are losing income; in others there are no (or limited) losses. While, as it recovered from recession, the U.S. industry paid overtime on a forty-hour week, avoiding new hires, there were and are proposals here, too, for a shorter work week. The debate centers on how it would be paid for—in lower salaries, lower profits, fewer taxes, or some combination?

One cannot predict the manner and the time for the solution of these issues in the context of the globalization of major economies and uncertainty as to how the discrepancies in both labor costs and nonwage labor costs between highly industrialized and developing economies will play out. However, we cannot conceive of a solution that lowers standards of living in the richest, most industrialized countries of the world. And adequate supports for parenting are part of that standard of living, certainly affordable in high-productivity societies. It is not unreasonable, then, to enact at least a "floor" for paid parenting time in the United States along the lines of current European provision. As opportunities present themselves in the future, many parents will do even more—on their own—in their personal responses to and investments in their infants and toddlers.

# 5

## A Healthy Start

If starting right is the objective, the health care system must be available and active in a baby's life, from the time of conception. The medical facts are clear, and public opinion polls show overwhelming support for giving child health services high priority. Access to health care is seen as more important than other key issues of child well-being. There is even some readiness to be taxed for the purpose, despite some differences about financing.[1]

Yet, whatever the miracles of American medical care for low-birth-weight and impaired newborns, the "standard" system is not doing well for significant numbers of infants and toddlers. Prenatal care and prevention services during a child's early years are often inaccessible or inadequate in the United States if measured by the standards of the advanced industrial world. Many American babies do less well than they should or could.

Since these poor results prevail despite the high competence of our medical professions and expenditure levels that lead the world, our deficiencies must be attributed to our access and service delivery systems and to our failure to develop prevention to the levels we have achieved for our admired and effective medical care, such as the care of children with severe deficiencies, injuries, and handicaps in the first twenty-eight days of life.

In this chapter we explore the reform of child health so as to guarantee every child an optimal start. After looking at indicators of deficits in the U.S. system, we discuss the context of child health services, especially the preventive components, and their importance. Then we seek some historical perspective on current patterns. Child health has had renewed and significant attention since the early 1980s, particularly through Medicaid enhancements, but we shall suggest that the improvements do not yet solve our problems. Popular U.S. child health "exemplars" are suggestive, but do not offer a full model.

Finally, we ask what the European experience contributes to the planning process. With the entire picture in hand, we offer some suggestions.

## What Is Wrong with the Present Situation?

In 1993 the National Commission on Children summed up its research as follows:

> Overall American children are healthier today than they have ever been. Yet in many key areas of health care, progress has been slow or halted altogether in recent years. In others, the nation is actually losing ground. Left unaddressed, these trends are likely to take a devastating toll on the health of the nation's children over the coming decade.[2]

The Commission and others cite higher infant mortality rates than those of the industrialized countries with which we compare ourselves and those of some countries so much "less developed" as to belong in another league. In recent years we have ranked number 19, 20, 21, or 22, a rapid fall in rank during each decade since 1950. The Commission reports that 40,000 children die each year before their first birthday. This could be cut by more than half if we could attain the Finnish or Japanese infant mortality record. The black infant mortality rate is more than double the white (7.3 per one thousand live births versus 17.6 in 1991), but even the U.S. white rate lags well behind the leaders (8.4 per one thousand live births in 1993, when the leaders were at 4.3 [Japan] or 5.4 [Finland]). Entire regions of the country and most large cities have infant mortality rates unknown in most advanced industrial societies.[3]

Low birth weight (under 5.5 pounds) is a major factor behind infant mortality and the many serious chronic conditions and disabilities with which children grow up—often after extraordinary costly and lengthy hospitalization and very skillful medical care. Again, the U.S. record here is very weak internationally: the proportion of infants with low birth weight is higher in the United States than in at least 16 other "advanced" countries. It remained at 7 percent in the late 1980s and early 1990s—long after adoption of 5 percent as a reasonable interim goal.

Infant deaths from injuries are high enough to cause concern, if difficult to document comparatively. The United States has the world's lowest mortality rates for low-birth-weight babies and pays the price. Approximately 7 percent of all babies consume 60 percent of newborn health care costs, given the high costs of life and care after rescue by the marvels of medical technology and skill. But many of the problems are known to be avoidable, detectable, and correctable—with the resulting improved lives for children—through prenatal care and related support service. Here, again, our record is most unimpressive by world standards.[4]

In 1990, one in four American infants was born to a mother who did not receive early prenatal care, and the coverage rate has declined since 1980.[5] A recent study shows modest progress between 1970 and 1980 in the number of women (about three-quarters) receiving prenatal care within the first three months of pregnancy, the medical standard. There has been no progress since that time. Data for black women showed a major spurt for a decade, but since, their coverage rate has been stalled at almost 20 percent below the rate for whites. Almost 11 percent of black mothers-to-be receive either no prenatal care or third-trimester care only. The rate for whites is 3.2 percent. We already have cited the differential infant mortality rates. [6]

The risk factors for inadequate prenatal care other than race also are well documented: teenagers, unmarried women, the poorly educated, the poor, those without medical coverage, inner-city residents, and residents of isolated rural areas.[7]

Clearly, prenatal care and the rest of the maternity care package (obstetric and neonatal care) are critical parts of the child health system. Early care, among other things, provides improved opportunity to deal with the mother's nutritional problems, exposure to harmful substances, exposure to sexually transmitted diseases, and physical problems—all central to the child's well-being and future. The questions of norms (timing and number of prenatal visits) and the delivery system will not be discussed in detail herein, given our focus. These matters must be part of the health care reform, defeated in 1993–94 but still on the national agenda; and there is ample U.S. experience with those who are medically insured. The fact that prenatal care works is well documented in the research literature. The success of any child health initiative, then, will rest on a successful outcome to medical reform in the form of accessible, affordable, high-quality medical services for all women.

In 1990 there were 27,672 reported cases of measles in the United States, part of a 1989-1991 epidemic, a completely "unnecessary" and sometimes devastating illness. There were 132 measles-related deaths and 11,000 hospitalizations between 1989 and 1991, among tens of thousands of cases.[8] Many diseases of childhood are preventable with routine immunization, yet our immunization rates for children in the years before they enter school—when immunization is required—are low. The last comprehensive immunization survey preceding these results showed that 21 percent of one- to four-year-olds were not immunized against measles, 24 percent were inadequately protected against polio, and 13 percent were inadequately protected against diphtheria, pertussis, and tetanus. Following an all-out special emergency campaign, the Centers for Disease Control noted that, for the first six months of 1993, only 175 measles cases were reported (and that the estimate for the first ten months was 260 cases), a virtual wiping out of the disease. However, in the same report (a 1991 survey), it was estimated that only about 45 percent of children had the necessary four doses of diphtheria-tetanus-whooping cough vaccine and only about 55 percent had the needed three doses of oral polio vaccine. The Centers' spokesman commented: "So, while we are winning one battle, the war is far from over." A few months later, the Centers reported that there had been 5,457 cases of whooping cough (pertussis) between January and December 4, 1993, the highest case total since 1967. Infants are the most severely affected by this illness that can cause pneumonia, seizures, and inflammation of the brain. Half of the afflicted infants require hospitalization; one in two hundred dies.

In a recent, expert review, the following observation was made: "Although these diseases are frequently not serious, deaths and significant neurologic morbidity have resulted from these outbreaks . . . failure to protect children from the risk of morbidity and possible illness at reasonable cost is further evidence of inefficiency in the health care system for children."[9]

Some 15 percent of children are affected by chronic and disabling conditions, including mental and nervous disorders, that limit their activities. While it is not possible to cite hard numbers here, the expert consensus is that "Some of these conditions may have been easily prevented or substantially ameliorated by timely health care and reduction in environmental risks."[10] Currently only half our children have the recommended nine well-child visits to a doctor or clinic by age 2.[11]

We do not need to elaborate on the well-documented fact that children living below or just above the poverty line have much higher relative frequencies of health problems of all sorts than do other children. Environmental exposure relating to deteriorated neighborhood and housing conditions, poor nutrition, inadequate preventive care, and poor access to medical care are all cited in explanation.[12]

The National Commission on Children has specified the consequences of nutritional deprivation during pregnancy and the early months of life in the form of damage "that can never be repaired." For infants and young children, slowed growth, greater susceptibility to disease, "risk of neuro-developmental problems that impair learning," and malnutrition resulting in "failure to thrive" are cited and documented.[13] We already have discussed the need to address problems of income and housing (Chapter 3). Here we focus on health care, broadly conceived. In a later chapter we look at family support and parent education, also relevant to the nutrition issue.

Equity in medical care access was proclaimed as the goal of the country's failed 1994 national health reform effort. Here we turn to the child health system as it should serve all children. We must confront the systematic research documentation to the effect that "a significant proportion of two-year-old children did not receive preventive health care" in the previous year. While many of those missed were uninsured or served through Medicaid, even some 20 percent of the medically insured had not had a preventive health visit. This is a reflection of a central problem in the several child health benefit packages and the related delivery systems.[14]

## Child Health Services

Child health services are not an independent factor when one deals with young children. A complex intertwining of nutrition, housing, poverty, parental competence, parental health, and life-styles determine child outcomes. Therefore, in some way, the medical supports and interventions must come from staff and a delivery system with a broad view of child development and a readiness to initiate other-than-narrow medical interventions. That delivery system must be planned with the understanding that "Especially for children, good health is essential for the multidimensional process of growth and development. Indeed, children's health status is in part manifested in the process of their development."[15]

A considerable amount of work is currently under way in an effort to define essential benefits for a child health reform package. Studies are pursuing dimensions such as "medical necessity," "insurability," and "cost effectiveness." Careful review of evaluations and other studies is helpful but not definitive in this process, which ultimately rests on what has been characterized as "consensus-of-medical experts," who are fully informed about the research but also are able to integrate contexts that the research has not controlled.[16]

The "package" developing out of work in the U.S. Public Health Service and the American Academy of Pediatrics of course covers traditional services for active and chronic medical conditions. Here, we need not elaborate. American child medical services are highly regarded in these fields, and the reforms of access, coverage, and finance currently under way in the American medical system will presumably fill gaps and increase equity.

It is the *preventive* component that needs major initiatives and will continue to do so under proposed reforms. Called "child health supervision", these are the services that distinguish health benefits for children from those for the rest of the population[17] and explain why child health is so central to starting right. Some child health supervision activities may involve other than the immediate family and health care providers, including child care programs, social service agencies, and government departments. The clinical elements, part of the personal health services needed, include "routine screenings, developmental surveillance, periodic medical examinations, counseling and anticipatory guidance, as well as referral and case management."[18] In one or another of these categories, and sometimes at the boundary of the clinical and the preventive, are the teaching of parents and information-giving with respect to physical and social development, environmental safety, nutrition, and even the modeling of adequate handling, bathing, and caring for babies. Inoculations that are timely obviously are central to a preventive regime.

The child health system may require an outreach component, varying by the backgrounds of populations served. As much should be said for the "maternity care system", defined as the network of publicly—or privately—financed services through which women obtain prenatal, labor and delivery, and postpartum care.[19] We already have noted that prenatal care must be conceptualized as a child health component, in effect shaping much of the environment for the child's first nine months of life.

These are the child health system requirements to the extent that research data, the public health record, and expert consensus come together. As shown in the previous section, many children do not have the benefits to be derived from protection by such a system. Given the more limited knowledge Americans have of the health care system as compared with welfare, it may be helpful before considering policy options to review, briefly, both the historical record in the United States and the events of the past several years. Why do we have so large a deficit in child health protection?

## Some Historical Notes

The Federal role in child health care is based on three pillars: one concerned with maternal and child health service delivery, the second with financing health care for the poor, and the third with providing a subsidy for health insurance for the employed nonpoor, through the federal income tax system. Over time, the importance of the first has receded and the second and third increased. As a result, far more children had access to health care in 1990 than in 1960, but there has been no development of nationwide or statewide universal "child health" (or "maternal and child health" or "child and family health") delivery systems.

Federal involvement in child health services began in 1921 with the federal Maternity and Infancy (Sheppard—Towner) Act, a state-federal partnership designed to provide services to pregnant women and children and not seen as a program limited to the poor. It was one of the first federal involvements in any social services. This legislation was passed at the end of a reform era in which there was much emphasis on children and in which women were in the national lead. Although the program was allowed to die in 1929 when the legislation was not reauthorized, its principles were incorporated into the second federal initiative, Title V of the 1935 Social Security Act (Maternal and Child Health and Crippled Children's Services).

Title V is the only broad Federal program concerned exclusively with the health of mothers and children. It provides support to States to enhance their ability to "promote, improve, and deliver" maternal and child health care and crippled children's services, particularly in rural and poor areas.[20] Guyer points out that the language of the Act reflected a perceived need to build a maternal and child health care delivery system that could assure quality services.[21] It was enacted in part in response to the dramatic rise in infant mortality rates that occurred following the demise of Sheppard-Towner and the onset of the Great Depression.[22] From its inception, the program was a universal one, applying no means test to service users, although targeting its services primarily on low-income women and children and those with limited access to health care by focusing on low-income and rural communities. At a time when health insurance was not available to ordinary families, Title V represented the only source of public funding for health care for many children.

As a result of the Sheppard-Towner Act and Title V, states developed maternal and child health divisions within their own health departments, with responsibility for financing or operating specialized services for pregnant women, well babies, and "crippled children" (later termed "children with special health needs"). No significant new federal child health legislation was enacted for almost thirty years, and there were only limited developments in the states.

Following World War II, federal policy encouraged employment-related health insurance, which gradually became the dominant pattern for most workers, and included some but not all dependents.

The poor and the others excluded from this major medical coverage system depended on medical care related to public assistance in some places; to city or county hospitals in others; or to public health clinics, and the charities of private hospitals.

The major health reform of the Great Society affecting the poor was Medicaid, enacted in 1965, at the same time Medicare was launched. The recipients of federal categorical assistance were made eligible, as were those defined by the states as medically needy. Because the reimbursement rate was affected by state-set income ceilings and the service package was subject to state options, Medicaid meant different things in different parts of the country, despite the potential to become a comprehensive health insurance system for the poor. Nonetheless, Medicaid became and remains the largest public medical program for children and their families. Initially, it expanded and made major progress; then, as Congress tried to limit costs and as state financial pressures and medical costs grew, Medicaid cut back. However, as noted below, Congressional mandates in the mid-1980s subsequently protected pregnant women and child health services with a series of federally mandated enhancements. A screening program within Medicaid, known as Early and Periodic Screening, Diagnosis, and Treatment offered an important prevention vehicle but was unevenly implemented.

A third group of child health programs also are traceable to the Great Society. A variety of special groups of children have been identified as needing care but as unlikely to receive it under existing delivery systems. Sometimes the defining characteristic is geography, other times it is the population group or the problem. During the War on Poverty, the Office of Economic Opportunity bypassed states and helped establish neighborhood health centers, which were eventually absorbed into a Public Health Service community and migrant care program (currently serving some six million of the thirty-eight million uninsured). Categorical programs also were established to deal with lead poisoning, adolescent pregnancy, sudden infant death syndrome, handicapped children, and so forth.

It may be said of the 1970s and early 1980s that legislatively stated goals were excellent but that program cuts in Washington and supervisory load-shedding left more children unserved. Some lost even Medicaid coverage. Studies, exposés and statistical reports on infant mortality and low birth weight became quite visible. The Congress had become aware of the barriers to prenatal care and the deficiencies in child health care. From the mid-1980s the states were permitted to end the linkage between Medicaid and AFDC and to adopt a series of enhancements for prenatal and infant health care. States continued to have expanded Medicaid mandates and options as Congress broadened coverage seven times between 1984 and 1990.

With this background in view, it is possible to offer a current coverage "overview" that defines the legislative and service delivery environments in which child health now operates and could be reformed.

## The Present Context for Maternal and Child Health Reform

We have already established that the sum total of available child health coverage is unsatisfactory, as is some of the substance. A review of what coverage is in place is a starting point for reform.

Most children have their medical coverage as dependents of workers with *private health insurance* at their place of employment. In the past several years, with high levels of unemployment and inflated health costs, these coverage rates have declined. According to Marilyn Moon of the Urban Institute, only 61.1 percent of children under age 18 had such coverage in 1992, down from 64.8 percent in 1988.[23] Another 20 percent of children depended on Medicaid for medical coverage. A shifting number had privately purchased family insurance coverage. Some 14.7 percent were uncovered.

The numbers are summarized in diverse ways. In 1992, 12.7 percent of children had no coverage for the entire year (8.4 million) but some sixteen million, one-fourth of all children, were expected to experience coverage interruptions at some point during 1993. Of the uninsured children, reported by some experts as totaling over nine million by 1993 (the determinant apparently being just when the counting is done), some two-thirds have parents who work but are not covered by employment-based insurance plans. Another 18 percent of uninsured children are in families with working parents who have employment-based coverage for themselves only. The rest are poor children whose parents do not work.[24] The research does not document all the consequences of erratic coverage or no coverage for primary care, but all observers regard it as a serious problem to be solved.

The Congressional Medicaid enhancements of 1984-1990 have, by all indications, improved maternal and child health access, adding coverage for four to five million children and one-half million pregnant women, according to the Urban Institute. By January 1, 1993, all states were mandated to offer Medicaid coverage to children under age 6 in families with incomes below 133 percent of the federal poverty level and to children under age 10 living in families below 100 percent of the federal poverty line. Further, the enhancements cover all pregnant women and allow the states to cover the children aged 0 to 6 in families up to 185 percent of the poverty line. Coverage is to include all children through age 18 by the turn of the century.

All this represents progress but does not take us far enough. Implementation of the enhancements is uneven. *Medicaid, private insurance, and employer-provided insurance often offer limited prevention service.* A U.S. Public Health Service study reported that only one-third of low-income preschool children received the number of well-child visits recommended by the American Academy of Pediatrics, and only one-half of those in more affluent families did.[25]

Where are we headed? It seems reasonable to assume that, when the country resumes its interrupted health reform efforts, currently "uncovered" children and those in areas where Medicaid services are very limited or inaccessible will have access to basic acute and chronic care medicine.

Americans know how to deliver such services, and the "uncovered" want what the well-covered or the purchasers in the marketplace can now get.

What this leaves unsettled is the preventive programs, sometimes called "child health supervision." There are many interesting U.S. ideas and initiatives and some demonstration exemplars, most of them state efforts over the last decade using Medicaid funds and mandates to reach the unserved—and in the context of either a full child health package (Minnesota)[26] or a delivery idea that deserves promotion (one-stop shopping for prenatal care).[27] A significant number of states support some home health visiting services with Maternal and Child Health funds, but most such programs are extremely limited because of financial constraints. As yet, there are no "child health supervision" models in the United States that are universal, have large-scale coverage, and have a track record of experience. Nor is there active consideration of the possibility that whatever the design for acute and chronic care, we should plan toward a semiindependent "preventive" or "well-baby" or "child health supervision" network. We introduce this possibility by referring to the European experience. It deserves weighing before the U.S. child health system becomes fixed.


## Some Possibilities as Seen in Europe

Without more specific information than is now available about a future comprehensive U.S. medical care reform and its implementation, one cannot predict the degrees of freedom available to design a "child health supervision" model. Our premise is that the pending reforms will ensure coverage for prenatal care and for acute and chronic services for young children. There is ample U.S. precedent for planning delivery systems for both.

All European countries have either national health services or national health insurance systems as the base on which their preventive child health services are developed. Such services are delivered through *two interrelated components: the equivalent of what we in this country identify as a "well-baby" clinic or service, and a home health visitor program.* The well-baby clinic or service may be either a special freestanding preventive clinic, apart from the family's pediatric coverage under the health plan, or a function of the primary care doctor under that plan. The home health visiting may be related primarily to the time immediately after childbirth, or may cover the entire first year and/or some contacts thereafter.[28] In general, these components at their best have a broad concept of "child health supervision" and intertwined medical and social components. This is what is of interest.

The "well-baby clinic" concept is familiar in the United States and has been since the Sheppard-Towner legislation of 1921 and the subsequent programs funded under Title V of the 1935 Social Security Act and the more recent Maternal and Child Health Block Grant. However, except in the earliest years, these programs and their many derivatives and supplements discussed in our historical view have targeted the inner-city poor, or inaccessible rural communities, or migrants. They could not assume that their child-patients had primary care coverage, and this, too, shaped their services. Thus, the United States has not had experience with universal or more broadly accessible well-baby clinics or services as part of a medical care system covering the entire population. Many children currently "covered" by parent workplace insurance do not have the recommended periodic checkups, and they are found among the uninoculated at age 2.

Similarly, there has been a "visiting nurse" tradition in the United States since the early days of the settlement houses. The well-known Henry Street Settlement in the lower east side of New York City began in 1893 as a visiting nurse service and had 92 nurses on staff by 1913.[29] All state maternal and child health programs support some home health visiting. Medicaid has financed home health visiting more recently as part of outreach efforts in many states. But the best available estimates cite a coverage maximum of two hundred thousand children who receive home visits—and many are not medical.[30] We in the United States do not have a precedent for *universal* home health visiting, although, of course, until recent decades, pediatricians visited their charges at home right after birth and during illness. Now, as in almost all countries, they see children in offices or clinics.

Therefore, it may be of interest to look at several European countries to consider the possible interrelationships among the primary care physician, the well-baby clinic or center, and the home health visitor as components of a delivery system. We include England and Denmark as best exemplifying the home health visiting service, and Finland and France for their child health centers (and not without home health visiting potential).

These presentations are introduced with some general comments about home health visiting, which explain the philosophy and prevention potential of such services.[31] Well-baby clinics, obviously of central importance, are more familiar in the United States currently. They are universal in Europe, see almost all children in some countries, and fewer elsewhere, where the primary care physician has a larger health surveillance (prevention) mission. We would assume that future U.S. developments also would be anchored by the family's primary care physician or pediatrician.

Home Health Visiting (HHV) exists to some extent in all the northern and western European countries as part of their national, universal systems of health care. These countries include Denmark, Finland, France, Germany, Great Britain, Ireland, Italy, the Netherlands, Norway, and Sweden. All the HHV services are voluntary, free, and not income-tested.

Each of these countries believes that preventive child health programs are but one piece of an essential network of economic and social supports provided by the government to families. There is strong conviction that child health goals require not only health services but also cash and non-cash benefits, housing supports, child care services, and social services, as needed by the family. In essence, child health care policies and programs are viewed as an integral component and interdependent with the other elements of good social policy for children and their families. A firm social infrastructure provides the foundation and building blocks for supplementary interventions for children and families with special needs.

In all countries, home visiting programs are carried out by professionals, typically registered nurses. The visitors in Britain are National Health Service nurses. In Denmark, home visitors also have pediatric hospital experience. In the Netherlands, paraprofessionals supplement the nurses' role. Where HHV occurs in Berlin, Germany, social workers are the visitors and encourage regular checkups with private physicians or public health clinics; often these professionals have supplemental public health training. Nurses visit in Munich.

Home visitors in each of these countries provide health education, preventive care, and social support services to very young children and their parents. Home visitors may be assigned to families according to geographic boundaries, or, in some countries, according to the general practitioner physician the family sees. In all countries, home visiting services are supplemented by more comprehensive health services available to children through the system of maternal and child health clinics or through private doctors under a universal health insurance system, or through both.

Each country focuses its home visiting programs on children under age 3 (or, in many, under age 1). All see the home locus as essential at the start. Home visiting allows the visitor to meet other siblings and the father, and provides a better opportunity to view mother-child interactions in a natural setting and to establish a close relationship with the mother on a one-to-one basis. However, European HHV programs vary along other indicia: whether special focus is given to specially identified families, whether visits begin prenatally, and whether the visits are supplemented with center-based support groups and care. In addition, these programs also vary in frequency of the visits. For example, in Denmark, Great Britain, Ireland, and the Netherlands, nearly all newborns and their mothers are visited at home by a public health nurse at least several times during the first year. In contrast, Finland, France, Germany, Italy, and Sweden offer only one or two postbirth visits, with additional visits on a discretionary basis as needed. These concentrate on encouraging child visits to child health centers.

Regardless of the frequency of visits, home visiting in each of these countries links the family, as needed, to social services, income maintenance, housing, and other government programs. Home visiting programs are often physically located within, or in close proximity to, the offices for broader social services. Regardless of location, they typically enjoy coordinated or integrated relationships with these other programs. Home visitors also help with early identification of risk of child abuse or neglect, developmental lags, or postpartum depression; they offer treatment or referral as appropriate for children, mothers, or other family members.

We begin with home health visiting, which is less familiar to most Americans than are maternal and child health clinics.

## *Britain*

Britain took the lead in health visiting and was of great influence internationally. In considering the British program, it is useful to recall that since World War II the British health service has provided all residents with coverage by a general practitioner (GP)—with whom they register—and who is the primary health care provider and the access point to specialists, hospitalization, medication, maternity care, family planning, and home nursing. The GP receives from the government an annual payment for all people on his/her list. This is paid for out of the general governmental budget. For participants, there are modest fees for checkups and prescriptions, but children under age 16 are exempt from fees. Thus, in effect, the GP may be seen by any child at parent initiative or if urged to do so by the HHV.

The British HHV role is the original model. HHVs in England and Wales are notified of every birth occurring within their district, by the physician or midwife in attendance, and visit new mothers and babies at home, usually within ten days after the child's birth. They offer an ongoing service of health education (about safety in the home, for example), advice (about nutrition), parent education (about child development), information and referral (concerning social benefits and other services), and social support (by the HHV or other mothers), and encourage attendance at the local neighborhood child health clinic. They make parents aware of the factors shaping their child's health that are within the parents' control to address, and ensure that all immunizations and screening procedures are carried out in a timely and appropriate manner.

Of particular importance, health visiting is a home-based outreach and

access service, opening the way to personal social service, income maintenance, housing, and other systems. In addition, HHVs provide an important case finding and early identification service concerning cases of incipi-
ent child abuse or neglect, developmental lags, or postpartum depression;
they offer treatment or referral as needed and as appropriate for children,
mothers, or other family members. (Social workers are required to report
incidents of child abuse, and multiagency child protection committees in
every area review potential or alleged cases of child abuse.)

The British HHV's contact with the mother is usually begun during
pregnancy when the HHV is contacted or referred by the GP or midwife,
and thus a relationship is established even before the baby is born. They
have no legal right to visit, only a legal requirement that they offer the visit.
Acceptance of the offer is up to the parents; the visits are strictly voluntary.
However, almost all parents welcome them because the service is popular,
universal, unstigmatized, and viewed as helpful.

British HHV has late-nineteenth-century public health origins, and by
early in the twentieth century the service was provided by almost all local
governments as a function of the local authority Medical Officer of Health,
as part of the maternal and child health service. Home visits were triggered
when the general practitioner or the midwife who was present notified the
Medical Officer of Health of a birth. Such notification, initially voluntary,
was later mandated.[32]

By World War II it was routine to visit every newborn within ten days
after delivery. The National Health Service (NHS) Act, passed in 1946
and implemented in 1948, formalized what was by then already a universally available service, by requiring that it be provided in every area to all
families with young children. In recent years, the typical, recommended
home visit pattern has been six visits before the child enters compulsory
education at age 5 (a visit immediately following childbirth, a visit just
after hospital discharge, and visits when the child is six weeks, eight
months, twenty-one months, and thirty-nine months old). However, most
HHVs adapt to individual circumstances after the initial visit. In fact, in
the two communities in which we carried out field visits, the practice was
seven and nine visits in addition to a predelivery contact with the mother.

All this is now in the midst of change. In 1974, local health authorities
(LAH) were established, leading to the reassignment of GPs who had
previously been affiliated with the local authority social services, to the new
health service. In 1990 legislation, the GP was given more comprehensive
responsibility for families on his list and the option of taking on (at an
additional fee) the regular surveillance of preschool children, at parental
request. Because the GP could refuse to accept families for his general list
who do not elect him for the surveillance, this becomes his decision, if seen
as attractive to him. (But some families will choose the HHV.) He can add

community nurses to his practice to implement the surveillance, or carry it out in his office. To the extent that GPs do not take on surveillance, the HHV role in the preschool years will continue. Or the HHV may continue as part of a GP practice, changing somewhat in the transition from a community to a GP-office base. It is too early to discern a trend. In a sense, in coming years, Britain could become more like the one- or two-visit countries, where the primary care physician or family pediatrician carries ongoing prevention responsibilities. In any case, the initial visit and outreach by the HHV along with some additional visits will remain, while more of the HHV's "reduced" time may become available for services to the elderly and other community functions.

## Denmark

Denmark's maternal and child health program has long been considered an exemplar in public health terms. Apart from the excellent infant mortality, maternal mortality, and morbidity results—much of it attributed to a generally progressive social policy and the related standard of living—the program has been seen as the nucleus of a family supportive health and social services effort, geared to case finding and early intervention. Its delivery system elements and the values that guide them could be of interest in an American discussion even though we will not, as a country, convert to a unified national health service and despite the fact that our size and diversity are in marked contrast to small Denmark.

The maternal and child health program, including the important home health visiting (HHV) component, is anchored in the country's general health service. Denmark, as did many European countries, began with occupation-related sickness insurance schemes. It gradually moved toward universal coverage, finally transferring all responsibility to public authorities. The National Health Security Act of 1971 abolished the remaining "insurance" (contributory) features of health protection, dissolved sickness insurance funds, and assigned their tasks to public departments. A uniform system of sickness, childbirth, and work injury payments was set up on the same basis as unemployment insurance. Medical care, whether outpatient or hospital-based, is a public service.[33]

A family chooses a family physician from among all physicians in its catchment area. If the family moves to another area, it has the option of continuing with its physician. Recent policy allows a change of physicians every six months if desired, and even more frequently under some circumstances. Here, as in Britain, the family physician is the route to specialists and hospitals. By all indicators the arrangement enjoys considerable popular support. Denmark does not experience the indiscriminate use of hospital emergency rooms and outpatient clinics known to the United States.

The Ministry of Health at the national level deals with fourteen county councils plus Copenhagen and Frederiksberg, which serve as both cities and counties. At the tier below the counties are the 273 municipalities. The counties carry responsibility for outpatient health services, hospitals, special services for the handicapped, and the nonmedical training of nurses and occupational therapists. The municipality is responsible for social services (under the Ministry of Social Welfare), which are closely linked with the health services, as well as for nursing homes, shelters, home nursing, and health promotion. In effect, the health care of infants, toddlers, and preschoolers to age 6 or 7, when compulsory school begins, is monitored by the public health nurse, who has links with the family physician (who provides most of the service to most of the children after age 1 or 2) and with the social workers in the local social service departments. The school health service takes over health surveillance when the child enters elementary school, but the local public health nurse continues to serve as a special liaison for families when there are special needs.

Danish public health nurse HHVs acknowledge the British lead, historically, but Denmark now has the most comprehensive program of this kind. The Danish program was enacted in 1937 following some years of concern about an infant mortality rate that was viewed as high in comparison to that of the other Scandinavian countries. The 1971 legislation creating the national health service assigned an important role to the HHV. The very first Danish public health visiting service, established in 1937, was based on voluntary cooperation of the municipalities and was universal from the onset. There were no advocates of selectivity, a program only for the poor. This would have been contrary to Denmark's general universalistic social policies. As the report proposing the service states, the HHV service was based from the beginning "on the principle that the advisory activities were offered to the homes without regard to their financial circumstances."[34] The HHVs were instructed to focus on infants under age one; even then, however, their instructions were to not limit themselves strictly to infants. At the beginning the services were aimed at improving the physical health of the child through routine and regular visits, but in subsequent years the focus shifted to include social factors as well.

The public health nurse is far more than the health visitor known in some countries. She (or he) completes training as a nurse, is required to have hospital experience, and then takes a year of special training. She is an experienced, well-qualified practitioner.

When a child is born, a message reaches the public health nurse through the hospital or midwife. (As is the case in many countries, midwifery is well developed and recognized as essential and effective in Denmark; almost all births take place in hospitals.) The public health nurse's first visit occurs during the mother's first week at home with her baby. On the first visit, there is much talk about the delivery experience (an opportunity for the mother to share her feelings and to express anxieties), the child is weighed and examined, the nurse deals with the mother's ability to breast-feed, and she gives any necessary guidance. If an alternative is needed, the mother is helped with the formula. There is an emphasis on understanding how the mother and baby are doing together. If there are older children, those relationships are looked at as well. If problems are noted with regard to the housing, a referral will be made; close social service links also exist and facilitate referrals. A handicapped child might be referred for special treatment or equipment. If special medical treatment seems to be needed, the public health nurse makes contact with the family doctor. The latter in turn has contacts when the baby is one week, five weeks, five months, ten months, and fifteen months old. Then there are routine checkups annually until the child is six years old.

Also visiting is the midwife, who will come to the home one or two times in the first week, particularly if the hospital discharge has taken place within fewer than five days. (There is current experimentation with shorter stays following childbirth, even one-day stays.)

If the public health nurse sees reason for concern about potential or possible neglect or abuse, she may discuss it with the family doctor or go to the social welfare office. From time to time there are multidisciplinary meetings at the local social welfare office about cases that are of concern, to develop a course of action.

All newborns are covered by the initial visits, although the mother has the right to refuse. The pattern for some time has been to individualize the visiting schedule after that, according to family circumstances, i.e. the mother's experience, the perception of potential problems or needs. Some homes will be visited only two or three times in the course of the first year, particularly mothers having a second or third child. A public health nurse, who at a given moment might have a caseload of approximately 140 infants, does not respond to a formal schedule (the earlier pattern) but rather is concerned with how the child is developing, whether the mother is an isolated single parent, whether the family is part of a network of family and friends, and the mother's health status. The nurse makes additional visits as needed. If concerned about a child's care, she does a lot via detailed demonstration, such as show how to bathe a baby, how to touch a child, how to give love, and how to express feelings.

When a baby is between seven and ten months old, usually in the eighth month, the nurse carries out a standard child development test and enters the result in the child's medical record. She checks eyesight, hearing, coordination, and responsiveness, among other things. The record, kept from the time of the first visit, is quite factual if all goes normally. The mother, in addition, is given a baby book for a record of the visits, in which the nurse makes an entry every time in the home. The family also brings this baby book on visits to the doctors. When the child is one year old, the nurses complete another form with the parents, and that becomes the record that the nurse keeps on file in the office for as long as the child is in the system (ten years). It is transferred if the child moves.

Another supportive or educational device emphasized is what the nurse calls her "open house." She invites several mothers with newborns to a gathering in an apartment, clinic, or other community facility close to where they live. Here she can talk to the group, look at individual children, and create subgroups (immigrants, parents of twins, young parents, single parents) for which she can provide help on a group basis.

Inevitably, all of this creates a complicated scheduling problem for public health nurses, but there is obvious enthusiasm for the role despite the frequent readjustments as birth rates fluctuate and special needs arise. The nurse maintains one office in the municipal public health office and another in the schools where she cooperates as a team member with the doctors. Although in theory she has a relationship to day care, day nurseries, and nursery schools, as does the family doctor, the practice of having the public health nurse routinely check children at these facilities was dropped some time ago. The district health officers supervise health practice in the nurseries; they go in on their own, in response to calls from the director, or in response to calls from doctors who have concerns. Some municipalities expect the public health nurses to give guidance to the child care staff. They also may be invited to speak at parent meetings.

As noted, when the child reaches elementary school age, the school health service takes over the surveillance, but the public health nurse continues to play an important part. The school physician examines kindergarten, first grade, and second-grade children once each year. All routine health care for children beyond the second grade is done by the school health nurse, who sees children annually, tests their sight and hearing, and provides health education.

Recent developments in research, and analysis of experience, have confirmed decisions to move the system of doctor, midwife, and nurse visits to the more individualized pattern, decreasing what were regarded as unnecessary routine visits to some families. The training emphasizes sensitivity to "special needs" groups, such as young single mothers, immigrants, people from other cultural backgrounds, the socially isolated, and first-time parents. The program features effective interdisciplinary collaboration, family-supportive "early intervention" that is both social and medical and includes parent education on a one-to-one and small-group basis. Staff regard themselves as still working to improve interdisciplinary collaboration and to develop better strategies for individualizing their work with families.

In the late 1960s an effort was made to assess the health visiting experience. Apart from the overwhelmingly positive assessments emerging from the counties, an important finding was that the average number of visits to infants could be reduced, permitting an increased number of visits to children with special physical and/or mental handicaps and to children in families with special problems. The 1970 report called for an effort concentrated on "homes with a first child and on the about 15 percent of the families in which the children are either not quite well or are living under conditions which may influence their physical and/or mental development."[35] This finding led to the subsequent curtailment of first-year visits from twelve to about six, with more frequent visits to families having just one ("first") child or living in situations requiring special attention.

In effect, the British HHV service began as a targeted service, became a universal service before World War II, and was mandated shortly after the war. It remains a universal service but is now becoming more targeted in the context of cost constraints as well as philosophical shifts. There is greater emphasis on expanding the preventive role of the GP (surely not a cost containment measure!), on reducing the alleged paternalism of the HHV service, on decreasing maternal and child isolation by forming mother/child groups at the local clinic, and on empowering parents. Despite this trend, the HHV seems likely to continue with four to six visits during the first year, to most families, and more to those with special needs.

The Danish system became more targeted after a late-1960s review and evaluation, but continued to sustain at least four to six visits a year to all, more to the firstborn, and still more to immigrant and other special-needs children and families. There has never been any serious consideration of anything but a universal service ("not for the poor alone"), given Denmark's general social policy. Within universalism, current targeting relates to the degree of need for service. The view is that more across-the- board visits are not needed. Most mothers are at work from the time their baby is six months old. As a result, more than half of all children are in out-of-home child care, whether family day care or centers, by age 6 to 12 months, and more than 60 percent at age 2. Case finding—of abuse, neglect, and/or developmental lags—can be carried out easily in these programs, which are community-based and municipally organized and supervised. In addition, all children are seen in neighborhood maternal and child health clinics, from shortly after birth; and if mothers do not appear for the appropriate examinations, the HHV calls and/or visits the home. Finally, there is strong conviction that mothers, especially those with just one child, are physically, socially, and psychologically isolated and benefit from mother/

child groups organized by the HHVs and carried out at various sites in the community, either at the home of a mother, at the clinic, or at some other community facility.

## Danish Home Health Visits: The System in Action

The summarized report elaborates on both context and process in the Danish system. Since Denmark is highly decentralized to the municipality, there are variations in how these services are implemented.

The city of Helsingör has a population of sixty thousand, with approximately 685 births each year. There are nineteen public health nurses, twelve of them full-time, who cover these births, resulting in a caseload of about forty babies per nurse. In addition, each HHV has responsibility for one school, having about six hundred children. In effect, the HHVs get to know all the families from the time a baby is born. Their offices are in an attractive, comfortable building along with the local social services department and the social work staff. The HHVs observed are well-trained, mature, self-confident professionals.

In the instance of a first birth, ten visits are offered from the time of the mother's pregnancy until the child is two and a half years old: late in the pregnancy, the first week after birth, two weeks later, three or four weeks later, and at ages 3 months, 5 months, 8 months, 1 year, $1^{1/2}$ years, and $2^{1/2}$ years. Paralleling these visits by the HHV, the doctor is seeing the child at the clinic for inoculations and checkups. At the time of the first visit, when the mother is nearing the end of her pregnancy, the HHV explains the services and offers them. Although parents have the right to reject the offer, none of the HHVs in this department has ever experienced a refusal. The first visit gives the HHV some sense of the mother's anxieties and concerns, her and her partner's attitudes toward the coming birth, and a review of how realistic she may be with regard to adjusting to a different life-style after the baby arrives.

The first visit following birth occurs after the return from the hospital. At the completion of this and all subsequent visits, the mother is given an offer of another visit. Usually it is a matter of the HHV having to set limits on the number of visits or having to phase down the visits over time—not a matter of the mother or parents refusing the offer. During the initial visit, the nurse makes a basic assessment, which she continues to make, and accordingly sets the frequency of other visits. Thus, she evaluates the quality of the communication between the parent and child, the extent to which the mother appears to understand the child's signals, how the child looks, and whether the mother really needs to have more attention.

In contrast to Britain (where the practice is actually disappearing), there is no such thing as an unannounced visit; visits here are all specifically arranged in advance. If the mother said she did not want any more visits, the HHV would concur; but the HHV would try to report any potential problems, either to the parent, physician, or even the social worker—if she had any serious concerns.

For a family with several children there will probably be six visits between birth and the first year, and that will be it. However, if there are social problems, parents with alcohol or drug problems, insecure young parents (sixteen to seventeen year olds), poor development, a mentally or physically handicapped child, or immigrant parents, the HHV will visit more often.

On a typical day, the HHV spent about one hour from (8:00 to 9:00 A.M.) in her office, responding to phone calls. On the day of our field visit, these included requests for an earlier visit, a postponement of an appointment, information about what to expect following a baby's vaccination, advice about starting a baby on solid food, reassurance regarding a baby's introduction to a new family day care situation, and advice on how to tell a two-year-old about a mother's pregnancy. This nurse has two phone-in periods each week, but parents also may call anytime between 8:00 A.M. and 4:00 P.M. and leave a message with the secretary, and the nurse will call back when she has time.

Following that, the HHV's first visit of the day was to a family living close to the center of town, in a small house with a patch of green in back. The home—two bedrooms, a living room, a kitchen, and a bathroom—was disordered and dirty. The parents are in their thirties; the father is a hospital worker and the mother an occupational therapist. The baby is their first child, ten weeks old, and cries frequently. The mother was concerned, called the nurse very often, and asked for as many visits as possible. The mother seemed insecure and asked the nurse, in person and over the phone, all kinds of questions about the baby's appearance, eating, and crying, and about how she should deal with the baby and whether she (the mother) was causing the problems.

After some informal talk with the mother, the nurse took the baby and put him on a table with a blanket underneath him, and proceeded to undress and examine him. She talked to the baby quietly, gradually undressing him, playing with him, touching him, and evoking a cooing response. She paid attention to a swollen part of his thigh, where he had been inoculated the previous day, and explained to the mother what had happened and how to deal with it and make him more comfortable. She then wrapped the child in a sling made of a diaper and weighed him; she used her tape measure to measure the child's body length and head size, and wrote the information down in the baby book—the baby's official health record, which all Danish parents have—which the mother presented when the visit began. The HHV compared this information with the data from the prior visit, commenting on the adequate growth. The HHV then took both her hands and ran them down the side of the baby's head, looking into the baby's eyes, nose, and mouth, examining gums and so forth. She carefully felt down the side of the baby's body, including his stomach, and looked at his legs, seeing if they were straight—all the time talking to the baby and watching for responses.

Along the way, the HHV responded to the mother's concerns about the baby's crying. Noting that the mother always responded to the cries by offering a breast, assuming the baby was hungry, she commented on how crying need not always be a signal of hunger. Maybe the baby wants to be picked up, talked to, played with, or walked with. Excessive breast-feeding could make the baby more uncomfortable and lead to crying. During the visit, she showed the mother how, when the baby cries, picking him up and talking to him and playing with him stops the crying. She modeled the child handling and relating, without saying much about it explicitly.

This was a very anxious new mother who did not seem to be able to respond to her child's signals. The HHV described a new mothers' group she was setting up with six other new mothers, and the mother agreed to come to the first meeting as soon as she was assured that this would not mean the end of the home visits. The HHV explained to us that she would launch a group, participate for the first few weeks, and then let the mothers continue on their own, usually meeting at one or another's home, providing support for each other. If they wish, subsequently, an "expert" in a particular subject of concern to the mothers may attend a meeting. The groups may last for a few months, a year, or even longer. Occasionally, a father's group is formed as well. She described one long-lived and very successful one.

### France: An Overview

Britain and Denmark were cited for their exemplar HHV programs, teamed up with primary care physicians. France illustrates an excellent service that would be called a well-baby clinic in the United States, operated with a preventive orientation and separate from the health insurance administration. We also shall briefly cite Finland's child health clinics to show a variation on the pattern.

Of the four countries chosen to illustrate child health protection possibilities, only France has an insurance system (rather than a health service). As we write, the United States has a variety of insurance systems and is moving toward a more uniform national coverage model. Therefore, it is of some interest that within its model France has developed and sustained an outstanding child health plan. Clinics offer an attractive, free option.

The French Maternal and Child Health services (*PMI* in French, *MCH* in English), which is separate from the health insurance system and administered under the Ministry of Health, began more than a century ago. MCH includes measures of both health and social protection. Current policies stem largely from the post–World War II years.

Since 1945, free well-baby or preventive health care has been available to children from birth to school entry (age 6) through the MCH clinics.[36] This care includes monitoring growth and development, routine vaccinations, and advice to parents on the care, feeding, and development of their children. Visits are recommended once a month from birth to six months of age, every three months from six to twelve months of age, every four months from one to two years of age, and then every six months until six years of age, when the school health service (much less satisfactory according to all reports) takes over.

There are seven "mandatory" prenatal examinations of the pregnant mother, and three infant examinations (one week after birth and at nine months and two years of age), in the sense that payment of certain family allowances is contingent on documentation of these examinations. Relevant information is kept on the *Carnet de Santé*, (the child's health passport, carried by the mother) and on each child's clinic health record, and a copy is sent to the appropriate MCH center to ensure necessary follow-up.

Earlier, each pregnant woman has received a copy of a maternity record that includes all relevant information about her pregnancy and her legal rights and entitlements during pregnancy and after childbirth as well as information about resources for help, advice, child care, and financial support.

Parents or caretakers may choose to have children examined either in an MCH center at no charge, or by their own private physician, where they will pay but be reimbursed completely or in part. About 30 percent of children have their preventive care at MCH centers and 70 percent with private primary care doctors or pediatricians. Since the early 1980s, administration of the MCH clinic service has been decentralized to the *département* level (similar to a U.S. county), and as a consequence, there is far more diversity and range in resource availability and allocation now than previously.

The clinics are community-based. The MCH team includes a doctor, a midwife, a nurse, social workers, and psychologists. Although a universal service, MCH is used more by lower- and working-class populations. Of the 800,000 pregnancies each year, resulting in about 760,000 births, about 20 percent of mothers go to MCH clinics, and the rest receive private care, which is covered under the French national health insurance program and is reimbursable. Immigrants and minorities make as much use of the MCH clinics as does the native French population.

The MCH is a preventive service, not a treatment service, although the line of demarcation is sometimes crossed, especially in low-income communities. Home visits may be provided if deemed necessary, but not on a routine basis as in England and Denmark. Nurses play an important role in the decision on whether to pay a home visit. Young mothers, those with large families, and immigrant mothers are the ones defined as high-risk and most likely to receive home visits.

There is an important and close link between the *crèches* and the MCH through MCH's responsibility for inspecting and regulating the quality of the *crèches* and providing health care services to the facilities.

### France: Two PMIs (MCHs)

We illustrate with reference to one MCH center serving a very deprived area in Paris and another in a suburb. One wonders whether we, too, in the United States, despite contemplated insurance availability, will want a well-baby clinic option in our pending health reform.

The first MCH to be described is located in one of the poorest areas in Paris. The buildings are old and dilapidated, and the streets are in need of major repairs. It is a neighborhood of foreigners, recent immigrants, mostly blacks from Africa, and of high population density. There are two hospitals in the neighborhood, one public and one private, that provide maternity services and tend to channel cases to the MCH. There is also an *École Matèrnelle* and a *Halte Garderie* (see Chapter 6).

Staff include one *puericultrice* (a pediatric nurse), an aide (individuals with one year of *puericultrice* training), and a receptionist/typist. Of the three, one helps the doctor who is doing the examinations, one staffs the reception area, and one serves children in the waiting room with their families. The staff also share the housekeeping.

The doctor with whom we talked confirmed what we have encountered elsewhere and not infrequently in the United States. The program is intended to be "preventive," but for the people in this neighborhood it very often provides the only treatment they are likely to seek. Either they are not in the health system, do not know how to use it, or whatever. If they are without health insurance and something special is needed, they will be provided with a signed form to obtain the service at the local hospital; and the city will pay for it, even if they are illegal immigrants.

Most of the activity, however, is the mandatory health checkups at the specified times following childbirth. These are essential, because they are preconditions for various child/family allowances. As indicated in the *Carnet de Santé*, the most important examinations are the ones during the week after childbirth, at nine months, and at twenty-four months. A form must be filled out and submitted to the National Child Allowance Fund

(CNAF). If the form is not received at the CNAF, the allowance will not be paid.

The entrance to the MCH is at the top of a flight of stairs, and at the beginning of the afternoon hours, parents and children assemble in the waiting room off the small reception room at the top of the stairs. Everything possible has been done to make the very limited, old reception and waiting rooms attractive. There are posters, children's drawings, and health posters that explain such things as the importance of sleep and of good nutrition. There are toys in the waiting room for children of different ages, and children's books as well.

Outer clothes are left in the waiting room, and then parents and children return to the reception area, where the children are weighed and measured. Five mothers and one father (and their children) were in the waiting room as we visited. All were black except for one Muslim woman and her baby. The black mothers chatted with their children while the Muslim mother remained impassive and silent. Three of the mothers had infants in their arms, and one was nursing her baby. Most of the children were toddlers, in animated conversation with their mothers or with the other children.

The aide engaged the children in play with the toys, in effect modeling for the parents what the children should be exposed to and how they can learn from play.

The doctor had an easy manner with the children and parents as he called them from the waiting room to go in with him to the examining room. He had the *Carnet de Santé* for each child and the child's medical record with him. When they left, he handed both to the receptionist, who filled them out and processed them properly, particularly the mandatory examination reports. The *puéricultrice,* who is the administrator for this MCH, previously worked at a *crèche* and a maternity ward of a hospital, and so was well trained and experienced for this work.

The typical examination takes about fifteen minutes, but the doctor is responsive to whatever may come up and whatever the mothers may bring up. A doctor sees about fifteen children in one of his sessions. In the last quarter of the year, in this MCH, well over a thousand children were examined.

The MCH serves children aged 0 to 6, and almost all the children in the neighborhood are seen; it is rare that any are missed. Mothers are told about the service in the hospital when they give birth, and by family and neighbors, subsequently. Everyone uses the service. At age 6, the children are transferred either to a private physician or the school doctor.

There is heavy emphasis on advice, in addition to the checkups and inoculations: advice about nutrition, sleeping, developmental issues, and family planning.

In contrast to the above, the second facility (in a town less than an hour from Paris) is in a middle-class suburb. The center is housed in a beautifully built structure, half of which serves as a *crèche* for one hundred children. The entry is very attractive, and the entire center is freshly painted, well furnished, and well equipped. There are posters, children's paintings, and other artwork on the walls. This is one of four MCH's in this town, which together serve about half the children under age 3. The other children are seen either in other clinics that have pediatricians, in hospital emergency rooms, or, for the most part, by their personal pediatricians. Nonetheless, for some part of the population, the preferred service is the MCH, perhaps because it is free but perhaps because there really is a great deal of warmth and attention and it is located near home.

This MCH is staffed by one doctor who is present four times a week for examinations and services: on Mondays from 4:30 to 6:45 P.M., on Tuesdays from 2:00 until 3:30 P.M., on Wednesdays from 1:30 to 6:45 P.M., and on Thursdays from 9:00 to 11:00 A.M. The Monday and Wednesday hours are by appointment, and the hours on the other two days are unscheduled walk-ins.

An MCH visit "costs" just over $21, which covers the staffing and ongoing expenses, not the capital investment; it is free to the families.

The doctor (like his Paris colleague) sees about fifteen children in each session, sometimes for the routine specified examinations, sometimes for problems or mothers' concerns. About three hundred children have follow-up each year. Of these, one hundred are North African and fifty-nine are black African, largely from Senegal or Mali. These are not the poor and marginalized families seen in the earlier MCH but rather those who have been in France for fifteen or twenty years and are now reasonably well socialized into French mores. They have steady jobs, have legal work status, have obtained decent housing, and have learned what their entitlements are and how to use the system.

The information provided parents by the *puericultrice* includes advice about feeding, nutrition, sleep patterns, and what can be expected in general behavior at different ages.

For the half days and full days when there is no clinic here, staff have organized a free play group that is a cross between child care and family support (see Chapters 6 and 7). Mothers come when the doctor is not here, to meet with other mothers, to bring their children to play with other children, and/or to talk with the *puericultrice* and aides.

## Finland

Finland offers a somewhat different pattern even though, as in Denmark, it has a largely publicly administered and delivered system of medical service (with a small private sector and the possibility of private insurance coverage).

What makes Finland of major interest is its current place, along with Iceland and Japan, as a world leader in conquest of infant mortality. And this status was achieved only after World War II. Finland's infant mortality rates plunged from 43.5 per thousand live births in 1950 to 21.0 in 1960, 13.2 in 1970, and 5.5 in 1990. Child health results are outstanding by all indicators, and contagious diseases virtually have been wiped out. All this was achieved during a period of late industrialization and the need for reconstruction of large areas and payment of heavy war reparations. After World War II, the country adopted an efficient and affordable health delivery system that worked well, became popular, and was continued into the affluent 1970s and 1980s.

The emphasis in Finland is on a free and universal system that integrates the family doctor, the health centers for children, the prenatal care and family planning in the health centers, and the hospital system, under one overall administration. It is all paid for out of tax funds.

People have the option of getting their medical care privately and receiving reimbursement through the public health insurance. Some do. Nonetheless, everybody joins the public insurance system, and practically everyones uses the primary public health care system. Some 80 percent of the volume of care and 70 percent of the costs are through the public system.

The local primary health care center is the core of the delivery system. Ninety-five percent of the population use it for maternity care and childbirth; most people also use the public hospitals for long-term care for children who need it, all without any fees. The exact physical arrangements for these services vary according to the municipality. For example, family planning, maternity and postnatal care, child health, mother's classes, and dental services could all be in one building. Nonetheless, there tends to be some separation of the child health clinics from the clinics serving others, or there might be one building with different wings.

In contrast to Denmark, the Finnish public health nurses do relatively little home visiting, except in rural areas, but they are central to the clinic preventive activities. Although historically the emphasis in the children's services was on following norms and procedures as defined from the medical end, there is more and more an attempt to go beyond the physical, into what might be thought of as family education, support, and cooperation with the social services. Inadequate physical resources, poor care, and possible difficulties in coping with one's child can be dealt with directly by the nurse. She has some discretion as to when she refers to the social workers, to the doctor, or to the family guidance setup. The same holds with reference to child abuse. Given a good basic and comprehensive child health service, here as elsewhere, there is less likelihood of setting up special detection units for child abuse and less need to refer to social services if the problem can be dealt with in the course of normal medical services.

The public health nurses are well trained for this work. They have four and a half years of standard training after secondary school, and some speciality training in addition to that. Some also are trained as midwives, and others have graduate training in public health. The pay is quite satisfactory but does not compete with engineering or other technical fields now open to women.

When there are problems that they regard as too complex for them or as requiring specialists, the nurses make referrals to the guidance personnel or the social workers. There are also outpatient clinics, and clinics in churches and elsewhere in the community. Public health nurses are encouraged to develop mental health understanding and not to refer too quickly. They know the family, know the situation, and are expected to try to help first.

To illustrate briefly: After her return from the hospital following childbirth, the mother is visited by the midwife, examined, and then transferred to the local public health nurse. All mothers and their newborns are visited two or three times. If there are problems requiring attention (alcoholism, a handicap, some other concern), there will be more home visits. Most children also are seen by the nurse (eleven times) and the doctor (three times) during the first year, at the child health center. The inoculation program begins at age 3 months. All future inoculations are given at the set center visits. Careful records are kept. For routine checkups after the first year, children see the nurse at the center annually and the doctor every two years. If the child is ill, he/she is brought to see the doctor (not necessarily the well-baby clinic doctor) in the other building. Should the mother be ill, a HHV may be sent. There is a "big" checkup of the child at age 5 or $5^{1/2}$ before compulsory school entry at age 7, and the intervening time is used to cope with school readiness and deal with whatever medical measures are needed.

The child health center sees every child and has a health record on every child. Moreover, if people do not come when expected for follow-up, the nurses will phone and then the parents comply. The stress is on monitoring the child and giving needed preventive advice. The nurse also meets with some of the mothers in groups, usually when the children are under age 1. They discuss everything about child rearing: eating, crying, colic, etc. The nurses arrange these groups for the mothers. Mothers also may go to "ready groups" in churches and elsewhere. The nurses are invited to make lectures before such groups.

A strong preventive philosophy dominates in Finland: A determination not to "lose" children in the system generates useful administrative and control devices, like the child health records that mothers in several countries carry from examination to examination until their children enter school, or the computerized national tracking system to ensure that children get preventive care and vaccination (as in the Netherlands and Britain).

We close this section with further brief reference to the Netherlands, where most families obtain preventive services f,om a national network of six thousand well-baby and well-toddler clinics, serving children to age 4. This network is separately organized and is financed with government funds routed to regional sickness funds and private insurance companies.[37] Some 90 percent of children attend the clinics for eleven recommended preventive care examinations and for immunizations. Problems detected during the checkups are referred to the child's GP.


## Some Possibilities for the United States

The future reform of health care in the United States challenges us to "get it right" for young children. It seems reasonable to assume, from all that is proposed and the nature of the recent debate, that maternity services and acute and chronic care for children will become universally available in the not-too-distant future. The medical system knows how to deliver such services, and the applicable standards are good. Professional bodies offer comprehensive outlines and guides. The challenge, then, is to organize as well for child health protection, the "prevention" component.

In 1921, and again in 1935, Americans launched a maternal and child health system, but subsequent developments defeated attempts to establish a broadly available, standard program. Nonetheless, within our public health systems we have some excellent programs and evidence that the health professions are not lacking in competence or capacity to design and implement a universally available child health protection model. The evidence is that we do need something that will offer what is done so well in Britain, Denmark, France, and Finland (and we could readily add to the list): a reaching-out preventive service with close ties to primary care but distinct and visible in its specialized mission. It would appear in a child's life nine months before birth in the form of a high-quality, universal prenatal service, with continuity into and out of the hospital. Early at-home visits would verify that the parent or parents is/are prepared emotionally and cognitively for a good start, and are equipped with the means, resources, and housing to cope and to function successfully. A home visitor or nurse/doctor in the child health center would advise, monitor, examine, teach, and refer to social services specialists or to income transfer, housing, and employment programs as appropriate, and would follow up. The philosophy would be what is expressed in the currently popular term, "empowerment" of parents, not taking over their roles. A system of available records would follow place to place, professional to professional, to ensure continuity and consistency of contacts. Computer systems would guard against losing a child in the system and against lapses in the inoculation schedule. The parents would carry their equivalent of the French or Danish child health booklet or "Passport."

All of this could be organized in a number of possible ways, but it is essential that, after debate, analysis, and perhaps experimentation/ demonstration, there be choice of what would eventually be a universal system (not for the poor alone, not dependent on one's financial means), recognized as a standard system, and integrated with the delivery options that the family will have for acute and chronic care.

We assume that the hoped-for U.S. health care reform will provide everyone with a primary care physician—but that there also will be state options, including offering all parents something like the Dutch, the Finnish, or the French PMI well-baby clinic. Thus, either the primary care doctor or the well-baby clinic would anchor the preventive care guarantee. (Pregnant women would have prenatal coverage guaranteed by the same system.)

It would be most desirable that this well-baby/well-toddler service be supported by outreach capacities. We refer to the HHV program, the broad view of what is relevant to child health and development that is seen in the United Kingdom and Denmark. Every child should be visited at home, at least once or twice, soon after return from the hospital. There could be as many as four to six visits in the first year (as in Denmark or Britain) at parental option. Other children should be visited more times, selectively, depending on the child's conditions, family problems, and status (risk factors)—especially in the first year. At the same time, there would be a set series of first-, second-, and third-year visits to the child health center, or the personal doctor, their number to be set by a professional expert group (The American Academy of Pediatrics?)—certainly no fewer than the recommended inoculation visits and geared to the times of such visits. The routine would include certain specialized screenings, along the lines of Medicaid's EPSTD, at specific intervals—with deliberately organized summing-up sessions with parents about their child's development.

A completely autonomous well-baby/well-toddler clinic system, at state option and covering all children (as in Denmark, Finland, and the Netherlands), is an attractive if probably utopian notion. Where preferred over complete reliance on the preventive role of the family doctor, it could be defined as a reasonable charge on the national budget, some of it financed out of what is now the Maternal and Child Health block grant. Or it might be considered a reasonable charge on the diversity of health plans and options from among which people will select their family medical plans following health care reform A fixed statewide per-child fee, perhaps adjusted by age, and covering the years 0 to 6, would be a not-expensive and certainly cost-effective investment. But the starting point would be a national decision to include the child health protection service in the basic health care package.

Two questions arise: Will parents be at home for the "outreach" efforts, the home visits? Will parents be able to bring their children to the private doctor or child health clinics for the inoculations and checkups? We must refer back to Chapter 4 and the issue of time for parenting. Income, services, and time are all components of a child policy strategy and they are intertwined. We note that France's female labor force participation rates are not unlike ours. Denmark and Finland lead Europe in the rates of full-time labor force participation by mothers. But these countries also manage maternity leaves, parental leaves, time to care for a sick child, longer vacations, and personal days. And, immediately relevant, this time for parenting means that parents are home for the HHV during the early months of the infant's life and that they can find time for the child health clinic visit or the trip to the doctor's office.

The proposal outlined above—home visits in the early months and set visits to the family physician or child health center in the infant and toddler years, all prevention oriented—is our best option. But we also must consider that, however desirable, a national delivery system may not be politically feasible. States will probably be the units for planning and organizing health coverage under future health care reform. There is a preference for decentralization in the entire strategy. It would be highly desirable for the Congress or a delegated federal entity that sets the coverage minimum for all plans, to specify the maternal and child health program (clinic and home visiting components) as part of the basic "insurance" package. One requirement might be the recommendation of the American Academy of Pediatrics of nine well-child visits to the doctor or clinic by age 2. State authorities, or regional purchasing alliances or cooperatives (whatever the eventual plan) could negotiate with potential providers and either finance a state-level public delivery system or contract for the inclusion of such components in HMO, managed care, PPO, and other health delivery systems with which they deal. Thus, the child health preventive staffs would have easy access to the family's primary care physician and to the other professionals in the family's basic health plan.

The latter may not be as promising an approach as the creation of a standard national plan, since it would take quite a while to ensure that the different types of entities can deliver what is needed, but it may be an easier road politically. Either option would provide a delivery system able to monitor and deliver needed inoculations, something not guaranteed by the 1993 legislation that provided vaccines for vulnerable groups.

Experts in service delivery may need to resolve yet another issue. Current interest in home visiting in this country recently has focused on developments in a number of fields.[38] There are reports of positive results focused on "parents as teachers" or case-aide "toy demonstrators," concerned with cognitive stimulation of deprived children. These, too, are home visiting programs. Family support and parent education programs, particularly those focused on low-income single mothers and their children, have found home visiting to be a valuable intervention. And, then, there is the experience with HHV. We leave to Chapter 7 further discussion of family supports. For present purposes we note that, whatever the other home visiting developments and the need to "coordinate" visits to "families with special risks or needs," there is strong endorsement of the notion of a "basic supportive visit to families of newly arrived infants [as] . . . a universally available service."[39] Such visits and services should of course be voluntary.

There is one further point: Impressed as we are with the excellent "coverage" capacity in Europe, where children are brought for health care and inoculations and not lost, we wonder about some related "carrots" and "sticks" as devices to support participation in the United States. It will be recalled that the French tie some family allowance payments to prenatal care and to checkup visits by mothers and babies to the PMI center. The Finns condition the birth "package" on prenatal care. Americans tend to oppose coercion or invasion of privacy even if the cause is a child's welfare. Yet we are concerned about a culture that permits infants to go without protective inoculations or without routine physical checkups. Therefore, we offer two proposals for discussion.

1. Almost all U.S. children now have their inoculations before they begin school, because it is required. Why not build into state child care regulations the requirement that all licensed centers and family day care homes must have proof of inoculations of all children in the program, lest they lose their licenses? This requirement already exists in some places. The federal government could (if legislation so instructed it) condition child care subsidies to the states on such regulations. (In fact, after we completed this manuscript the federal government issued proposed regulations that would enforce such requirements for programs funded by the Child Care and Development Block Grant (CCDBG), which is described in Chapter 6. It remains to be seen whether these regulations will be approved and whether similar regulations will be applied to other federally funded or state-funded programs).

2. Since infant/toddler care covers only part of the cohort, an alternative or supplementary device would use the income tax system to ensure inoculations and/or enrollment in a child health protection system. One could condition eligibility for Earned Income Tax Credit or the child tax exemption on the filing of a certificate verifying the child's inoculation

status or participation in the child health system. (We recently required a social security number for claimed dependents on the income tax return for the first time.)

The latter proposals are of course at the margin. The central recommendation is strongly made and supported by the record: we should launch a child health protection system, ensure well-baby clinics and physician and home health visiting components, and anchor it in the health service reorganization currently under way. It is part of what is required for "starting right."

# 6

## Infant and Toddler Care
## and Education

Over the past two decades, child care has moved to the forefront of the national child and family policy agenda, and the issue has been redefined. Child care has been transformed from a concern with children with "special" needs in the late 1960s and early 1970s (children who were abused and neglected, cognitively deprived, from dysfunctional families, or of poor, working mothers) to a primary concern with that majority of children who have a working sole parent or two parents. The child care system as a whole continues to take account of special needs as well.

For our purposes here, child care services include all types of out-of-home, nonrelative care of children under compulsory school age, whether in centers, family day care homes, or schools. In the United States, the major functions of these services, in no particular order, have been to provide care for the children of working mothers/parents generally; to provide care for the children of welfare-dependent and low-income mothers so as to facilitate movement off the welfare rolls and into the workforce; to provide special help, care, or compensatory education and socialization experiences for dependent, troubled, deprived and disadvantaged children; and to provide children with an opportunity for early childhood education, socialization, and development. We shall emphasize the new interest in infant and toddler care with respect to even the last of these functions.

Good-quality child care services can make a major contribution to child development and school readiness. At the same time, child care programs are a critical link in the family-work nexus.

Infant and toddler care services, as distinct from care of the 3- to 5-year-olds, was not a significant issue in the United States until the end of the 1970s. Before then, child care policies were thought of largely in relation to 3- to 5-year-olds. It was assumed that younger children were at home, cared for by their mothers, who were also at home; the small number of children with employed mothers were assumed to be taken care of by relatives, or by nonrelatives, in the children's own homes. It was assumed that poor, single mothers with very young children were supported through AFDC and thus did not need nonparental care arrangements. Children with "special needs" might be in day care—but usually not the under-threes. Head Start, the major child care/compensatory education program established in the 1960s, was explicitly focused on the three- to five-year-olds (especially the four-year-olds) and was premised on "participation" by an at-home mother. The long debate about the never-to-be-implemented Federal Interagency Day Care Regulations (FIDCR) did not even involve care of the under-threes; it was only in 1975 that standards for infant and toddler care were included.[1] Several states even refused to license centers for children of this age.

Indeed, it was not until the 1980s that significant attention was drawn to the issue of child care for the under-threes, and this was largely in response to the growing trend among married women with children of this age to be in the labor force. By 1986, half of such women were in the labor force, and by the beginning of the 1990s almost 60 percent were. In 1987, for the first time, half the children under age 3 had "working mothers," and 57 percent in 1993; and more and more of them were being cared for outside of their homes, by nonrelatives.

By the late 1980s, infant care had clearly become an issue. There was serious debate among researchers and child care experts about the consequences for infants of out-of-home child care.[2] The two other major foci were the supply shortage of infant and toddler care and the quality of the care provided. With a significant proportion of available care for infants and toddlers made up of family day care, either unregulated or unlicensed, or, if regulated or licensed, operating under low standards or unenforced standards, the problem of quality assumed special importance. In contrast to care of the three- to five-year-olds, which continued to be pulled in two directions—by the education system (nursery schools, prekindergartens) and the social service system (day care)—infant/toddler care was viewed only as a social service for working parents, albeit sometimes under education auspices and sometimes social welfare.

The auspice issue initially appeared less important for infant/toddler care, in part because the subject appeared to be ancillary to the main focus—care for the three- and four-year-olds. (By 1980, most five-year-olds were already in kindergarten, for at least part of the day.) Yet now, the auspice question, too, is emerging as an issue for infant and toddler care, along with the question of whether center or family day care is the preferred mode.

Both child care and family support services (Chapter 7) are now aimed at helping parents care for and rear their very young children successfully. The focus of this chapter is on the present status of infant and toddler care in this country; the need for improvements in supply, accessibility, quality, and affordability to meet present and expected demand; the options in programming; and the urgency of a major federal role in coping with the situation.

## The U.S. Scene

In the United States, most child care and family support developments occur at the state and local government levels, where most prerogatives reside. Nonetheless, federal policy is a major force shaping what occurs in the states.

With the Head Start exception, major federal child care involvement is via financing rather than direct provision or involvement in program detail. It now includes funding for child care for AFDC beneficiaries and low-income working families, compensatory education programs and Head Start, and child care tax credits that benefit the middle and upper classes primarily. State and local government funding goes toward some child care services and most preprimary education. A large part of child care is also a market service and as such is heavily financed by parents themselves—with, at most, modest tax credit or employer subsidies.

The first significant, exclusive federal child care program, not a by-product of social service funding and not Head Start, the Child Care and Development Block Grant (CCDBG), was enacted in 1990, providing substantially increased funds for child care for low-income families. Despite many proposals and long debate over several years, the issue of standards was left largely to the states, except for rules relating to physical safety and health. In authorizing $2.5 billion in new funds for three fiscal years, 1991–1993, the legislation designated 75 percent of the total for sliding-scale fee assistance to help poor families meet their child care needs and for state initiatives to improve service availability and quality (with much latitude allowed). A small set-aside—about $470,000—is reserved for early childhood education and after-school programs.

About $7 billion in federal funds was expended in 1990 for child care, almost half through the tax credit, benefiting middle- and upper-income working families, and the remainder through Head Start, the CCDBG, and social service funds, benefiting low-income families, both working and nonworking. This was more than triple the 1986 expenditure in current dollars. Subsequently, President Clinton proposed full funding of Head Start.

But the federal policy is unchanged. The response to working parents and to children awaiting group experiences is quite inadequate. There has not been a significant move toward more federal support for child care for working- or middle-class families going beyond the child care tax credit, a modest assist. Quality issues have not been addressed nationally. Preprimary school programs are continuing to grow in numbers, albeit slowly, in response to state and local government initiatives—constrained by funding problems but reflecting concerns about the future labor force and, especially, school-readiness of poor, minority, and non-English-speaking children. Kindergarten coverage for five-year-olds became universal in the 1980s and is steadily increasing for three- and four-year-olds. However, universal coverage for the latter groups is still very far away, and there are substantial shortages of child care resources for children under age 3 whose parents seek out-of-home care arrangements.

Much national attention has been focused on Head Start during the early Clinton years because of the President's public commitments, the strong complaints about program weaknesses by Congressional critics, and a subsequent major report by an Advisory Committee to the Department of Health and Human Service. Head Start, which may be school-connected or related to social service agencies, offers its enriched, compensatory program to 720,000 children out of 1.8 million estimated eligibles. Most participants are four years old and they are served in a comprehensive program featuring child care, health, social services, and parent-participation components. Most Head Start programs are part-day and open only during the school year, so working mothers are not well served unless they can manage the complex packaging with a "regular" day care program.

The voted expansion, following the debate and the advisory committee report, is expected to coincide with major efforts to upgrade Head Start staffing and management and to develop more all-day, all-year programs. Especially relevant to our under-three concerns, there are to be serious if modest beginnings in services to infants and toddlers. In addition there is to be major encouragement as well to development of more family support services, especially those involving parents and the youngest children.[3] However, the "policy" victory of advocates of a Head Start for under-threes was a modest one. Of the 1994 major Head Start expansion, only $20 million is earmarked for new child care programs for the zero to three age group.

The continued existence of what is in effect a dual child care system—social welfare child care and preschool education—makes it difficult to provide a fully accurate and complete statistical picture of current provision. Often the data published relate to only one system (social services or education), or to only one level of government (federal), or to only one category of children (those with working mothers). Supply, usage, and expenditure data that integrate preprimary school programs with social welfare child care are not available in systematic form. Nonetheless, we offer some specifics.

Kindergarten for five-year-olds has become universal (and provision is mandated in some states); coverage is complete, at least for part-day programs. By 1990, about 75 percent of four-year-olds were participating in a preschool (56 percent), a center (7 percent), or Head Start (12 percent), as were more than half the three-year-olds (33 percent in preschool). An additional small proportion of three- and four-year-olds were in family day care. According to the National Child Care Survey, in 1990, 37 percent of three- and four-year-olds (43 percent of those with working mothers) were in centers and 11 percent were in family day care (17 percent of those with working mothers).[4] (These data are not fully compatible with Census Bureau data on preprimary school enrollment.)

Among children under age 3 in 1990, the Hofferth data indicate that about 26 percent were in out-of-home care: 14 percent in center care and 12 percent in family day care. Among those with working mothers, approximately 40 percent were in out-of-home care, almost equally divided between family day care and center care, reversing for the first time the previous pattern in which family day care was the overwhelmingly dominant pattern of out-of-home care for the under-threes.

Disaggregating the data still further to account for age differences among the infants and toddlers of working mothers in 1990, the primary child care arrangement was an in-home provider for 3.4 percent of the under-ones and 3.0 percent of the ones and twos. In contrast, 13.6 percent of the under-ones and 22.7 percent of the ones and twos were in center care. Family day care was the primary mode for 20.4 percent of the under-ones and 22.6 percent of the ones and twos. The latter totals include both registered/licensed family day care and informal arrangements with a woman caring for several children in her home. The remainder were cared for by parents, relatives, or their own siblings, or were in informal neighbor exchanges.

Despite significant increases in supply during the 1980s, infant and toddler care remains scarce in relation to the proportion of children this age with working mothers. National studies and reports have stressed such shortages since the mid-1980s, but especially of late. Many states, cities, and corporations have responded with targeted recruitment or funding initiatives. Most recently, in early 1994, a federal welfare reform task force, projecting work, training, and education opportunities for parents of infants and toddlers, said that this could not be undertaken without improving the child care supply. If, indeed, the Family Support Act's exemption of welfare mothers with children under age 3 is changed to include them, federal concern with the supply of infant/toddler care will be essential. Even without such shift, the work patterns of many working mothers clearly have made a supply increase urgent.

In reporting the results of a 1990 survey of child care settings, the researchers found that[5]:

The average enrollment in centers under *all* auspices (Head Start, public schools, social services, religious organizations, for-profit providers) is sixty-two children (but it is ninety-one among the for-profit chains);

62 percent of the children enrolled are aged three to five (95 percent of those in Head Start, 83 percent of those in school programs, and 48 percent of those in for-profit chains), and the remainder are under 3; the for-profits play a particularly important role in infant and toddler care;

22 percent of program funds are public (3 percent in for-profit chains);

The average group size for three-year-olds is seventeen, and the staff:child ratio for three-year-olds is 1:10; the average group size for infants is seven and the staff:child ratio is 1:4 (Table 6.1).

The average proportion of staff with a college degree is 47 percent (99 percent in school programs and 31 percent in for-profit chains);

The average annual teacher turnover rate is 25 percent (14 percent in the school-based programs and 39 percent in for-profit chains;

The average wage is $7.45 per hour, ranging from $5.43 in for-profit chains to $14.40 in school-based programs.[6]

**Table 6.1** Average Group Size and Staff/Child Ratios For Children Under Age 6, as Reported by Centers

| Age of Child (yr) | Group Size | Staff:Child Ratio |
| --- | --- | --- |
| <1 | 7 | 1:4 |
| 1 | 10 | 1:6–7 |
| 2 | 12 | 1:7–8 |
| 3–5 | 17 | 1:10 |

*Source*: Willer et al., Table 9, p. 38.

Public schools were the base for 8 percent of the total group of centers in 1990, and for 6 percent of for-profit chains. Most centers are nonprofit, including those in voluntary social welfare agencies, churches, and synagogues.

U.S. child care policy is focused largely on three- and four-year-olds. Coverage is not yet adequate for this group, nor is quality; and it is abysmal for younger children.

One general criticism of the U.S. situation has been that the diverse and fragmented delivery system is confusing for parents to navigate, even if they can gain entry. Whether a family, especially a low- or modest-income family, enters one system or another is often a matter of luck, yet the type and quality of care varies greatly from program to program, as revealed in the data just presented. Child care provided through the welfare system in many communities does not begin to compare in quality and comprehensiveness of services with that provided by good Head Start programs (also serving poor children), and public school and for-profit care also vary significantly in quality.

A special study for the National Research Council/National Academy of Science documented at the beginning of the 1990s the problems of inadequate supply, and poor quality, difficulties in access, as well as the lack of "a comprehensive array of coordinated policies and programs responsive to the needs of families in different social, economic, and cultural circumstances and to children of different ages, stages of development, and with special needs."

The National Commission on Children noted subsequently that despite years of public discussion, the country has only begun to respond to these issues and to the social changes and concomitant needs that drive the debate. There seems to be a growing consensus that all families who need it should have access to high-quality child care and early childhood services and that parents should be able to choose the type of care that best suits them and their child. Underscoring this, the report reminds us that the quality of care children receive is critical to their health and development and that high-quality programs can support, stimulate, and enhance the physical, social, and cognitive development of all young children.

The more recent Carnegie Task Force (1994), in a synthesis of available research and reports, found that U.S. infant and toddler care today is seriously deficient in quantity and quality. However, one could not expect otherwise given the lack of standards, or low standards, and defective enforcement in many states, the poorly qualified or trained staffs, salaries so low as to create high staff turnover, and insufficient public subsidy to improve the supply for those unable to pay expensive fees. By contrast, according to the Carnegie report, the Army has expanded programs to meet needs, and in 1990 it carried out a major reform of program quality.

The problem is not limited to child care *centers*. In a recent study, the Family and Work Institute documented serious quality problems in much of family day care and relative care.[7]

Thus, the concern continues. With more than half the mothers of infants (under age 1) and higher proportions of the mothers of toddlers (ages 1 and 2) working outside the home, there is an acute shortage of child care for these children. And what *is* available, both center and regulated and unregulated family day care, is often of poor quality. For the family that wants to make a child care plan in this environment and is concerned with convenient location, cost, and some aspects of programs and setting, there is also a problem of access and affordability. American tradition limits the federal role, and, Head Start excepted, recent funding does little about quality and quantity issues in infant and toddler care.

Americans know how to run child care. Our best programs would be regarded as impressive anywhere. But that does not solve the problems of coverage, quality, cost, and access for the typical parent.

What does the European experience have to suggest about these matters?

## The European Backdrop

The European countries, almost unanimously, have elected universal but voluntary preschool for children from age of 2, 2½, or 3 until age 5, 6, or 7, varying according to a country's age of compulsory schooling.* The infant/toddler care developments need to be understood in this context.

These preschool programs are variously justified as preparing children for school, as enhancing child socialization and development, and, somewhat less frequently, as offering good quality care while parents work. So important are the school readiness concerns and so highly valued are the socialization and developmental opportunities that participation is in most places unrelated to parental employment status, family income, cultural backgrounds, or judgments about parental capacities. Indeed, just about *all* children in the three-to-five group attend in some countries (France, Belgium, Italy), *almost* all in others (Germany, Denmark, Finland, Sweden). These programs are heavily subsidized, operate largely in the public sector (or with extensive public subsidy), and cover at least the normal school day (in the Nordic countries the full workday is covered). Countries have various arrangements for supplementary care, to match parental work hours. Where the preschool and school day are short (Germany), there are problems.

---

*The exception apparently is Luxembourg, where recent legislation makes preschool compulsory for four-year-olds.

In most of Europe the preschools are part of the education sector, but there is an alternative pattern, as seen in Denmark, Finland, and Sweden, in which a separate child care system covers all children until age 7, when elementary school begins. The United States, Canada, and Britain represent still a third pattern, in which some children in care (ages 2 to 4 in Britain, where compulsory school begins at age 5, and ages 3 to 5 in the United States and Canada, where school begins at age 6) are in what has been known as "day care" in the social welfare sector, whereas others attend preschool or nursery school, under educational auspices (either part-day or full school day). (Head Start, we have seen, appears in both.) Both types of programs may be publicly subsidized but not necessarily so; in the United States, a significant portion are under private auspices, both nonprofit and for-profit. The programs under social welfare auspices give priority and subsidy to children alleged to have special needs because of abuse, neglect, parental and familial problems, and, in the United States, parental involvement in work-training designed to end dependence on public assistance. Preschools more often serve middle- and upper-income children, who may or may not have two parents in the workforce. In the United States the preschool/day-care "split" is increasingly disappearing for this age group.

With this backdrop, an important distinction for Europe should be introduced. If child care for the three- to five-year-olds now has a large school readiness and socialization/developmental rationale, care for the zero- to two-year-olds remains an essential response to female labor force participation. Yet, as we shall see, there is also increasingly an affirmation of the importance of offering even the youngest children an experience providing cognitive stimulation and socialization with peers and other adults, even if there is a parent at home during the day.

Apart from the explicit policy regarding children aged 3 to 5/6 in most of Europe, and the almost universal preschool coverage for this age group, two other differences between the United States and Europe should be noted. First is the explicit, special concern with child care policy for the under-threes in much of Europe, dating from the mid-1970s; second is the universal policy of paid and job-protected maternity or parental leave that directly affects the age at which nonparental infant care is needed by a working parent.

The flavor of European developments and the excitement over achievements, possibilities, and challenges, are best conveyed by illustration.[8] We will refer to Italy, Denmark, England, Finland, France, and Sweden. Table 6.2 also provides data on several other countries.

*Denmark* has the highest coverage of child care provision for the under-threes in all of the "west," combining center care and family day care of high quality. (East Germany had higher coverage after extended maternity

**Table 6.2** Child Care Coverage for Children Aged 0 to 3
and 3 to 5 in Selected Countries, 1990–1992

| | *Percent of Children in Child Care, Full and Part-Day by Age* | |
|---|---|---|
| Country | 0 to 3 | 3 to 5 |
| Belgium | 20 | 95+ |
| Britain | 2 | 43[a] |
| Denmark | 58[b] | 75 |
| Finland | 48[c] | 72 |
| France | 29 | 97+ |
| Germany | 5 | 80[d] |
| Italy | 6 | 91 |
| Japan | 21 | 52 |
| Sweden | 29[e] | 79 |
| United States | 26 | 71[d,f] |

*Source:* Compiled from country and international sources.

[a] Since compulsory school begins at age 5 in the United Kingdom, this figure is for 3 and 4 year olds only.

[b] This figure is for children from age six months (when the basic maternity leave ends) through two years.

[c] This figure is for one- and two-year-olds, after the conclusion of the $10\frac{1}{2}$ month parental leave.

[d] These are largely part-day programs.

[e] This figure is for the zero-to-three group. Since the parental leave is fully paid for one year and partly paid for another three months, only toddlers (one- and two-year-olds) are in care. Thus the "real" coverage rate for one and two year olds is probably similar to Finland's.

[f] Almost all five-year-olds are in either kindergarten or first grade; 44 percent of three- to four-year-olds are in pre-primary programs.

leaves, but following reunification and with unemployment and resource constraints, infant/toddler care services have been curtailed.) Of particular interest for our purposes, infant/toddler care is delivered under social services auspices, with programs including children from six months of age(when the Danish paid parental leave ends) through six years, when compulsory schooling begins. With the 1993 enactment of legislation permitting a one-year parental leave, paid for through unemployment insurance, infant care may become largely parental care, as it is in the other Nordic countries. Some programs—and some groups—are age-segregated, some integrated. Active parent involvement is emphasized.

*France* has the highest coverage for three- to five-year-olds internationally, and the highest coverage of under-threes after the Nordic countries. With its brief (ten-week) postchildbirth maternity leave, babies aged three months and older are seen in *crèches* (day care centers). France's services for children under age 3 are under health auspices, whereas its preschool programs, serving children aged 2 to 5, are under education auspices. Thus, two-year-olds can be served in either system, but most of those in out-of-home care are in preschool.

In *Italy,* almost all three to five year olds are enrolled in preschool, but there is only limited coverage for the under-threes. Program creativity in north-central Italy with regard to the three- to five-year-olds has inspired many countries. There is also, especially in these areas, recent and significant expansion in programs serving the under-threes (largely aged 9 months and older, when the Italian maternity leaves end)—and a strong case is made for ensuring access to infants and toddlers even if a full-time adult caregiver is available at home. For our purposes, of special interest, all child care programs in several regions in north-central Italy are under education auspices, even though there is a clear distinction between services for the under-threes and those for the three- to five-year-olds; and the programs for the under-threes include under education auspices both full workday and part-day child care.

*Finland* and *Sweden*, in systems covering all children to age 7, have pioneered in offering parental at-home options for infant care, while also legislating a right to a guaranteed child care place (in the Finnish case, for the under-threes). Like Denmark, their child care services are all under social service auspices, in a separate, special system. With programs covering the full workday and with the highest labor force participation rates in any country of women with children of this age, the number of places available is still not sufficient to meet need. Nonetheless, as in Denmark, the quality of these programs is extraordinarily high.

Among this group of countries, *Britain,* has the smallest proportion of very young children in out-of-home child care, perhaps in part because of its low (but recently rising) labor force participation rates for women with children of this age. Although compulsory school begins at age 5, and almost all four year olds are in a program somewhat similar to kindergarten in the United States, coverage for the under-threes, and especially the under-twos, is almost nonexistent, apart from informal child minding (family day care). Moreover, England provides child care through two parallel systems, one a social service for children "in need"—who are deprived, disadvantaged, or troubled—and the second an education-based program for middle-class children whose parents seek an enrichment experience for them. For our purposes, England is of special interest because several local jurisdictions are now attempting to integrate the education and social service programs into one child care system, under education auspices.

We turn now to a more detailed picture, focusing on issues of particular salience to the United States but limiting our observational reports to two countries.[9]

## Infant and Toddler Care in Europe

In contrast to preschools for three- to five-year-olds, infant and toddler care is far less likely to be universal in Europe and access far more limited. Moreover, just *when* the postchildbirth parental leave ends has a significant impact on coverage rates. For example, Denmark and France have similar overall rates for the under-threes (see Table 6.3) but once the Danish six-month paid and job protected maternity and parental leave is taken into account, almost 60 percent of the children aged 6 months to 3 years are in subsidized child care, 25 percent more than in France. Similarly, the Finnish coverage rate is substantially lower than the French, but in reality is the same once the babies (under age 1) are excluded, since they are cared for at home by a parent on a fully paid and job-protected leave. Nonetheless, even the "high-coverage" countries such as the Nordic countries, France, and the north-central part of Italy, continue to have significant gaps between demand and supply; and this remains so even when focusing only on providing enough places to meet the needs of children with working parents. Given that criterion, these countries meet about 67 to 75 percent of the "need," not enough, but far more than in the United States.

In the light of continued scarcity, priorities for the limited places are similar across countries: children of single working mothers; handicapped, immigrant, disadvantaged, or deprived children, or others with special needs; children with working parents.

Nonetheless, given the greater supply of infant and toddler care in these countries than in the United States, how is it paid for, and what kind of financial burden is carried by parents?

### *Costs, Financing, and Affordability*

Child care for the under-threes is an expensive service everywhere, largely because it is labor-intensive. However, in many other countries, the society views such care as a worthwhile investment and shares in the costs to a much greater extent than in the United States. The Danish picture underscores this.

In Denmark, where the quality of care is uniformly high, operating costs are also high. At a time when the average salary for a male production worker was $38,423, the average for a female production worker,

**Table 6.3** Infant/Toddler Care by Country and Type of Care (Percentages)

| Country | Supervised Family Day Care | Centers | Nursery Schools | Age-Integrated Centers |
|---------|---------------------------|---------|-----------------|------------------------|
| Denmark | 60 | 28 | 4 | 8 |
| Finland | 56 | 44 | | |
| France | 52 | 16 | 26 | |

$32,461, and the average income for a two-parent family with one child was $55,068, the annual operating costs of a place in a day nursery (*crèche,* i.e., center for under-threes) were $12,324, according to a Danish study. A family day care place for an infant/toddler cost $6,708; a place in a preschool for a three-to five-year-old cost $6,552. The higher infant/toddler care cost is typical internationally. (See Appendix A for explanation of currency conversions and equivalents in purchasing power parities—what these incomes purchase and thus their real equivalence in U.S. dollars).

What portion of this do families pay? By public policy, parent fees are not to exceed 30 percent of operating costs, and some municipalities manage to keep them a bit lower. In fact, parent fees met 22 percent of costs in 1990. Earners with incomes under $7,270 paid nothing at all; full fees are collected from families with incomes over $22,604. In between, there is a sliding fee scale. There are decreased charges for second, third, or additional children in a family. If parents have more than one child in a preschool program, there is a 33 percent fee reduction for each. A two-earner, one-child family with average wages would pay about 5.3 percent of family income for a child in a day nursery, the most expensive mode. For family day care it would be 4.8 percent of income, and for a nursery school, 3.5 percent. The day care place costs society about 22 percent of the total earnings in a two-earner family. The family day care or nursery school place costs about 12 percent.

Despite the high costs, child care services are far more affordable for families in the continental European countries than for those in the United States. Preschool programs in many countries, including France and Italy, are free for the core school day, with income-related fees for meals and the extended-day coverage, if needed and used. In France, almost half the two-year-olds are in such programs. Income-related fees are charged for the whole program in the Nordic countries.

The U.S. Bureau of the Census reports that the average child care expenditure for a child under age 3 in 1991 was 8.5 percent of family income. Expenditures were 11 percent of family income for families with monthly earnings of $1,500 to $3,000. For families with above-median income, it was 7.3 percent for those earning $3,000 to $4,499 per month and 4.8

percent for those earning over $4,500. If they paid for child care, families with below-poverty income expended 27 percent of earnings for such; those with above-poverty income expended 7 percent.[10] A 1990 survey found that child care fees accounted for even higher proportions of family income—10 percent generally, 23 percent for poor and modest-income families.[11]

Costs for families are lower because preschool programs and infant/ toddler care services receive far more extensive public subsidies in the European countries than in the United States. Even where parents pay income-related fees, they expend smaller shares of family income on child care as a result of these subsidies. Most important, some of these programs are free for all children (the preschool programs), and all are free to poor and low-income families.

In the United States, according to the Willer et al report of findings from the 1990 national child care survey, parent fees accounted for 76 percent of the operating costs of child care centers.[12] Since the mid-1970s, parents' share of child care center costs has risen from 70 percent to 76 percent, while government subsidies have declined from 29 to 19 percent. A review of the European pattern offers a dramatic contrast. Parents' fees accounted for 11 percent of child care operating costs in Finland, 26 percent in France (and 38 percent of family day care costs), and between 5 and 36 percent in Italy. For example, a place in a center in a northern Italian city cost 1.8 million Lira per month in 1991, or $1,450 ($17,400 a year). Parents who paid the full fee were charged 250,000 Lira, or $200 ($2,400 a year), less than 15 percent of costs, again for a high-quality program. The Danish parent portion, as noted, was 22 percent in 1990.

The remaining costs are picked up by government—the local government in Denmark and Finland, a combination of local and regional government in Italy, and a combination of local government and the family allowance fund in France. Capital costs are borne by either the local government (Denmark and Finland), the regional government (Italy), or the local government and the family allowance funds (France).

Administrative responsibility for these programs is public. Two-thirds of the centers and nursery schools in Denmark are public; the remainder are publicly funded and subject to the same regulations and standards as the public programs, but operated under contract with voluntary (private nonprofit) agencies. All child care programs are public in Finland, and almost all programs for under-threes are public in Italy. The French pattern, like the Danish, is a mixed picture, but largely public. Except for Britain, which in any case has places for only about 2 percent of the cohort, there are no for-profit centers in any of the other countries.

In effect, these are expensive programs, but as a matter of public policy, parent fees are kept at an affordable level for all, and quality is not sacrificed to achieve this.

## Quality and Staffing

Quality, as a function of group size, staff:child ratios, staff qualifications, and center size, varies across and within the countries. However, some countries appear to have uniformly high quality, while the situation is far more mixed in others.

Denmark, like Sweden (not described herein, but described in earlier work) has the highest quality of care for both under-threes and three- to six-year-olds.[13] Focusing here on the under-threes, Danish infant and toddler centers typically have thirty to forty places, with three to four groups of ten children each, and with two staff members for each group. (The preschools, which serve children from about age 2½ to 6, are in facilities that can enroll forty to eighty children in two to four groups of 20 children each, with three staff members per group.) For purposes of staff:child ratios, each child under age 3 is counted as two children aged 3 to 6. Family day care mothers may care for a maximum of five children, including their own.

About half the staff have special pedagogical training—a three-year, post-secondary-school course. The others are assistants without this training, but often having taken a variety of special courses. The municipal family day care mothers are required to have between two and six weeks of special training, depending on the municipality, before beginning to care for children.

Salaries of child care *"pedagogues,"* the term used to describe the professional early childhood educators, are relatively high in Denmark, equal to the average female wage. Since, in addition, female wages are much closer to male wages in Denmark than in the United States, child care staff earn much better wages than comparable U.S. staff. One result may be the much lower staff turnover rate in Denmark, about 10 percent a year, in contrast to 25 percent or higher in the United States.

French centers range in size from forty to eighty places, with a national average of forty-seven. The staff:child ratio is 1:5 for infants and 1:8 for toddlers. In the kindergartens and part-day programs (Jardins d'Enfants and Haltes Garderies), serving two- to four-year-olds, the ratio is 1:20 (plus "helpers"). France has long had larger groups in its preschools than Americans are comfortable with.

In Italy, the picture is slightly different. Emilia Romagna, a region with an extensive supply of high-quality infant/toddler care, has a policy supporting a three-group center of sixty children in attendance (sixty-six registered), staffed by eleven teachers, four auxiliary staff, and two cooks; there would probably be fifteen "babies" (under one) among the sixty children. In a smaller center with forty-two children and no infants, there would be six teachers, two auxiliary staff, one cook. Staff work thirty hours a week directly with the children and six hours in preparation and meetings. They are all public employees, and salaries are pegged at a civil service middle level, and at about the same level as that of preschool and primary school teachers. In the past, most staff have been secondary-school trained. There is a growing trend to use college graduates but not necessarily those with a child development specialization. There is some concern about this lack of specific substantive training. Nonetheless, there is great emphasis on in-service training, and the jobs are relatively well paid.

## Program Models and Curricula

*Denmark: Centers and Family Day Care.*  Danish children aged 6 months to 2 years may be cared for in day care centers serving the under-threes, in age-integrated centers that usually serve children under age 6, or in supervised family day care.[14] The early childhood educational philosophy in Denmark stresses age integration and relatively unstructured curricula. Because many children spend long days in care most of the week, while their parents spend a full day at work, the program staff realize that they are part of a dual socialization experience for children—yet they also agree that they should not and do not wish to replace the family or take over the child's socialization. As a result, they have developed a program philosophy that emphasizes psychological and social development, rather than formal instruction.

The child care staff, in the child development tradition, are called *"pedagogues,"* not teachers. They work with children, without preparing specific curricula or day-by-day programs. The children are offered activity choices, and the pedagogues are trained to respond to children's leads and to encourage success and development of skills. Each child's care is highly individualized. Indeed, recognition of the long "care" day and tight midweek family schedules supports the effort to create a family-like environment for center care. Or, put somewhat differently, the feeling is that children with two working parents often have all their daytime activities organized and that what they really miss is time to just "hang out." The Danes appear to have institutionalized this concept by making it possible for children to "hang out" in their child care programs, to be with siblings, if possible, and to have the span of opportunities for interaction provided by participation in a program with children of various ages.

Age integration is a concept now being worked out. One sees different versions in action in different cities and in different program forms. It is said that young children benefit from play with slightly older children and that the age range permits the organization of activity groups that correspond to children's interests and development. These arrangements also make it easier for authorities to cope with fluctuating demand, as birth cohort sizes fluctuate.

In Denmark, family day care is not regarded as secondary to group care programs, despite the less-formal staff training. The large public family day care system began as a temporary measure, developed to cope with serious shortages in the supply of center care and the unsatisfactory nature of the informal day care system, which was filling the gap. Now it is a public service with salaried personnel, who receive job-related benefits and who are selected, guided, supervised, and made ever-more-qualified by assigned and qualified supervisors. By now, municipal family day care, the most commonly used resource for the under-threes, is a firmly established alternative, to which authorities give the same status as centers and which many parents of young children consider preferable to the institutional facilities. Many centers have linkages with family day care providers in the community, and there are also community facilities that bring together, on a regular basis, family day care providers and the children they care for. In fact, providers and children share group experiences in a special setting regularly, and on trips with other providers and children. A backup system is organized as well. Family day care mothers are "paired," ensuring a degree of security often absent in family day care.

In sketching how some of this looks in action, we note, first, that the lack of a formal "curriculum" does not mean disorganization. Child care programs have a basic structure with regard to opening and closing times; times for breakfast, lunch, and snacks; and nap times. Children and adults engage in interaction, as do children with other children. There is involvement with materials and activities. The settings are warm, safe, very attractive, and stimulating. No one is lost in a crowd. In any comparative context, or on its own terms, this is splendid child care.

For example: In a working-class suburban community just outside of Copenhagen, three child care facilities have been built in a cluster arrangement, two separate day care centers for children under three and one age-integrated center that includes a group of under-threes. Two are on one side of the street, and the third is across the street, in a sort of mini childcare "park." Individual centers are deliberately kept small and administratively separate. The two under-three programs have forty children each, while the age-integrated center, with sixty children, has one group of ten under-threes.

All three centers are in one-story U-shaped buildings with a small, paved, innercourtyard and a surrounding large grass area (except for the paved entrance). These buildings, constructed within the past five years, are designed for possible conversion to nursing homes or old-age facilities should the demand for child care decrease. Although the general ambiance is urban, two of the centers have vegetable gardens to teach children about planting and growing and to provide food. The age-integrated center has decided to add rabbits. Despite the cold climate, the grounds are extensive, the equipment is good, and the children are outdoors a good deal of the time.

All three facilities open at 6:00 A.M. and all close at 5:00 P.M. They are open twelve months a year, and closed for only a few major holidays. They are publicly operated; staff are municipal employees.

At the entrance to one center, there are two shedlike rooms on the side, one for strollers left by parents in the morning or for center strollers used to take children on a "walk." The other shed protects staff bikes from the weather. Beyond the entrance is a large room, the base of the facility. A Danish equivalent of the Italian "piazza," this community meeting place and activity center is larger in some facilities and smaller in others (varying even among the three in close proximity) and leads to the group home rooms, two in each direction. Each group's home space includes a larger room for active play and eating, a second room for quiet play and sleeping, and its own toilet/washroom.

The central space is important to the program. Children are not kept strictly in their own room. At various times during the day, they are allowed to wander out and play in this space, which at various points has mattresses, little chairs, large blocks of a foam-rubber material that fit together like a puzzle but can be sat on, and games. Children have plenty of opportunity to interact with others, and the interaction is ongoing, comfortable, and clearly enjoyed.

Here (and throughout Denmark) there is strong conviction about the value of fresh air, even for sleeping. The youngest children are placed in carriages and wheeled into the garden area (or in some centers, into shedlike areas with protection but open windows). On the coldest days, they are in sleeping bags in the carriages. During the summer, the carriages are covered with netting. While sleeping, the children are closely monitored. The carriages are used deliberately to distinguish outdoor sleeping from the indoor cribs.

The normal routine in this facility is that the children arrive between 6:30 and 9:30 A.M. Most arrive in time to have breakfast, between 7:30 and 8:30, and by 9:00 there tends to be a somewhat more "structured" series of activities. When they first arrive, the children play in the large open room. Group rooms are opened one at a time, as needed, when enough children are present. The children have lunch at 11:00, a nap between 12:00 and 1:00, and outdoor play in both the morning and afternoon, every day, unless the weather is very bad.

Parents are expected to call by 9:00 A.M. if they are not bringing their child. They also are expected to call if their child is ill. Children may attend if they have head colds, but not if they have a fever or an upset stomach, for example. If a child gets sick during the day, staff call the parent to take the child home. Parents are expected to pick up their children by 5:00 P.M., and most pick them up before 4:00.

A group's main room typically has two large tables, a floor mat for sitting and playing, and a child-height mirror on one wall, along one side of the mat. There is an enclosed section, equipped for playing house. Another area can be converted to a store. On top of that area, a playpen, about five feet above ground, allows infants to see what is going on in the room. Shelves on one side of the room hold toys. Doors lead to the central room, the group's smaller room, the toilet/washroom, and outdoors. There is eye-level glass in the door to the central room so that small children may see what is going on. Although no two group areas are exactly the same, they all are light, bright, colorful, and have ceiling mobiles and wall hangings—and are very attractive.

On each side of the building, the changing areas in the toilet/washroom are back-to-back and have a see-through window. The rooms have two toilets, a long low wash basin, changing tables, and supply cubbies. A child's name or a symbol identifies personal clothing, pacifiers, toothbrushes, cups, and washcloths—all strategically located in the different rooms. Each group's main room contains a list of the children by name, birthdate, and parents' names.

The outdoor space is ample for the play period. A shed containing kiddie cars, trucks, wagons, ropes, and balls is beautifully painted, and the equipment was in active use. What is particularly impressive is that children are pretty much on their own in playing with peers. An adult is present all the time, but the adults do not lead or play with the children. They simply provide the opportunity for the children to play and interact with one another.

This center has a staff of fifteen, including the director, plus the cook and a cleaning woman. Each group of ten children has three staff members assigned to it. In addition, there is a substitute who fills in when someone is absent. About half the staff members are professionally trained; the others are helpers.

In this same community there are three centerlike settings in which family day care mothers and the children in their care assemble for a half day or full day of activity, biweekly, weekly, or even more often. The day is enriching for children and caretakers, and the relationships established simplify "coverage" when caretakers are ill. These occasions also offer valu-

able contact and guidance opportunities for responsible staff consultants.
*Italy: The Asilo Nido.* The Italian infant and toddler care center (*asilo nido*)
is an educational and socialization service appropriate for all very young
children but now designed for the children of working parents. In contrast
to the universality of the preschool program, the quantity and quality of
the programs for under-threes vary widely across regions, with north-
central Italy playing a leadership role in coverage and quality.

A range of program forms (part-day to full-day) and a close relationship
to a diversity of child care–related family support programs (see below)
suggest the distinctive quality of these programs. There are no formal
family day care programs and there is very little informal provision. The
centers are open from 7:30 A.M. to at least 4:30 P.M. and sometimes 6:30.
Few children are younger than nine months. Groups are age-related (three
to twelve months, twelve to twenty-four months, twenty-four to thiry-six
months), have socialization, developmental, and cognitive objectives, and
have a much more deliberate "curriculum" than their Danish counterparts.

To illustrate: Modena is a prosperous mid-sized city with a female labor
force participation rate on par with that in the United States. The *asili nidi*
in Modena follow the standard pattern, they are open five days a week,
except for holidays (Christmas and Easter), from 7:30 A.M. to 6:30 P.M.,
eleven months a year (they close in August for one month, although sometimes one center in the city may remain open in August).

One center serves forty-eight children, in three groups of sixteen, organized by age. There are two teachers for each group, with a third for the
middle group, who helps out in any group if a teacher is absent. Thus,
overall, there is one teacher for every six children aged 9 months (approximately) to almost three years; and there are two cooks and one helper,
who also cleans and assists with the children as needed.

The program begins in September of each year, with a new entering class
of babies. The first week is just for staff to prepare for the year. From then
to mid-October the new children are phased in, about two or three each
week.

The building is a low-rise, half one-story and half two-story. There is a
large open area off the entrance (the "piazza" or "village square" concept),
and near the entrance are strollers and baby carriages. There is a climbing
area in the back of the room, and several small tables for painting or for
play with clay, dough, or other materials. Each group has its own smaller
room located off the piazza, and each of these is subdivided into three
areas: one for active play, with tables and chairs, one for quiet play and
eating, and one for sleeping. The rooms are colorful and spacious. There is
also an office for a pediatrician, who holds a health clinic at the center, once
a week, for the children in the center. There is a small kitchen as well, and a
room for washers and dryers.

Children have their own cubbies, with their names or pictures on them, for putting away their outer clothing when they arrive each day, and for keeping a change of clothes as well. Each group has its own menu, posted at the entrance to the group room so that parents can see what their child has eaten. The children are deliberately introduced to different types of foods, including those not served at home. At the same time, there is great sensitivity to cultural differences regarding food and special diets. There are Muslim children, a child from Sri Lanka, and several from Turkey—and diversity is accepted and supported.

Children have the same crib each day, when they rest; and they have their own transitional objects as well—a stuffed animal, a blanket, or a piece of a blanket. The children who will attend the preschool in the fall spend one day each week, from January to July, with the youngest group at the preschool, to facilitate the transition.

Almost all the children have working mothers, although, as is typical, there are a few children with at-home mothers but special needs, including one handicapped child (with Down's syndrome). There is great emphasis in Italy on mainstreaming handicapped children.

In the room for the under-ones, there is space for crawling, low mirrors to look at oneself, and a place for water play. Changing tables, in a separate room, have windows at a level that children can look through to the playing area and watch the other children while they are changed and cleaned.

In the room for the one- and two-year-olds, there is more equipment for active physical play, including climbing toys and steps, and there is more opportunity for drawing, painting, and water play. There are also low windows between the rooms, one-way mirrors for adults to observe, and low mirrors for children to look at themselves. Child-sized toilets and sinks are in a separate room.

Center staff here have completed a three-year, post-high-school vocational training course and a fourth-year special course in early childhood education. Staff turnover is very low, in part because these are civil service jobs and are relatively well paid and secure, with good benefits. Staff are paid the same as preprimary and primary school teachers, and only a little less than a secondary school teacher.

In general, whenever feasible, the recommendation is that the centers be located near a preschool and near several part-day child care centers and family support centers as well. In Italy there is great interest in the philosophy and curricula of these programs, which emphasize socialization, education and development as an integral part of good child care from birth on; there is emphasis on verbal interaction and on close links between and among the centers, the preschools, the family support programs, and the health and social service programs, and between the preschools and the primary school.

Although the coverage of the under-threes is modest even in this region (about 20 percent in center care), the quality is very high and there is conviction about the need for a universal program albeit not necessarily for hours equal to a full workday. The family support (family center) programs established in the 1980s are designed to satisfy the latter objective and to meet the needs of both very young children and their mothers and care-givers for socialization-development-education experiences.

The Danish and Italian infant and toddler care programs offer contrast-ing illustrations of high-quality, affordable, exemplary programs. With very different philosophies, both strive to respond to the needs of children in their societies. The children may have different family lives and daily experiences, and the countries may emphasize different social values, yet clearly these children are experiencing intellectual, social, and physical stimulation and enhanced development while being cared for outside their homes. Our observations in many other countries convince us that none of this is beyond our capacity in the United States, if we are prepared for the resource, personnel, and policy commitment.

## Conclusion

Infant and toddler care services are expanding in almost all the western European countries, albeit modestly in most. As seen in Table 6.2, the United States ranks in the middle with regard to coverage, but quality is generally inferior, and places in center care are in very short supply. The dramatic difference is that the European developments are premised on a paid and job-protected maternity or parental leave following childbirth (see Chapter 4). Therefore, much of infant care is tending to become at-home parental care that is publicly subsidized in one way or another. Except for a small number of places for under-ones, most of what is pro-vided in family day care and centers is "toddler care," for one- and two-year-olds. In times of economic recession and high unemployment, de-mand pressures ease; nonetheless, the development is rapid, and shortages exist in all countries, including even Denmark, which leads in coverage with places for almost 60 percent of the under-threes. As in the United States, supply, quality, financing, costs and parents' share of costs, staffing, and curriculum are all issues that are discussed and sometimes debated; and the results could inform the U.S. debate.

Only in Denmark, Finland, and Sweden is there an explicit, consistent, and coherent policy and a kind of "Nordic model" in place, with some variations. These countries provide heavily subsidized, publicly operated centers and family day care, covering the usual workday, with the major country difference involving the type of groupings, i.e., age or "sibling groups" (from infants to three- or six-year-olds). Denmark, for example, is increasingly moving toward age integration, emphasizing socialization/

developmental experience, even as Sweden, long featuring age-integrated sibling groups, moves toward age grouping to strengthen cognitive content.

In the other countries (France, England, and Italy), despite the uniformity of programs for three- to five-year-olds in France and Italy, there is much greater diversity of models and program types for the under-threes.

School readiness, an important issue in the United States, is equally important in these countries. All stress the value of preschool in achieving this objective and emphasize the negative consequences for children in primary school if the earlier experience has not been available. However, of particular interest, is the growing concern with "preschool readiness" in some countries with universal preschools (France, Italy), and the conviction about the importance of a still-earlier group experience for very young children. In response, there is emphasis on the cognitive and socialization aspects of these programs and on helping children and parents adjust to transitions—important factors in a successful preschool and primary school experience.

Program auspice varies significantly across the countries, and there are interesting implications for the United States. Except for the Nordic countries, there is clear consensus that preschool programs for three- to five-year-olds should be under education auspices. Even the British are moving in this direction. And all stress the need for close linkages between pre-primary and primary school as well as the necessity of preschool for ensuring primary school readiness, as discussed above. For infant/toddler care, auspice is more varied; and it is not clear whether or how the variations make much difference.

Child care costs and who pays clearly constitute a critical issue. Child care services are expensive to develop and operate in all these countries, indeed often far more expensive than in the United States; but the costs for good-quality programs are apparently an accepted and acceptable expense for the society. Services are paid for by some combination of government expenditure (national and/or local) and parent fees. The latter cover a maximum of one-quarter to one-third of operating service costs, depending on the country, and far less in some jurisdictions, including Finland, where the government pays about 89 percent. Programs for the three- to five-year-olds are completely free in several countries. Parent fees elsewhere for three- to five-years-olds and everywhere for infants/toddlers consume less than 10 percent of the average income of families with children, and only 5 percent in Denmark and Finland, a far lighter burden than in the United States, where child care costs can claim close to one-quarter of the income of working poor families. Full fees in these countries for those able to pay are less than the comparable fees in the United States, for much-better-quality care than is typically available here.

What, then, needs to be done in the United States? We begin with the fact that although our focus is the under-threes, infant and toddler care cannot develop soundly in the absence of universal preschools for three- to five-year-olds. Federal incentives should be created for helping states move the public education system in this direction, to provide developmentally appropriate, high-quality programs covering the normal school day, with extended-day, wraparound services available at income-related parental fees. Many states have made good beginnings on their own, and the move would have popular support.

As is clear in our discussion of "time" (Chapter 4), infant/toddler care and maternity/parental leave work best as an integrated package. We therefore have urged early reform of the Family Medical Leave Act (FMLA), to include an improved, paid parental leave. Eventually, but hardly on the horizon, the United States should establish a one-year paid parental leave for working parents.

Thus, the premise is: a viable plan for maternity/parental leave and a preschool program for the three- to five-year-olds, educationally connected, serving "caring" and developmental needs, and available (on a voluntary basis, of course) for children whether or not the mother works outside the home. Infant/toddler care belongs in the niche between the two, and must be conceived of as providing an age-appropriate socialization, developmental, and cognitive experience, as well as "care."

We cannot know what the demand for infant/toddler care will be once there is an adequate, paid maternity/parental leave available, but it is clear that a supply expansion is certainly needed, its ultimate dimension to be discovered empirically. Such expansion requires federal funding, through an infant/toddler care block grant and/or by making the child care (dependent care) tax credit refundable (e.g., "nonwasteable", paid to the eligible whether or not they have income tax liabilities). Then, to achieve the needed progress in quality, national standards must be connected to receipt of federal funds. They would refer not only to health and safety (provided in the 1990 block grant) but also to group size, adult:child ratios, and staff qualifications. We assume that the most feasible system would involve state standards and state enforcement, under a national umbrella code, and appropriate certification, accreditation, and licensing systems for programs and staff.

Just as there are individual child care centers in the United States that match in quality *anything, anywhere,* we also have research and experts available to guide quality development in a nationally supported effort involving standards, staff quality (including the compensation essential to recruitment and/or stability), and program content. Indeed, there has been a flurry of research and related creative work in the nineties related to quality.[15] The generally poor standards in many of our child care programs reflect the lack of a policy commitment, not ignorance or incompetence.

From all that has been learned about parental preferences, and on the basis of the significant exemplars cited in Denmark (there are similar ones in France and Sweden), it is necessary and possible to do family day care well, not to turn it into a cheaper and very inferior mode for those who cannot demand something better. These countries set tight requirements for caretaker qualifications, guide and supervise them, offer some training, provide materials and supports, ensure available and sound backups when family day care mothers are ill or unavailable, guarantee that the quarters used are safe and stimulating—and pay decently (including the fringe benefits that go with employment) so as to encourage staff stability. In the U.S. vocabulary, these are family child care networks, well organized, responsible, and recognized as offering good care and respectable work. We identified the quality enhancement and program enrichment possibilities of family day care networks in an earlier study.[16]

One important additional under-three program development could be a refocused Head Start program. It does not diminish the accomplishments of Head Start to note, almost thirty years after its beginnings, the need for adaptation to change. Head Start began with the concept that for disadvantaged children to enter primary school ready to learn, they required an earlier preschool experience that would offer the stimulation and enrichment provided by an excellent nursery school; compensation for earlier social and cognitive deprivation; access to health care, good nutrition, and social services; and the active involvement of parents in their children's experience. If child development experts have taught us anything since then, it is that waiting until ages 3 and 4 to provide children, especially poor children, with such an experience, is too late. The real need is for a program designed to meet the developmental needs of all children, but especially the poor, to optimize their competence in social and school settings from birth to age 3. As we saw earlier, it is the first three years of life that are especially important for a child's later development. A refocus on the earliest years, with Head Start seen as a core component of the growing cluster of family support services (see Chapter 7), would make a significant contribution to the needed growth in infant and toddler services and would make sense for Head Start, given its mission. This would require a phased shift from the four-year-olds who now dominate the program to toddlers (one- and two-year-olds) and their mothers who now are in greatest need of the program and who could benefit from it most and would constitute the best client-consumers for such a program. We refer to a more drastic shift than the modest under-three add-ons that will be supported by the recent legislation.

Head Start was never conceived of as a static, uniform, rigidly designed program, but rather as an "evolving concept . . . that illuminated new pathways leading toward the goal of better serving children and families."[17] It has already played a role in developing programs for very young children (Parent and Child Centers; Parent Child Development Centers). Given that more than half the children in Head Start now come from families receiving AFDC, and that AFDC serves, overwhelmingly, families with children under age 3 (42 percent) rather than those aged 3 to 5 (21 percent), it is clear that the mothers who are most available as active program participants are those with very young children.

If a phased transition from the current to the future Head Start model were needed, we would recommend beginning by guaranteeing the four-year olds a place in a public prekindergarten, with wraparound services available for the four- and five-year-olds, for a full workday and work year. Focus Head Start on the two- and three-year-olds while (1) expanding prekindergarten for the three-year-olds and (2) planning an appropriate Head Start program for infants and toddlers.

For parents who use infant and toddler care to support their employment and do not require the costly add-ons of the Head Start intensive intervention, a federal block grant (details in Chapter 8) could sustain a sliding fee system, making good-quality care affordable. Further, the child care tax credit, one of the current major federal financial commitments to the support of child care for working parents, could become a more important support for low-income workers if made refundable.

Why would or should our government and taxpayers take on this burden? First, the most readily accepted rationale: work is the best and the favored route to income. If parents are at work, children need good care, or the children, their families, and society will pay a sorry price. Also, while we recognize more immediate priorities, we would hope for increasing agreement on a second rationale—because we care about the quality of our children's lives and their environments, whether nor not there is a parent at home.

At various points in history, as economies have changed, as have family sizes, residences, and relationships with relatives and neighbors, the locus of experience for very young children has changed as well. Traditionalists in many countries (we might cite Germany, Austria, or parts of the United States) feel that the normal/natural milieu for an infant and toddler is the home with a nonemployed mother present. Others prefer a group experience for their children, whether in child care or a type of family support program such as those described in the next chapter. A policy that respects differences would attempt to buttress both options. A modern industrial society certainly can afford to do so.

# 7

## Family Support Services: Helping Parents to Be Better Parents

The theme of family support has been sounded frequently over the past decade. Thus, the report of the National Commission on Children, in discussing the social, economic, and demographic changes of recent decades, addresses the increased stress and social isolation of families raising children. It notes that all parents need support, whether it takes the form of advice on child development and child rearing, of help in managing the family budget, of information about other types of help available, or of opportunities to form friendships with other parents. The Carnegie Task Force on young children notes that such activities are of great importance and, to be effective, require a local community base.[1]

### Background

Paralleling the emergence of infant and toddler care as a significant development in the United States, there is a new and growing interest in providing supportive services to families with very young children, in patricular those with "special needs." These new, so-called family support services do not constitute a single, specific, uniformly delivered program; rather, they are a cluster of services, delivered in a variety of ways, under different auspices, sometimes supplemented by additional services. Together, they are a developing component of preventive services for children and their families, and potentially an important early intervention into problems.

151

Their design is only beginning to emerge. Our approach, therefore, is exploratory.

Family support services are broad-brush programs, often with multiple goals, and they employ multiple, somewhat diffuse interventions. Their major focus is on educating and helping parents to be more successful in their child-rearing roles. The ultimate goal is to improve child and parent outcomes. More specific announced goals may include better physical health of children, enhanced child development (cognitive and social), greater school readiness, better parenting skills, facilitation of parents' independence (reduced use of welfare; obtaining jobs), and prevention of child abuse. Most U.S. programs are targeted primarily on preventing the kinds of family crises that lead to removal of a child from his or her home.

Like the infant and toddler care programs described earlier, family support service programs are usually community-based and always focused on the parent *and* child or the family. Most offer information and referral services, parent education classes, adult basic skills classes (e.g., literacy, high school equivalency courses [GED], job training), and drop-in child care services. Some also provide home visiting services, child care beyond drop-in services, toy and book lending services, and counseling.

Family support services are voluntary, often involve parents as volunteers, and are established under diverse auspices—education, health, social welfare, and child care—or as a freestanding service. Regardless of the auspice, however, all emphasize close links with all these different service systems.

In addition to auspice, family support services vary in the frequency and duration of contacts, the interventions/services/activities provided, program goals, and the type of staff used (paid or volunteer; professional or paraprofessional). Home visiting (both home health visiting as well as home visiting with other orientations) is an important but also non-uniform intervention within the overall cluster of family support services.[2] Alternatively, home visiting may constitute a strategy for delivering a cluster of family support services to the child and family at their home. We have already looked at some home health visiting programs in Europe (Chapter 5).

The first national recognition of family support program developments occurred in the course of several conferences of program directors and interested researchers in the early 1980s.[3] The first formal federal recognition emerged in legislation enacted as part of the Omnibus Budget Reconciliation Act of 1993 ("The Family Preservation and Support Services"), making $900 million available to the states, over five years, for the two related initiatives. Family support has become somewhat of a social movement.

Although family support services and child care reflect the same social trends, they have been somewhat independent in their development in this country. Infant/toddler care, we have seen, is largely involved with working families, whereas most family support services address vulnerable and high-risk families or ones with identified problems, usually without an employed parent, or headed by a very young and inexperienced mother, a single mother, or a parent considered "at risk" of neglecting or abusing his/her child. But there also are programs targeted on families without such problems. Whether the emphasis is remedial and therapeutic, or much wider, the family support services are grounded in a philosophy that attends to parental as well as children's needs. Our particular interest in this chapter is the early intervention or more basic prevention programs in this field, and those with clear educational, socialization, and developmental content. Like the infant and toddler care services discussed in the previous chapter, we see these as programs aimed at helping parents care for and rear their young children successfully. At best, they will support the diversity of parenting options, among which parents must find their way.

Prior to the 1993 funding, family support services were largely a state and local government activity—or they received their financial support from private foundations, individual contributions, and/or voluntary organizations. The impacts of the new program will not be immediately visible because the states have been urged to undertake a broad child welfare planning process.

Inevitably, there still are no systematic national data on family support services. Kagan and Shelley, characterizing family support programs as "as yet an undefined phenomenon" refer to "thousands of such efforts," whereas Powell[4] notes that a total of seventy-five U.S. family support programs were listed in the "1991 Family Resource Guide" (one-third of which have a home visiting component). The Roberts and Wasik survey obtained responses regarding two thousand home visiting programs (one type of family support service), about six hundred of which served young children and their families. Perhaps because these programs are so diverse and ill-defined, authorities are counting different things. As yet, there are limited evaluations of the programs' effectiveness in achieving the desired goals.[5]

In 1993 the National Commission on Children recommended the development and expansion of "community-based family support programs to provide parents with the knowledge, skills and support they need to raise their children." The Carnegie Task Force spoke along similar lines.[6] Family support services clearly are relevant to the under-threes. But what does this imply? Both Europe and the United States are groping for direction, and no one format is clearly dominant. It is a time for exploration.

We begin with some brief illustrations of family support services in the United States. Then we turn to the European scene. Finally, a possible U.S. initiative is proposed.

## Some U.S. Family Support Programs

There are now several published compilations of descriptions of diverse U.S. programs and various task-force reports cite exemplars. These are listed among our references. However, it may be easiest to introduce some of the issues by reporting some of our own observations.

### *Avance: San Antonio, Texas*

Avance is a family support and parent education program targeted on a Hispanic Mexican-American population characterized by low income, social isolation, and the presence of very young children, under age 3. By far, most participants are single, young, at-home mothers who are high school dropouts with no skills, often welfare-dependent—and sometimes with recognized parenting problems as well. At best, it is a poor, high-risk mother/child population.

Avance currently operates forty-two Family Centers, twenty-two of which are at six sites in San Antonio, Texas. It prefers to serve the young mother from the time of her pregnancy through the child's second birthday, and also to serve the child directly, from the first weeks after birth.

The program was begun as a parent education course for Mexican-American mothers in 1972–1974. It was initiated and continues to be directed by a charismatic Mexican-American woman, who based the program on the federal Parent-Child Development Centers that grew out of Head Start, but modified the model over time. The program currently is one of about twenty-four federally funded Comprehensive Child Development Programs. It is somewhat more controlled and didactic than the original model.

The core of the program is a nine-month, three-hour-a-week parent education course. The first hour each week is devoted to making a toy (and learning multiple ways of playing with it) that the mother will bring home and use to play with her child. The second hour is a formal parent education course. The third hour is devoted to lectures and discussion regarding a variety of alternative topics, including good nutrition, job counseling, and so forth.

While the mother is in class, her child is in a child care program designed to provide cognitive and social stimulation and enrichment, along with good physical care. This child care program is also highly structured (perhaps in part to counter the tendency toward disorganization in many of these families), with a detailed curriculum and lesson plan for each session, a detailed daily activity plan, and menus. Recently, the organization has been trying to get the child care programs formally licensed in order to qualify for certain funds.*

The weekly three-hour course and the socialization experience for the child are supplemented by a monthly (sometime more often) home visit that is designed to assess how well the mother has integrated what she has learned in the class about playing with—and interacting with—her child.

The focus of the first year (core) program is to improve the mother's parenting skills; educate her about child development, the child's needs, and appropriate parental responses; and build her self-esteem. It is designed to affect both her behavior and attitude toward her child as well as her parental role. For some parents, the program is viewed as either "preventive" with regard to child abuse, or remedial in relation to this problem, but this was not an explicit part of the original concept. The second year supplements the first, building on the mother's increased self-esteem by providing job-skills training as well as literacy, GED (high school equivalency) and ESL (English as a Second Language) courses.

In addition, the program offers a case management and case advocacy function, helping parents learn about and use community resources. The program also provides an employment opportunity for some of the more successful "graduates," by hiring them for staff positions and providing a kind of apprenticeship experience for them. It also has a special Fatherhood Program. In addition, the leadership is increasingly trying to deal with job placement assistance and medical benefits for the adults and to become more cognizant of the formal school experiences of the six- to eighteen-year-old children in these families.

The overall program seves two thousand mothers (families) and at least one child per mother. Of every one hundred mothers recruited to fill a "class" each year in each center, about fifty complete the course (the first year). A still smaller group continues during the second year and takes a GED course. Some mothers leave because they obtain job—on their own—before the program ends; others discontinue for other reasons.

The estimated incremental cost of a center for one year, serving an initial class of one hundred, is $100,000 to $150,000. Depending on how one calculates, this means between $1,500 and $3,000 for each mother or mother/child. These totals do not include the considerable overhead and administrative costs.

As a retention incentive, Avance assures participants' children of priority

* Our program descriptions in this chapter refer to 1993. Our purpose is to identify patterns, not to offer updated evaluations.

for Head Start, promises families priority for new low-income housing, and offers a guarantee to mothers and their children of tuition for college. It is too soon to know whether they can deliver.

The center environment is pervaded by vitality, enthusiasm, and much activity. A limited, early formal evaluation of the program suggested that it could be effective in changing mothers' attitudes toward their children and child rearing, thus changing their parenting behavior. Something more rigorous and longitudinal will be needed to fully document effectiveness.

To conclude: Avance is a model that is explicitly designed to serve a low-income, poorly educated, largely young and socially isolated group of Mexican-American mothers who are not effective mothers and are often very depressed, and their very young children. It assumes the mothers are at home. It does not provide strong health care links, and it assumes that enrollment in Head Start will follow. It stresses education and the value of education and of work. This is not a model for a universal family support program, but it seems to be valid for the subpopulation it serves. Senior staff are of high quality and appear very committed. Many of the lower ranking staff are former parents in the program, and they too seem very competent, committed, and enthusiastic.

### Parents as Teachers (PAT): Independence, Missouri

PAT is a state-mandated program, something rare in this program field, located in every school district in Missouri, funded partly by the state and partly by the local school districts and private sources. It is designed primarily to enhance child development, provide a better foundation for school readiness, and prevent or identify early a miscellany of problems through the use of various parent education strategies for parents of children under age 3. The program is widely publicized and now exists in some jurisdictions in thirty-eight states but is not operating statewide in any except Missouri. Even in Missouri, at best only 30 percent of families with young children are served. PAT also has been introduced in Australia and New Zealand.

The "model" program includes at least the first four of these five elements:

1. *Home visits* by a "Parent Educator" (PE) on a monthly basis for eight months—the basic school year. In reality, few sites carry out this many visits, not even the Independence, Missouri "headquarters" where the first pilot program was established, which now makes five visits a year. However, in programs specifically designed to serve teen mothers, more than eight visits are scheduled; and in low-income neighborhoods, with high-risk families, even more visits may be scheduled. When funds become

available, the Independence leadership hope to reestablish the eight-visit program, with which they began.

2. At least *one monthly group activity* with age-appropriate material for parents with children of the same age. The sessions are mostly during the day, but there is a growing demand for evening meetings, and all new PEs are now hired to carry out evening and Saturday home visits and to participate in evening group activities. (Also, there are some recently established fathers' groups.) In Independence, there now are about six to eight evening meetings each year. These usually involve lectures and responses to parents' questions by pediatricians, nutritionists, preschool educators, and child development experts. Recently, PAT has concluded that these sessions should include more parent/child interactive programs in which parents and children play together in group settings, where parents can observe other parents playing with children, and where professionals are present as well. Other group activities include child play groups that may meet once or twice a month, another type of activity that the national staff would like to see expanded. Thus far, fewer than one-third of the participating parents (those receiving home visits) have joined in the group activities.

3. *Developmental screening* for hearing, vision, and dental problems, per a state mandate. These crude screening efforts are not viewed as a substitute for medical screening but rather as a link with such programs. PEs urge parents to go for medical screening.

4. *Information and referral services* to establish links with community resources.

5. The *children's play groups* are now expanding and may emerge as a standard component.

PEs are mandated child abuse reporters under state law, and the service is viewed as a case finding device for child abuse. The program is said to be an effective preventive strategy in dealing with abuse/neglect, because it teaches parents to have more appropriate expectations regarding their children's behavior.

One person in each school district office has overall administrative responsibility for the program, usually a local assistant superintendent, and there is a district coordinator for the PEs. The state is divided into five regions and each has its own coordinator who also has responsibility for in-service training within that region. (About fifty PEs qualify as regional in-service trainers.)

PAT National Center, located in St. Louis, is a training resource and clearinghouse for PAT programs throughout the country. About ten trainers at the national center and ten from elsewhere around the country do training nationally.

The program serves about sixty thousand families in the state, the maximum number that can be served given the state's policy of reimbursing only the cost of serving 30 percent of eligible families because of budget constraints. School districts are urged to match state funds, and some private sources contribute as well. In effect, PAT offers full coverage nowhere, but it is far larger than all other family support programs.

The service is universal and free, although some other states that have adopted PAT are targeting high-risk families only. Targeting has been rejected in Missouri, but several districts make a special effort to recruit "hard-to-reach" families. There also are special programs for teen mothers and programs on Indian Reservations under the aegis of the Bureau of Indian Affairs. Overall, however, the state wants the program available to all families. Staff are not willing to state which families would benefit most from the program; they do not know.

PEs are primarily well-educated women, between thirty-five and forty years of age, who have had their own children and are now available for part-time work. They are drawn largely (75 percent) from among former elementary school teachers and, to a lesser extent, from former nurses and social workers and secondary school teachers. Most work fifteen to thirty hours a week, during the day, but the program is recruiting a growing number to work evenings and Saturdays. Average earnings are $10 to $15 an hour, with a maximum in some districts of $20 an hour and a minimum of under $10. In addition, all PEs get social security coverage but not other fringe benefits. There is very little turnover and no difficulty in recruitment; the program has very high quality staff. The only other requirement is that PEs participate in a one-week training workshop that is also used to screen out some inappropriate people. Once hired as PEs, they also are required to participate in ongoing, in-service training, on an annual basis. This training includes twenty hours during the first year as PE, fifteen hours during the second year, and ten hours for the third and each subsequent year.

The key role of the PE is that of home visitor. Some more-experienced PEs also participate in recruitment, group activities, and training. Formal supervision is limited, typically to about two sessions a year; informal supervision is on an "as-needed" basis or through a formal mentoring relationship with an experienced PE, also as needed.

There is a structured curriculum for each lesson for the (maximum) eight monthly home visits. These plans differentiate seven stages of child development between birth and age 3. Each lesson plan—and each home visit—involves a form that the visitor completes, regarding focus, aspects of cognitive, social, physical development, and self-esteem, as well as general comments. Each lesson also involves a "handout," a printed sheet with developmentally appropriate descriptive statements as well as indicators of what is ahead. The handout is both reviewed with the parent and left behind for the parent to read. For parents with limited literacy, there are handouts that have pictures primarily, accompanied by a few simple words.

Each home visit is scheduled in advance, to suit the parent. The parent views the PE as a "teacher," closely linked with the school. The visits are not viewed as a form of surveillance, but rather as instructional. Most are scheduled during the day because, until recent years, most Missouri mothers of young children did not work. Increasingly, however, with more women working, more visits are being scheduled for evenings and/or Saturdays.

The visits are very structured. The PE has been trained in advance and is given a very detailed "lesson plan." The visit includes demonstrated play with a brought-along or homemade toy and some observation of the parent and the child in interaction. The visit also includes a didactic section wherein the PE gives a brief lecture on child development to the parent. Finally, there is opportunity for the parent to ask questions, which the PE answers. The typical visit takes one and a half hours.

The curriculum is clearly oriented to white middle-class Americans. The senior staff realize this and have made their first significant adaptation for families on Indian Reservations. They realize that other adaptations would be needed for other types of communities.

The curriculum is based on the work of—and consultation with— Burton White and Berry Brazelton, plus input from Board members. Despite the presence on the national advisory board of other experts, such as Edward Zigler, senior staff seem quite uninformed about family support program models other than their own.

Watching the PE at work in the home, one wonders about the compatibility of playing with the child and modeling appropriate playing behavior for the parents, on one hand, with following a strict outline for a didactic lecture on the other, while the child is being engaged. The alternative of the one-hour Avance class/lecture comes to mind. It is not feasible here to refer this child development content to the group meetings because the majority of parents do not attend them. It is not clear whether the parents read the material left with them, and whether they understand it and find it helpful. Although parents may call their PE between visits, this is not encouraged and indeed is seen as a kind of "dependency"; as a result, parents do not do this often. Such a policy raises questions about the nature of the basic relationship between parent and PE and about the goal of the service.

PAT costs amount to about $20,000 for a PE for one year of visiting thirty families plus some group activities and recruitment; almost all of this goes toward salaries. It is not clear exactly what the other costs are. In general, it appears that there are no precise cost data available. District programs are funded by the state, at $180 per family per year, and they try to get a district "match" for a total of $350 per family per year. This level of funding clearly would not sustain eight visits per family.

Parents are recruited through announcements made on television and in newspapers. Teachers also recruit parents through older siblings in school. Efforts to reach the hard-to-reach are carried out by recruiters going to WIC (Special Supplemental Food Program for Women, Infants, and Children) sites, welfare offices, hospitals, Medicaid M.D.'s, and clinics. Eligible parents are admitted on a first-come-first-served basis.

The only evaluation thus far has been an assessment of the original pilot program. There are no systematic data on the variations of actual operating programs or the differential impact of more or fewer visits, the group activities, and so forth.

If there were more funds, there would be interest in establishing parent support groups and more part-day play groups, especially for three- and four-year-olds, but *not* full-day, full-week preschool. Yet one unanticipated result of the program is that more parents want more preschool for their three- and four-year-olds.

To conclude: This is a low-cost home visiting program, oriented in content and method largely to middle-class families and using one-on-one but relatively structured parent education as its primary intervention. At best, there is coverage of only about 30 percent of the families because of resource constraints. PAT is viewed largely as an alternative to preschool programs. The group activities—meetings designed to provide additional support—are used by only about one-third of the participating parents, and the program has not been evaluated to assess whether different activities would make a difference in outcomes/impacts, whether more or fewer home visits would make a difference, and how children in this program compare with those who are in a preschool program, when they enter primary school. There is much conviction but not much data. There are no firm cost estimates for the service.

PAT is the largest of a significant number of home visiting programs, which display both philosophical and program variations. The Mother-Child Home Program, operating on a far smaller scale, at twenty-eight sites in six states (and abroad), is another. It has an impressive body of rigorous research documenting that this type of intervention with two- and three-year-olds "at risk" has lasting impact on school performance, high school completion, and cognitive development. There are measurable positive impacts as well as mothers' verbal behavior with their children.[7]

The program features twice-weekly half-hour home sessions (continuing for about two years, with children aged 17 months to 4 years) with "Toy Demonstrators." Recruitment is from among "poorly motivated, low-income (often welfare-aided), low-educated single parents, usually mothers." The Toy Demonstrators may be paid paraprofessionals or unpaid volunteers. The Toy Demonstrator brings a toy or book each time and "models for the parent a curriculum of verbal and other positive interaction with their children." Weekly guide sheets, given to the parents, contain the core concepts as illustrated by the book or toy. The visitor demonstrates but does not teach. The parent may or may not follow the program as delivered. The key objective is to encourage mother-child verbal interaction around the toy or book. The mother helps her child to school readiness in a natural way.

Toy Demonstrators do not counsel families but do alert their coordinators, to whom they report, to families possibly needing more help from community agencies and resources. The coordinators visit and, as appropriate, offer referrals.

This, then, is a remedial program for high-risk families, but an effective one.

## New Mothers Project: Memphis, Tennessee

The New Mothers Project is a time-limited demonstration project with a strong research and evaluation component, serving low-income, low-skilled and poorly educated first-time mothers and their children, from pregnancy through the child's second birthday. It was specifically designed as a methodologically rigorous experiment in the "randomized trials" category.[8] The program's objectives are (1) to enhance child development and the mother's personal development; (2) to improve maternal and child health, and (3) to enhance the general well-being of the mother and child in the broad sense of physical, cognitive, social, and emotional health.

The major program concept is that intervening with the mother will enhance both the mother's and child's health and development. The strategy is intensive, regular home health visiting: weekly for the first four weeks during pregnancy; biweekly for the rest of pregnancy; weekly for the first six weeks after birth; biweekly until the child is about eighteen months old; and then monthly for the last four months. The visits are carried out by a registered nurse (with at least a B.A.) and usually last one to one and a half hours. The program is neutral as to whether the mother should finish school, get a job, or stay on welfare.

Mothers must be residents of Memphis, seeking medical care at the center and having their first baby; they must have a low income (below 200 percent of poverty) and be either unemployed or a high school dropout. Most are teenagers. The final sample is slightly under two hundred. There is a control group as well. There has been a very low attrition rate.

The program is an effort at replicating an earlier successful program developed by the same researchers (Dr. David Olds and collaborators), in

Elmira, New York.[9] The Elmira program was carried out in a small city with a largely white and middle-class population. The Memphis program, in contrast, is focused on a largely black population in a large city (about seven hundred thousand population in the city and about one million in the county). Also, this program is based in the Department of Health; it is not a freestanding program such as that in Elmira. The Elmira program's apparent success raised additional questions and pointed to the need for replication. It was hoped that this program, if a demonstrated success, would be sustained, but this already seems doubtful because one of the senior health officials has indicated that only some "elements" of the program, if successful, would be integrated into the existing Memphis program, but not the whole program. Nonetheless, an important research contribution seems likely.

The demonstration project began in 1988 and ended in the spring of 1994; the systematic analysis will follow.* It is a preventive, case finding, and health promotion program. The premise is that the targeted population of adolescent first-time mothers provides very little stimulation for their babies, and that without appropriate stimulation the babies will show serious developmental lags in language by eighteen to twenty-four months of age. Also, many of these young mothers are likely to be depressed, and this too has negative consequences for their babies. Thus, this is a deliberately designed, early intervention program aimed at reducing developmental delays. In addition to the limited capacities of many of these mothers and the large number of major problems confronting them, another problem is their limited access to many social services in the city. As a consequence, the visiting nurses act as information brokers, advocates, counselors, and case managers.

The caseloads of the home health visitors (HHVs) are five to six visits a day, three when the relationships are being established, and five when they already exist. (In the Department of Health, "normal" routine, HHVs make six to ten visits a day.) The core program involves intensive visits to the mother's home, on a weekly or biweekly basis, to observe mother/child interaction. The visits during the first four weeks are intended to establish a relationship. Five areas of assessment guide each visit: the personal health of the mother; her life course development; her role as mother and the child's development; her use of community resources; and family, friends, and personal/family supports. During a given visit, the nurse may focus more heavily on certain aspects than on others, depending on the mother's needs. The guidelines are not formally structured "lesson plans" like those in the two programs described earlier.

As relevant, HHVs provide health education, social support, counsel-

* The demonstration part of the project ended before this publication went to press, but our sketch was written at the time of the program visit.

ing, crisis intervention, case management, case finding, information and referral, and diagnosis and treatment.

The visits tend to be more mother-focused than child-focused. Nonetheless, a great deal of child abuse has become apparent during the visits and must be dealt with. The mother remains the focus even when a child is removed and in foster care; then, the nurse sees the child separately.

All the nurses are professional and well trained. They are more flexible than the paraprofessionals of the other programs, but nonetheless they seem much less spontaneous than the Danish HHVs discussed in Chapter 5. They also focus far less on physical health than do the European HHVs, and do not carry out the kind of health examinations done by HHVs in Europe. They spend more time on formal didactic "teaching." The argument is that it is more important to get the mothers to go to the clinics. The program is not intended to be a substitute for clinic visits, nor to make the mothers "dependent."

The visits are carried out between 7:00 A.M. and 8:00 P.M., but most occur between 3:00 P.M. and 6:00 P.M. because many of the women are in school.

On the basis of a review of developments elsewhere, one might wonder whether these very intensive interventions (1) are too frequent, (2) perhaps need to be supplemented by weekly mother/baby or mother/toddler groups and other types of family support and interactive parenting groups, (3) are too structured and didactic in their child development components, and (4) make too little use of the visitor's nursing skills. Inevitably, the randomized-trials design required structuring early in the project. No detailed cost data are available yet. Nonetheless, given the high quality of the professional staff and the rigorous experimental design, this is an impressive home visiting service, and research results will merit serious attention.

### *Family Focus: Chicago, Illinois*

Family Focus began as a service to teen mothers and their children under age 3. In short, the organizers and sponsors decided that it was a mistake to provide a rich complement of services only to teens who became pregnant or had babies, so they also began serving both preadolescents and adolescents who were neither pregnant nor parents. The preadolescents were included because it increasingly became apparent that children in the community who were aged 10 and 11 were already sexually active. The sponsors and organizers also found that the teen mothers wanted to continue to participate even as they got older, because they still needed help. It was not considered right to leave them on their own, since the issue of subsequent pregnancies and child bearing/rearing was also a potential problem. Consequently, the program has gradually expanded to include children, youth, and young parents. Other programs at different Chicago and suburban sites make community-specific decisions as to the age group served.

The present objective of Family Focus is to establish a kind of modern-day settlement house. In this context, the major gaps in the programs are viewed as (1) the need for full-day child care rather than just drop-in child care and (2) the need for a somewhat fuller range of services.

The central office of Family Focus is in downtown Chicago and includes a development office for fund-raising, a program director who provides programming assistance to the several centers, a finance department that handles budgets for all the centers, and staff developing training packages for family resource programs around the country. The Family Focus leadership see themselves as conceptualizing models for different types of communities and do not consider any one model as definitive. The centers follow a core model but adapt to community variations, depending on location. There are significant variations in black, Hispanic, and suburban community programs.

One Chicago center is located in what looks like a war zone—a poor black inner-city neighborhood with some single-family dwellings and some low-rise multifamily dwellings. Across the street is a dump for wrecked cars. The sidewalks are torn up; there is trash on the ground.

The low-rise center building itself looks like a series of remodeled old stores. The center is on the main floor, and there is a basement area as well, with a small kitchen, staff office space, and a group meeting room. The main floor is narrow and deep, with a long narrow corridor going almost the length of the center. There is a small entry area off the street, with a receptionist, coatrack, and desk. The hall leads down the middle of the center. Off to one side is a small area with a playpen and crib, which can be used for babies if needed, and a group play room for toddlers, with three low tables and chairs as well as low shelves with toys and books. Opposite is a room for discussion groups; the room can be extended further by opening sliding doors to another still larger room that covers the whole width of the center and can also be divided into two rooms for different activities. The rooms are used for parent activities: parenting groups, literacy and GED classes, learning how to use a computer, learning to type, parent education courses, and drop-in child care.

The center is open from 8:30 A.M. to 7:30 P.M., five days a week; however, in crisis situations staff stay longer and may be reached at home on weekends. The family literacy program operates Monday through Thursday from 8:30 A.M. to 2:30 P.M. and is for the "older moms" (i.e., usually late teens or early twenties). From 3:00 P.M. to closing, the center serves teens and teen parents and their children.

Funding is close to $1 million; a large part comes from a state program for at-risk teens and teen parents and a state Board of Education program for teen parents. In addition, there is funding from the Illinois Department of Human Resources, private foundations, and others. At the core, the concept is that to properly serve parents and children there must be integration of the schools, the relevant social service agencies, and the health care services.

There are twenty-eight staff at this center, fifteen of whom live in the community; seven are former program "graduates," and fifteen are home visitors (paraprofessionals who are supervised by a professional). The home visiting curriculum is parent education. Two staff members are placed at local schools two days a week, to do case finding and case management of complex situations involving the families they are working with at the center. The teen moms and/or their children are in the school.

The center served thirteen hundred families in 1991, about half through information and referral services and half through direct services. It is a voluntary program. Few adolescent parents are referred for reasons of child abuse. Those who are usually do not end up getting involved in the program but do participate in short-term parent education groups. These parents usually have many needs, often well beyond what can be met by this program or the other resources it has available.

The Family Literacy program deals with the basic skills, GED, and ESL. It serves about ten to fifteen mothers (late teens or early twenties) in a morning program. The younger teen moms are usually in school then; they arrive at about 3:00 to 4:00 P.M. Several days a week there is an after-school program for teens, dealing with their issues, and possible job opportunities.

There is a home visiting program for teen parents for whom the home visits constitute both surveillance as well as a parenting education service and a demonstration program/intervention. In addition, a large group of mothers gets only home visits; they do not come to the center. All the older mothers have a home visit initially; the number and frequency of contacts depend on the home visitor's assessment of need and risk (of abuse). There are three home visitors assigned to this program, and each sees thirty-three families. The teen mothers may be referred from school, a social service agency, a clinic, or word of mouth, or are recruited off the street by staff who see a pregnant teenager or a very young mother with a stroller and decide she looks like a likely candidate.

There are parent groups for support and parent education purposes. The group discussions focus on topics such as safety in the home and avoiding accidents, a subject of frequent attention in other family support programs as well as in the European home visiting and family support services. There are monthly parent groups for extended families as well.

There is a program for teen males too; a job club program, which meets twice a week; a weekly discussion group on issues such as AIDS, self-esteem, role models, and parenting; and a twice-weekly recreation program.

There is an after-school program for elementary school children in which staff provide help with homework. There also is growing interest in scouting, and there are now thirty girls in a Girl Scout group; there is talk of beginning a Boy Scout group as well.

Staff carry out "family needs assessments," job training referrals, and referrals for entitlements. They have an activity program for teens including taking them to theaters and concerts, skating, and on overnight trips.

The group for pregnant teens stresses as its major theme: "Every decision you make—what to eat, whether to stay or leave school, and so forth—affects your child." There are two home visitors assigned to this program, each responsible for a caseload of twenty mothers and their children. Despite staff preference for a good child care/Head Start experience, most of the children of these teen mothers are cared for by grandmothers or other relatives. A big emphasis in working with these girls is getting them to complete their education, and for some, getting them to go beyond high school; but there is also concern that their children need more stimulation than they are now receiving.

Teens who are known to be members of gangs are not permitted to participate in center activities, and staff reject gang accoutrements such as caps, earrings, and jackets.

Each program has a "module," a plan for about ten weeks, but it is implemented flexibly. If a special issue emerges, the plan is put aside and the immediate issue is addressed. At the end of each module, the staff get together and review how things went, what needs to be changed, and what new issues have emerged.

To conclude: This is an increasingly comprehensive, settlement-house type of program, serving children, youth, and young parents in a variety of ways. Counseling, advice, information and referral services, parent education, adult basic skills, drop-in child care, job clubs, and recreational activities are provided. The lack of a full-day child care program is a big gap; to have a positive impact on these children, a rich, stimulating, and consistent environment is needed from the beginning. In contrast to other family support programs, this is more comprehensive, less didactic in its teaching, but also more chaotic and less standardized.

There is a local advisory board, but it is only beginning to be active. Major policies are set by the central organization, while the programming seems to be done at the center. One big question remains: if universal preschool coverage were available for all, and universal health care as well, would all of this be needed?

## Family Support Services in Europe

We began with four U.S. programs, all under the "family support" rubric, but very different from one another. We turn now to the European scene, asking as well about the relationships between family support activities and infant/toddler care.

We start with a brief description of the situation in the selected countries.

*Denmark* places great emphasis on parent "participation" in child care programs, but, perhaps because of the greater availability of infant and toddler care, the extensiveness of the home health visiting services and related mother-baby groups, and the availability of high-quality extensive municipal personal social services, it shows no visible additional development of formally defined family support service programs.

*France,* in contrast, has a small but growing "family support" service development, especially in and around some of the larger cities (but does not have an extensive home health visiting program). Like the Italian programs (see below), the French "family support" programs are emerging out of either a child care or health care base, as a universal program, sometimes targeted on deprived, disadvantaged, immigrant children and their families, but also meant for average "French" children and parents.

*Italy,* in the child care–rich north and north-central area, has developed an innovative and diverse group of family support services, under education, and as part of its infant and toddler care system.

*Finland and Sweden,* like Denmark (and perhaps for the same reason), do not appear to be developing family support services yet, although there are some activities in Sweden that might come under this rubric.

*In England,* in contrast to Italy and France where family support services have developed out of the child care and or health systems, family support services are currently emerging from the social service/social welfare system, and are targeted on high-risk families. Similarities to the United States are immediately apparent in this regard.

During the latter part of the 1980s, a series of new initiatives began to emerge in several European countries, linked to child care in some countries but independent in others. These developments suggest the formation of a more extensive system of child and family services, focused on meeting a broader range of child and family needs—not just the need for child care when mothers work. The objective is to meet the diverse needs of very young children and the preferences of parents who might not need or want to participate in a formal day care center but are convinced that they do need and want a group experience for their children and, often, for themselves. Further, the intent is to provide this experience at much lower costs than those of a center program.

Leading French and Italian child development researchers and child care policy and program experts, seeing themselves as working for the enhancement of childhood rather than just the improvement of child care services, have taken a new and different approach.[10] They see their agenda as improving the conditions of childhood; responding to social change, including changes in family structure and gender roles; facilitating the new interest in educational reform; trying to be sensitive to the needs of parents who have limited knowledge of parenting; and, most of all, responding to the needs of children.

The result is a new concept of a diversified system of child and family services for the under-3s and their families, a system that includes child care centers as one component, but adds to it a variety of other types of group experiences for children with different needs. The "target group" includes children whose parents are not in the labor force, children with part-time working parents, and children cared for by grandparents, other relatives, or nonrelatives. These children need different types of experiences. The new programs are designed for *children and their parents as well as their grandparents and other caregivers;* and they are designed to be used part-day or even irregularly, to supply the kinds of group experiences that are essential for good child development. These new developments are seen also as providing opportunities for parents and other caregivers to exchange experiences and concerns with other parents; obtain expert guidance from professionals if they wish, including information, help, and support in their parenting role; and ultimately, to contribute to parents' socialization and education as well as that of their children, through peer interaction and interaction with staff. None of this is being proposed as an alternative to or substitute for existing "traditional" good-quality center care, but rather as a supplement to and extension of such programs.

Recent Italian research found that children from better-off families are the most likely to be provided with intellectual and social stimulation by their parents and also are the most likely to be in an infant/toddler center and thus benefit from the high-quality care provided in these programs and the experience of being with other children.[11] These children end up better prepared for preschool—and later for primary school—than those who come from families with fewer resources, whose mothers have more limited education, have lower-status jobs, are less likely to have knowledge about child development, and are most likely to use informal child care and to have their children cared for in situations where they will receive limited stimulation. Inevitably, the latter children are likely to be less well prepared for preprimary and primary school.

These child development researchers are convinced that given small family size and the paucity of children in neighborhoods, the social isolation of many of these mothers—and their children—can be devastating.

Supplementary and supportive group experiences are essential. They need not be full-day, and they should not be limited to the children; but they must provide some opportunity for children to interact with other children, separate from their mothers, and for mothers/parents/caregivers to interact with one another and their children and staff. Wherever these new centers have opened, there has been enormously enthusiastic response by mothers and grandmothers.

Although these Italian and other European child development/child care leaders would like to see center care available as a universal counterpart to the preschools, for a full or part day at parents' preference, they recognize that current resources make this impossible. However, what can be done, instead, is to expand the range of offerings beyond the traditional centers in order to make some of this experience available to a wider range of children, including those whose mothers do not work full-time.

The goal is complete coverage of all children under age three (as now exists for the three- to six-year-olds), but not all in a full-day program. A secondary goal is to establish a cluster of universal services that will link children and families, as necessary, with health care and other social services, but not specifically services for children or families with "problems."

Unfortunately, these developments are too recent for there to be any systematic data regarding supply; and even less is available by way of outcome data. No longitudinal studies are planned, nor are any rigorous evaluations. There are some studies of preschool impacts, however, which strongly suggest positive results.[12] Nonetheless, government officials and the public generally are becoming increasingly aware of the potential for learning that very young children have and how this needs to be nurtured.

## *Time for the Family Centers, Italy*

Time for the Family Centers are one of several new initiatives that have emerged in north and north-central Italy over the past five or six years, focused primarily on providing socialization and education experiences to children under age 3 and their mothers or caretakers. The purpose of the new developments is to approximate the value and universality of the preschool for the children who are not eligible for formal day care centers. They are designed to attract the shy, insecure, isolated mothers, as well as the young or single mothers, to offer them and other caretakers (child minders, grandparents) opportunity to meet one another, to discuss common problems, to participate in activities with their children, and—under the guidance of professional staff—to offer their children opportunities for socialization, peer interaction, and cognitive stimulation. Initially, this was a demonstration program, but now the city of Milan has taken it over and is establishing others.

To participate in the program, the children must be accompanied by a member of their family or a nonrelative caretaker. The premises are designed to allow individual free play as well as large-group activities. Mothers can participate in their children's activities, observe their children, read, or chat with other mothers or the staff. Participation is free, although parental contributions may be sought to buy special equipment or supplies.

One center is located in a working-class housing development that includes among the residents drug addicts and others with a variety of social problems. It serves mothers with children who are from a few months old up to three years old. Some mothers are not in the labor force; some are home on maternity or parental leave; and others work part time. In general, women with children under eighteen months old tend to come out of their own needs, whereas those with children aged eighteen months and older come in response to their perception of the child's needs. Two or three very experienced, full-time professional staff are available in the center for each fifty children, plus the same number of part-time staff, a cleaning woman, and several volunteers from among mothers who previously participated in the program. Recently, some of these mothers have begun to organize themselves as family day care mothers, a type of caregiver that did not exist in Italy until the last few years.

Mothers, caregivers, and children come from 9:30 or 10:00 A.M. until 12:30 P.M., or from 3:00 P.M. until 6:00 or 6:30 P.M. No lunch is served, and therefore there is no all-day participation. About 150 families use this center, not all at the same time, of course. Mothers/caregivers are expected to come with their child at least two times a week; fewer times make it more difficult for the child to adjust to the group. Most come three or four times a week, and under special circumstances they may even come every day. After a period of visiting, the mother chooses the morning or afternoon sessions, or a combination, and is scheduled. The center's capacity is about twenty-five mother/caregiver/child pairs, thus there is a need for some modest scheduling. Also, staff do not believe that a larger group is helpful for either the mothers or the children. Mothers are not held to a fixed schedule and can come in response to their own needs, but it is not a drop-in center. It is believed to be better for the children to find the same children—or at least some of the same children—whenever they attend. There are regular parents' meetings, and issues of concern to the mothers/caregivers are addressed in sessions led by a professional.

Some see these Time for the Family Centers as "preventive" programs. Nonetheless, a repeated theme is that the programs are designed to serve average, normal families with children, not problem cases. They are located in a wide range of communities, middle-class as well as poor and working-class. However, there is a parallel assumption that in a big city, such as Milan, in some sense all families with young children have problems. Moreover, given the limitations in the number of spaces, priority is given to children with special needs (handicapped, immigrant) or families with special needs (lone mother). However, the problems that tend to be the priority cases are more likely to be social or physical handicaps rather than family pathology (e.g., child abuse). Children who are neglected or at risk for maltreatment are more likely to be served in full-day center care. The general assumption is that no more than 10 to 20 percent of enrollment in either the infant/toddler programs (see Chapter 6) or Family Centers should be "problem" cases. There is general conviction that a higher proportion is likely to distort the program and, therefore, as the 20 percent ratio is reached, the pressure for establishing a new center becomes intense.

These programs are expanding because they are less expensive than full-day centers and there are many families who would not qualify for a center but want a group experience for their child and for themselves. There is response to the demand in part because the theory is that mothers who are more inadequate, insecure, inept, or isolated will learn from exposure to other mothers, even more than they will learn from the professional staff; and even these very young children will learn from other children, and from their mothers' enhanced parenting skills as well. (In this connection, American research showing the ability of young infants to learn from other young infants is quite supportive.)

A second, very important potential problem that these programs deal with is that of mother-child separation. At many preschools in France and Italy, this is viewed as a major problem for three-year-olds, in particular those who have not attended a center earlier. This can create problems for the child's adjustment and learning.

A third function of the centers is social and cognitive stimulation and enhancing the children's development. Mothers see their children playing with other children and begin to understand the value and importance of this experience. The children respond to other mothers, to staff, and to other children.

A fourth function of these centers is to provide a substitute—or surrogate—for what was earlier provided by the extended family. Information, advice, role modeling, encouragement, concern, and support are all provided here. In contrast to the U.S. (and British) focus on pathology and high-risk families, the Italian focus on average families builds on a social infrastructure that is already in place: preschools, child care centers, and health services.

Parents apply for places in this program just as they do for the centers, making formal application in the local district office. Parents must provide proof of the child's age and vaccinations. Here, too, demand far exceeds supply.

Although our illustration is European, we pause to note that the needs and responses are not totally unfamiliar in the United States. Several years ago, in the context of a U.S. child care study, we reported on a family support activity based in a child care "resource and referral (R and R) agency," Resources for Family Development, in Livermore, California:

> This organization's parent education and support efforts, based at a special location about a mile from the main office and known as Parent's Place, are particularly noteworthy. Most of the AP* recipients are working single mothers. Many others who call for R&R information are at the point of transition involving divorce or separation or some family crisis. The centrally located Parent's Place, in a refurbished old building, is staffed by a young mother who recently had her second child. She is interested in parents and in child development and is obviously relaxed, sensitive, and supportive. Mothers may come with their children to the "living room," and the children may play. There is a small parent library and a small toy library. A mother may come for respite, relaxed conversation, or for information. A family day care provider may find books, toys, or guidance. The Parent's Place is also used for lectures, support groups, and meetings. Materials are disseminated.
>
> The child care field has sought a family support model for many years and has invented several in the context of Head Start. The support services tied to R&R programs here and elsewhere offer intriguing possibilities. Interestingly, they are all encompassed within the R&R budget and some of the administrative overhead from the other programs, as is a social service component.[13]

### Family Support Services in France

Family support services are increasing in France, too, especially in the large urban areas, emerging under the aegis of different systems: child care, maternal and child health, and social services. The trend in France is toward the establishment of a variety of community-based programs serving very young children (under age 3) and their parents. The focus is on both "welcoming" the child and "awakening" the child by stimulating his/her development in a variety of ways. The overall objective is to enhance child development and parent/child relationships. More specifically, the objectives are (1) to encourage parent/child interaction, (2) to reduce parent-child conflict, (3) to refer those with special needs to appropriate resources, and (4) to facilitate adult/adult (mother/mother) as well as mother/child interaction.

The program concept was first launched in middle-class communities

*AP denotes Alternative Payment, a state child care voucher program.

but then moved to a focus on the more deprived and on immigrants. It is now expanding once again in middle-class communities, where it is viewed as important for all children under 3 whose mothers are not in the labor force, and who would otherwise not qualify for *crèches*. These programs are not a substitute for *crèches* but rather a complement and supplement. They may be open five days a week, all day or part day, or even part week. Staff often include volunteers as well as paid staff. Thus far, despite the growing popularity of these programs, there has been no systematic evaluation of the extent to which they are achieving the desired goals.

The programs stress parent/child relationships and a family focus: in particular, helping inform and educate mothers and parents regarding appropriate child development and behavior by staff "modeling" such behavior. "Inadequate" parents are helped to become more adequate, to learn how to talk to and with their children, and even to play with their children. Similarly, the parents who have difficulty with the French language are helped to recognize that this is not a unique experience for them, but rather an experience that is shared by many others. Second, there is focus on reducing the social isolation of some of these mothers by placing them in a setting where they can develop relationships with other women in similar situations and from similar backgrounds, through informal contacts. Third, children are helped to become more independent and to learn how to separate from their parents, an important aspect of subsequent adjustment to preschool.

Basically, the only requirements are that the programs be community-based and child-development-centered, and that the child be accompanied by an adult who remains with him or her while at the center. There is no formal registration or formal program, and there are no required activities. The programs focus primarily on children aged 3 months to 3 years. They are all publicly financed, but the funds are usually supplemented by other sources, whenever possible.

The programs are considered "preventive" in the sense that they are designed to stress school readiness (and therefore to reduce the potential for school problems), to stress educating and socializing the mothers (to reduce the risk of child abuse), and to help mothers develop social networks, so as to reduce the risk of depression among them. They are increasingly popular wherever available.[14]

### Family Centers in the United Kingdom: A Focus on High-Risk Families

Like those in the United States, British family support programs (Family Centres) vary in auspice, in range of interventions, and somewhat in philosophy, and are targeted on high-risk and vulnerable children and families, on young parents and young children, and (like many in the United States) are equally diffuse in the ways in which they "intervene" and in their impacts.

A 1989 survey[15] identified 495 family centers nationally, ranging from public programs to voluntary agency programs; from projects under the auspices of large voluntary agencies to small, informal grass-roots organizations; from residential facilities to home-based services; from intensive professionally staffed, therapeutic programs to informal self-help groups; and from "deficit-oriented" treatment services to developmentally oriented or supportive mutual aid and self-help groups. Most (84 percent) are under voluntary agency auspices.

Regardless of the "model," almost all characterize their mission as strengthening family functioning through the provision of supportive services designed to help and enhance parenting skills. And almost all are located in communities with high rates of social pathology, poverty, and unemployment. All provide some kind of child care service. All include some home visiting and some outreach services. Indeed, some child care centers seem to have simply renamed themselves "Family Centres," as a new kind of "marketing" device. All are relatively informal, as compared with more traditional family service agencies. All use a broad-brush approach to intervention and rarely carry out any rigorous evaluation or impact studies. Most focus on families with young children (under 5). Most are under social work auspices and, as mentioned earlier, are voluntary agencies or are attached to such agencies.

The population served varies, however. Some accept only "at-risk" families who are referred by other professionals. Some accept all families living in an "at-risk community." Some take children (and their families) who are listed on child care service waiting lists. And some take any child or parent who wants to participate.

The types of services provided and interventions used also vary. Some have focused on intensive, "family preservation" type work (avoidance of placement) and crisis intervention. Many carry out remedial and treatment interventions with abusing parents or very disorganized families. Most offer at least drop-in child care services, information, advice, counseling services, and parent education.

Staffing patterns vary as well. Some are highly professionalized. Some use paraprofessionals or a combination of professionals and paraprofessionals. And some use lay volunteers or "indigenous" staff—parents who "graduated" earlier from a family center program. One criticism heard is that often as a condition of getting other more practical help, more and more inadequate parents are being made to participate in parent education classes run by untrained staff, with no evidence of positive outcomes.

Despite the developmental rhetoric, most centers seem to offer problem-oriented treatment, rather than developmental services, and they are focused increasingly on problems of child abuse and severe neglect. The centers seem to have moved away from the earlier stress on broad-brush preventive work "towards the targeting and surveillance of families deemed to have failed."[16] Nonetheless, they are viewed by some as reducing social isolation, giving support in crises, and providing enhanced opportunities for children to learn, play, and relate to peers. The last is of special importance in a country where most child care for the under-fours is limited to care for children in need—and children with employed mothers are not defined as "in need."

The best exemplar is briefly described in what follows.

## Pen Green Centre for Under-fives and Their Families

The Pen Green Centre is located in a heavy industrial and mining town in England's midlands, which has a very high unemployment rate. It is described now as a "women's working town" because many of the men remain unemployed and the women are working irregularly or on off hours or on shift work in the service sector.

Pen Green has an extraordinarily strong child orientation, deriving from its child care base, and therefore goes beyond the U.S. family support centers in that it includes a child care program among its core components. It is a family support and parent education center with a day nursery (child care center) at its very heart, serving two- to four-year-olds primarily, and with a strong commitment to active parent involvement and empowerment.

The center opened in 1983 as a "demonstration project" in the integration of early childhood education and social welfare day care—combining a nursery school, day nursery, and social services. The funding and administration are jointly shared between education and personal social services, and there are meticulous efforts at implementing a balanced joint administrative and policy-making perspective. Staff include five fully qualified child care workers, two nursery school teachers, and a group of five other staff who have miscellaneous experience and qualifications (e.g., cook, kitchen assistant, part-time "dinner supervisor," group-work leader, support staff, etc.). The full complement would be about twenty-five in staff; currently they have the equivalent of about twenty full-time people. Each child care (or family) worker follows the progress of ten children very closely (four in each session, including two who remain for the full day); this worker, who plays the central caregiving role for a few children, is known as the "key worker." A number of British child care programs employ this concept.

The child care day is largely unstructured in the sense that the staff try to follow the child's lead, the child being free to play indoors or outdoors and to play in various parts of the room where the group is meeting. The key worker makes a point of remaining close to "her" children. Twice during the day, once in the morning and once in the afternoon, the key worker will initiate activity (11:00 A.M. and 3:00 P.M.), which might take the form of story reading, discussing something on the children's minds, and/or asking the children's opinions about something—somewhat like the approach taken by the Danish pedagogues.

Before the children enter school, when they are four years old and leaving the program (children qualify for school if they reach age 4 before August 31 of the year they will be entering school), there is a formal program of preparation for school, in which the schools participate by inviting the children and their mothers to come and visit once, twice, or three times in the spring of the year before the child enters. In this program they discuss concerns regarding the transition to school, such as getting lost, being bullied, and being approached by strangers.

The program at Pen Green has some qualities of a settlement house for young families and children. In addition to the child care center and some other related activities, including the drop-in service, a play group, and the crèche services, there is a health visitor who comes regularly to the center, social workers who carry out counseling as needed, and a home visiting program. Another core component at Pen Green is an active and extensive parent education and support program with high rates of participation. Parents are extraordinarily active in all phases of the program and often are not distinguishable from staff. It is an environment full of happy, engaged, active children and adults.

Pen Green staff clearly see themselves as being at the forefront of an important development. The center is viewed as an exemplar among both social service and education professionals. How much it will influence future developments in the British family center movement remains to be seen.

## Conclusion

Several developments have led to the emergence of what we have characterized as "family support" services, however labeled in other countries. First, there is a growing conviction regarding the universal need of infants and toddlers and their mothers for a group experience regardless of whether the mothers are in the labor force. Given the high costs of good-quality infant and toddler care, the current constraints on economic resources, the increased provision of leaves permitting infant care to be at-home parental care, the diverse attitudes toward out-of-home care for very young children, and the country variations in labor force participation rates of women with such young children, it is not surprising that only in a few countries is there significant expansion of the supply of child care services for the under-threes now.

Nonetheless, what is expanding in some countries is at the interface of child care and family support, premised on the assumption that the very young and their mothers or caregivers need a group experience that will facilitate and enhance child development and meet the needs of the mothers at the same time, but that the children may not need this on as extensive or as sustained a basis as do slightly older children. There appears to be a growing assumption that part-time, part-week group experiences will offer an important transition to a fuller program subsequently, for the children of working parents, and that this may be all that is needed for others (when mothers work part-time themselves, for example, or when mothers are at home). Thus, whether in part-day child care or in family support services, these youngest children are increasingly being exposed to groups providing cognitive, physical, and social stimulation while their mothers are offered information and advice (if requested) about child development, parenting, child care, as well as education and training opportunities for themselves and opportunities for socializing, cultural integration, and making friends. As part of this process, and because of the interest in enhancing preschool readiness, not only is there a growing trend toward family support programs, but in several countries there are close links and even integration between the two types of programs—infant/toddler care and family support services.

Indeed, this linkage between the two seems to ensure that in the countries where it exists, both types of services will develop along universal lines rather than as a response to children with special needs and problems. Of some interest, among the European countries it is only in Britain, where there is little in the way of infant and toddler services, that the family support services are emerging with a "special needs" orientation. The result is a program targeted on the poor, the troubled, and the high-risk. In contrast, in France and Italy there is conviction about the universal need for these experiences and there is implementation that supports this concept. Priority may be given to children or parents with special needs, but the programs are not designed for this purpose nor limited to this population. Indeed, the absence of family support services in Denmark may be a function of the far greater availability of other universal "family support–type" services: infant/toddler care, home health visiting, and broad personal social services.

To conclude: The care of very young children and support for their parents are both receiving growing attention in Europe. Several countries have a more extensive supply of infant and toddler care services than we do in the United States, and these countries all have far better quality services and far more extensively subsidized services, which, as a result, are far more readily accessed and afforded by parents. At least as important, in a few countries there is conviction about what very young children and their parents need that goes beyond child care for the children of working parents. The goal is to respond to a broader set of needs—cognitive, social, physical, psychological—and to parental as well as children's needs, to move toward a more holistic child and family service. In this context, child care, early childhood education, maternal and child health care, and family support services are emerging as a comprehensive and integrated young child and family service system. Could this be a model for the United States?

The last decade witnessed a dramatic increase in the number, diversity, and visibility of family support service programs in many places. Despite the lack of uniformity, the absence of any distinct "models," the diffuse nature of the intervention, and the very limited evidence of success in achieving improved child and parent outcomes, there appears to be a kind of family support "social movement" emerging in much of the advanced industrialized west. There is growing consensus that new parents need help—information, advice, practical assistance—and that infants and toddlers need stimulation as well as care and nurture. The rhetoric surrounding the U.S. developments stresses the need for a developmental and universal program rather than a deficit (treatment) oriented, targeted model. The Italian and French developments and the Danish child care and home health visiting services have implemented such a program strategy.

We would encourage continued experimentation in the United States but urge some systematic evaluation and long-term monitoring and assessment of outcomes, in particular regarding the alternatives of universal and targeted programs, and of developmental and treatment-oriented programs. As part of this (as noted in Chapter 6) we also would urge a refocus of Head Start, from a narrowly targeted program serving poor four-year-olds to a universal program for one- and two-year-olds, with priority attention given to children and families with special needs, including poverty, handicap, immigrant status, first children, young parents, and child protection against abuse, neglect, and other social risks.

Zigler and Styfco note that the most important insight gained from the last three decades of child development research is that

> Child development is a continuous process: physical and psychological growth build upon earlier stages, and each stage influences the next. There is thus no magic period during which we can inoculate children against the developmental threats imposed by poverty. Intervention during the preschool years is certainly important in preparing children for school, but the social and emotional foundations for learning have been

laid long before this age. . . . The social policy implications of this . . . are clear. A nation committed to having all children enter school ready to learn must do more than offer them a preschool program. For at-risk children to have a genuine head start toward school success, intervention must begin prenatally and continue throughout the early years of life.[17]

We would suggest the possible validity of this for many or most children in modern societies; voluntary family support resources as well as diverse child care services should be available for their families—and selected in accord with the family's election of a parenting mode that reflects their economic and social realities and their preferences.

# 8

## Getting Started on Starting Right

Behind the statistics, the observations, and the exemplars there is a clear and simple message: this country needs to get its priorities right with regard to young children. Children have a claim to a decent life, and a decent life requires a good start. No moral society will allow children to be born and then strive for any less for them. Time, talent, expertise, resources, and organizational capacities all have limitations, and this is a world of many uncertainties; but our failure should not reflect a lack of commitment, our unwillingness to make the necessary effort. And if we do make the effort, we will make significant progress. We already achieve much with some of our children; other societies show results for larger proportions of theirs. Moreover, sound policy for little children—as we have seen with regard to health, child care, family support, and income transfers—can be hand-in-hand with social policy for their families, particularly their mothers. Indeed, lack of sensitivity to mothers and their needs would undermine the potential benefits to children of the measures we have outlined.

If the fundamental moral argument does not suffice, there also is a case from the perspective of societal self-interest. Society needs "good" children because it needs responsible citizens, competent and creative workers, and attractive members for the kind of civil society that enhances the daily experience of all.

These results do not occur on their own in a complex, modern country, without forethought, policy, and effective action. There are perhaps some extraordinary parents with adequate personal and financial resources who could do all that is needed to launch their children from within their own sheltered havens. For almost everybody else, the reality is a different one. For low earners, the difference between poverty in one country and resource adequacy in another is tax and income transfer (income maintenance) policies of government. If there is to be effective, efficient, affordable, and accessible medical care, there must be governmental interventions via supports for training, regulation, monitoring, and service delivery machinery—as well as the enactment of health insurance or direct service commitments.

The same observations apply to child care services, family supports, and much else. Complex modern societies cannot forgo government, even though governments retain important options. They may subsidize, mandate, regulate, operate, or delegate to lower-level jurisdictions. The American mixed economy of social welfare has demonstrated the strengths of a public-private nonprofit mix, of a division of roles between Washington and the states, of sharing with or relying on the for-profit market. To urge a major commitment to starting right with our children is not to upset the values and preferences that create the particular American "mix." It is, however, to stress the primacy of governmental policy as the beginning point and generator. We need a national governmental lead because of the strategic nature of the required actions, the scale of resources involved, and because children have a right to "territorial justice." It should not matter where one lives and who one is. Our proposals refer to all the children.

If the government is to act, it will be because of public insistence. We already have in the public debate the carefully researched and documented proposals from two recent commissions. The bipartisan National Commission on Children (chaired by Senator John D. Rockefeller IV), created by public law "to serve as a forum on behalf of the children of the nation," did not limit itself to the under-threes and published a rich menu of proposals.[1] We have referred to several. The Carnegie Task Force on Meeting the Needs of Young Children focused more sharply, involved leading experts and research scholars, and issued its report shortly before this publication went to press.[2] Now, the specialized substantive organizations, the professional associations, the voices of parents as expressed throughout their associations, and the women's groups need to be heard and the issues raised taken up in Congressional hearings and new Executive Department initiatives. The goal should be targeted, coherent policy attention to the under-threes and their families.

Our argument is not that we should ensure our children a good start because the Europeans do. Or that we should import European programs to the United States. Our children should have that start because it will improve their lives and life-chances and strengthen their families, and also because it is a good investment in our own society. The European experiences have been reported because, along with important new developments in the United States, they enable us to draw upon the best of societal learning in lining up the options, so as to plan American reforms.

Will it be expensive? Of course. The economic supports, the infrastructure, and the various programs and benefits described must be paid for— out of the national product. The programs cited have developed in countries prepared to allow government to tax and to spend at a needed level, within their constraints. Referring to data for the latest years available (1988–1991), we note that while the United States was allowing government to spend 36.4 percent of its gross domestic product (GDP) (while collecting 32.2 percent and thus adding to the deficit), all the countries illustrated herein were spending significantly more through government: Denmark, 57.2 percent; Finland, 56.2 percent; France, 48.5 percent; Germany, 44.4 percent; Italy, 53.1 percent; Sweden, 59.8 percent; and the United Kingdom, 39.7 percent. (But some of their governments operated utilities, railroads, or other industries.) Within the government budget, the United States also was assigning a smaller proportion of funds to social welfare (but here we note imprecision because comparable data are not available in other countries on the private sector, which is high in the United States). We clearly were spending less than the others on cash family benefits.[3]

As much may be said about taxes leveled to pay for the budgets. In 1992, when the United States' tax receipts from all sources totaled 29.9 percent of the GDP, the European Community average was 40.8 percent and the OECD average—covering the major industrialized pluralistic democracies—was 38.8 percent. To illustrate the range, Canada's tax receipts totaled 37.1 percent of their GDP, Denmark's, 48.6; Finland's, 38.0; France's, 43.7; Germany's, 37.7; and Italy's, 39.1. With the possible exception of Japan, we are the lowest taxers.

Any discussion of learning from exemplar countries must include learning about costs and the willingness of citizens to defer some of their potential personal market consumption for public programs and public resource consumption. Inevitably, this would involve some degree of redistribution from the more affluent to the totality, through payment of graduated income taxes. We have been impressed with the public ethic that supports such an approach in the countries cited. The particular ideology varies, but it is of great interest that most of these countries are governed by conservative regimes that sustain the basic family policy. "Solidarity" and "equalizing of family burdens" for those with children reflect deeply felt societal values. Analysis of the histories of these countries does reveal some shifts in policy, as there are shifts to or from conservative or social democratic party control, or as coalition balances change. Nonetheless, the shifts tend to be at the margin with regard to the core child and family supports that are part of the society, the civic culture, and the social environment. They are no longer debated as reforms, experiments, or marginal enhancements. Thus, with their variations, and even occasional cutbacks responding to economic pressures, they do add up to a secure start for most children.

Governments periodically regroup their priorities. The health and welfare initiatives and the claims made for children do call for some adjustments in the United States at this time. And it is an appropriate time as we ease some of the military commitments that long constrained domestic budgets and explore quality-of-life issues.

The proposed new expenditures do not ask Americans to lower their standards of living. They do involve some very modest constraints for middle- and upper-income people with good personal disposable income, in favor of societal initiatives and guarantees of medical services, child care, and other essentials to all children.

Before turning to specific proposals, we wish to return to a theme also buttressed by the European experience: the need to move away from fragmented, disjointed increments that may not add up, in favor of a holistic under-three policy. We add to the arguments already made some testimony from Europeans whose formal responsibilities are related to child health.

A World Health Organization (WHO) official remarks that "Infant mortality is not a health problem. Infant mortality is a social problem with health consequences. . . . The first priority is not more obstetricians or pediatricians or hospitals, nor even more prenatal clinics or well-baby clinics, but rather to provide more social, financial, and educational support to families with pregnant women and infants."[4] His conclusion is that what is critical, if infant mortality and morbidity are to be reduced, is to guarantee all American families with pregnant women and young babies a basic economic and social standard of living. This, he argues, is what children need for a good start in life.

From a somewhat different but related perspective, many European child health experts stress the integration of child health with economic and social well-being. For example, home health visiting in Europe is viewed as a key component in some countries' overall systems of child health care. At the same time, however, both this service and the child health care system are viewed as a key part of the overall social policy for children and their families.[5] Or, put in more general terms, there is strong conviction that child health goals will not be achieved in the absence of income transfers (direct cash benefits and taxes), housing policy (subsidies and homes), child care services (subsidies and programs), social services (family support and services for children with special needs), as well as health care (insurance and services).[6] In effect, child health care policies and programs are viewed as an integral component and interdependent with the other elements of good social policy for children and their families. A comprehensive, holistic view of "health" is considered to require this perspective. A firm "social infrastructure" provides the foundation and building blocks for supplementary interventions for children and families with special needs.

Thus, for example, a "table" listing the major maternal and child health legislation in France includes laws on family allowances (cash benefits for families), guaranteed minimum income, maternity leave, child protective services, and child care services, as well as laws regarding maternal and child health, birth control, compulsory health examinations, abortion, prenatal care, and so forth.[7] In describing child health care in France, a French public health expert concludes that "Child health policies and programs are necessary but not sufficient [to produce a healthy child]; to be efficient they must be part of a comprehensive welfare policy."[8]

Similarly, in her overview of child health services in England and Wales, the former Head of the British National Health Visiting Association describes child health services in Britain as being rendered largely through the National Health Service *and* the Department of Social Security. She notes that central to child health are the various income transfers provided by the Department to families with children, including Child Benefit (a universal child allowance), One-Parent Benefit (a child allowance supplement for single parents), Family Credit (a refundable tax credit for working parents with children), Income Support (the means-tested public assistance benefit, like our Supplemental Security Income [SSI], but unlike SSI, for *all* low-income individuals), Unemployment Insurance, Housing benefits, and so forth.[9]

Family Support services in Britain, France, Denmark, and Italy also are all predicated on the adequacy of the foundation on which they rest: monetary family benefits, child and maternal health care, parental leaves following childbirth, and child care services. Except in Britain where they are oriented more toward helping disadvantaged families cope better and toward providing "treatment," the focus is on a universal helping service designed to aid mothers and children, especially in the very early years, before the universal preschool programs begin. They are viewed as both an access service (linking parents with a variety of other social benefits and services) and a support service. It is assumed in all these countries that they can only function well when the other more basic forms of social protection are in place.

The same is true for services for troubled children and their families. U.S. participants (government officials, academics, Congressional staff of all political persuasions) at a National Academy of Science meeting on child welfare internationally[10] concluded that, without attention to the establishment of a broad and firm social infrastructure that includes adequate income (supplementing wages; assuring child support), health care, housing, and universal preschool, any effort at protecting deprived, vulnerable, high-risk children would end up dominated by investigative, adversarial, and adjudicative procedures, as in the United States, the United Kingdom, and Canada—and not meeting the full range of child and family social services needs, as in Germany, France, and Denmark.

Conviction that a holistic approach is essential and recognition of the interdependence of strategies guide our proposals. We recognize that a balanced strategy is hard to achieve because the debate as to whether policy should stress services, or adequate income, or parental time, often goes on without any recognition that these are linked. The child care planners do not consider parental leaves. The medical planners are unrelated to the child income questions. The advocates are separate; the professional associations are separate; the disciplines that deal with each are separate; the Congressional committees that make the policies are fragmented; and the delivery systems are divided. Moreover, the call for a multifaceted strategy can sound like a desire to slow action on one side or the other.

Nonetheless, an Administration, or advocacy group, or Congressional committee that would be of maximum aid to the under-threes would do well to hold on to the total picture and to move the strategies forward with careful phasing and consideration of the problem of resource competition.

We attempt, in what follows, to summarize our specific recommendations in this spirit.

## The First Stage

Our cluster of major proposals consists mostly of items already on the public agenda but in need of energetic action and visibility as an investment in the under-threes. Here we refer to:

A major child health prevention component as part of medical care reform ("child health supervision")

A $1,000 per-child annual refundable tax credit (or the equivalent if a child/family allowance is preferred)

Child support assurance.

Several urgent AFDC enhancements

A first installment on an improved Family Medical Leave Act (FMLA)

Implementation of a first installment of an infant/toddler concentration in the enhanced but reformed Head Start

A modest infant/toddler care block grant appropriation to allow state upgrading and some expansion of centers and family day care

## Child Health Supervision

We begin with health because of its urgency and because what we propose is within grasp. This country debated and dropped a major reform of its health care system in 1993–1994; there is widespread conviction that the effort must be renewed. We see in this reform a strategic opportunity to develop a national system of child health supervision, the prevention component in child health, with broad social and developmental perspectives. This is a matter of saving lives, avoiding disability, protecting against serious diseases, and enhancing lifelong well-being.

The international experience makes the case for a prevention system separate from, but with close operational ties to, the system of acute and chronic care for children. On the other hand, it needs to be fully integrated with the "maternity care system," the network concerned with prenatal care, labor, delivery, and postpartum care.

The child health supervision program for infants and toddlers and for children in the preschool years calls for a network of child health (well-baby) clinics, supported by an outreach system of well-trained public health visitors and serving all children. The alternative is an insurance plan in which each child has full access to a family doctor or pediatrician responsible for preventive as well as acute and chronic care services. Set visits to the home immediately after the baby's return from the hospital and in the early months (at least two visits to be offered to all families, and more where there is defined "risk") would have enormous health payoff and serve as a major case-finding and outreach service. Other scheduled visits to the family doctor or clinics—with outreach to nonparticipants—would assure completion of essential inoculation series and checkups at specified intervals. (We have proposed that admission to child care be conditioned by proof of inoculation, just as admission to elementary school is.) A reasonable goal would be the minimum of four to six contacts in the first year, divided between the home and the clinic. The acceptance of the visit "offer" should be voluntary, but complete nonparticipation would alert personnel to the need to explore a possible child protection problem, because it is rare for parents to reject health care for children.

We see this as a matter of planning in the context of the current commitments to health reform, not a call for still additional resources. The price tag of that reform will depend on many decisions made in the broader national debate; children's services are among the less expensive part of the health budget. Recent proposals would finance the reform out of cost controls and savings in current Medicaid and Medicare programs. Present commitments, especially to the Maternal and Child Health block grant, could provide core financial resources for the federal contribution to costs of a separate network of well-baby clinics, if that is one of the options adopted.

We in fact do see great merit in creation of one maternal and child health (or "child and family health") preventive service, based in a national network of centers, probably state administered, with a home health visiting capacity. The alternative, which probably is the best fit with our diverse delivery systems and the likelihood of state options under health reform, would be the requirement that state authorities (or other regional contracting authorities or cooperatives that are established) include these services in the "package" to be negotiated on behalf of all participant families and delivered by a diversity of providers. From the user's perspective, the payment should be part of the family "insurance" guarantee, not involving special costs or copayments.

There are few things that a society can do with immediate payoff for children that match a well-organized prevention initiative in the health care field. Together with improvement of economic underpinnings, this could be a historic step.

## *Income*

*A Tax Credit or a Child Allowance.* We have stressed throughout (see Chapter 3) that "families need money if they are to manage well with young children." We now summarize and specify further our proposals for a child tax credit or child allowance; child support assurance; and urgent AFDC benefit upgrading.

The case has been made for a child (or family) allowance as a basic societal contribution to the costs of child rearing, recognized everywhere but in this country. In fact, the allowance is only a modest supplement, not an alternative to a salary or wage or, when appropriate, social insurance or public assistance (transfer) income. However, income supplements (among which the child allowance is the most important internationally to families with children) make low-wage incomes or low transfers viable. A family can rear a child decently if society helps out in this way.

The most active child allowance proposal already on the U.S. public policy agenda is the proposal for a $1,000 refundable tax credit as suggested by the National Commission on Children.[11] In the past, we and others have made similar proposals from time to time. A tax credit may be a form of child allowance quite compatible with the American ethic. However, because low-income families should not have to wait for the money until tax time, there are some implementation problems to be solved.

This is our most costly recommendation. The $1,000 tax credit, as noted by the Commission in 1991, is equivalent to a $3,225 exemption for an individual in the 31-percent marginal tax bracket, then the highest, and a $6,666 exemption for people in the lowest (15-percent) tax bracket. It would do more for upper-income earners than do the present personal exemptions for children, much more for middle-income families, and would for the first time provide a benefit for those below the tax threshold. After elimination of personal tax exemptions for children, the annual cost, as computed for 1992 and before 1993 reforms, would be slightly above $40 billion.[12]

We noted in Chapter 3 that a child/family allowance is the standard income supplement in Europe to assist families with the costs of child rearing. Such an alternative initiative would be welcome. It is easily administered because checks are automatically mailed out monthly and could be deposited directly in people's bank accounts. In a plan developed by University of Wisconsin researchers, it could be either more expensive or less expensive than the proposed $1,000 tax credit.[13] The tax credit may prove to be more attractive politically and already has some impetus. It is, in a sense, a U.S.-style child allowance.

Several presidential candidates and others made more—and less—generous tax credit proposals in 1992. Action in the near future would require negotiations in the context of deficit-reduction concerns. It would be important to have a first installment as part of any initial overall child policy package for the under-threes to give such "package" credibility. Courageous proponents will need to argue that there are some things that even justify tax increases—and that such increases, if properly targeted, need not interfere with economic growth.

*Child Support Assurance.* Although important to many nonwelfare families, child support assurance (as described in Chapter 3) tends to be discussed in the context of welfare reform, with an eye to removing families from the welfare rolls. In this sense, the calculations are intertwined with the issue of a federal floor under the AFDC benefit, or complete federalization. This analytic and advocacy process is under way, and action will be taken independently of an under-three initiative.

Cost estimates depend on the generosity of the guarantee, whether or not there will be a means test, and whatever else is expected to be done at the same time to affect child support collections. One "low-option" plan "costs out" at $0.6 billion, and a more generous proposal at $1.6 billion.[14] We suggest use of the latter; a successful child support system is more likely to evolve if it continues to consider the economic needs of millions of "nonwelfare" children in divorced families and if it avoids the stigma of a welfare connection. Not on the same scale as the other two income proposals, child support assurance is very important to many children and essential as a strategy for helping single-parent, mother-only families to avoid welfare.

*Urgent AFDC Reform.* The child tax credit or child allowance is a supplement, not a full income support program. Child support assurance offers modest aid to children, and the potential for avoiding welfare when coupled with a child allowance and a wage. But for some families, sometimes these will not be adequate—or a job will not be available. Many under-threes, albeit far fewer than now, will still be dependent on AFDC grants. While there has been much staff work within the Clinton Administration directed to welfare reform, and considerable political maneuvering on all sides of the debate, none of the publicly discussed proposals or scenarios visible (as this publication went to press) suggest a major enactment very soon. Major policy changes such as limiting the duration of grants while guaranteeing public employment as a last-resort fallback for younger single mothers would, in any case, be phased in on a modest scale, because a massive launch is deemed too expensive. Those with children under age 1 probably would not be required to take part, and any except the younger mothers would not have priority space in the education/ training/job search/work programs. Most children in the five million families on the AFDC rolls will continue to depend on the program.

In Chapter 3 we expressed outrage at the notion that second and later children born into AFDC families could be kept off the food budget at state option, according to one proposal. We also noted that if most or some mothers of infants and toddlers remain home on AFDC grants, it is unconscionable to provide AFDC and food stamp "budgets," which keep almost everybody below the poverty line. We suggest instead that it is time to do for AFDC what was done for the adult assistance categories (aid to the aged, blind, and disabled) in 1972 when the SSI program was created. That reform involved federalization, to end geographic inequities, and an indexed benefit minimum with an eye to the poverty line. Making a variety of conservative assumptions about a moving target, we have estimated that an AFDC benefit increase to bring all recipients to the poverty line (including food stamps) would add $10 billion to federal and state costs—on the premise that current state expenditures would be "captured" in some way by a "trade" as part of federalization. This sum ($10 billion) is equal to the Clinton Adminstration's most recent estimate for its welfare reform proposal. We have no basis for optimism about this notion because there has been an emphasis in public discussion on the JOBS program and on punitive measures toward AFDC families, not on achieving a more adequate standard of living for them. Yet for some, this may be all there is.

## Parental Time

It is difficult for parent(s) and child(ren) to have a good start together without unhurried time for the mother to recover physically from the immediate effects of childbirth and time for baby and parents to develop their complex and vital relationships with one another. Later, there is the need for a parent to be at home for the health visitor, or to go to the clinic or doctor's office, or to care for an ill child. "Preventive" child health involves parent and child.

A modern, industrialized child-and-parent-friendly society allows time for these things in the form of job-protected leaves. It makes leaves possible and protects income for the time away from work. The United States is unique in its failure to offer even the most modest of packages. Its first installment, the FMLA, passed in 1993, did not cover the majority of female workers and left out the wage-replacement component. We have summarized the practice in other countries (Chapter 4).

The conversion of the truncated FMLA into a modest but useful piece of legislation would require, at the minimum, as we have noted, lowering the firm-size criterion to cover more female workers; making eligibility work-history requirements more realistic and relating them to female work patterns; decreasing substantially or eliminating exemptions for the top 10 percent so-called key employees; covering, on a modest basis, care for a sick child upon medical certification of necessity; and ensuring income replacement at least at the level of unemployment insurance.

We already have offered a rationale for these proposals (in Chapter 4). We need to note, as well, that the legislation creating the FMLA also designed a vehicle for its evaluation and enhancement; the Commission on Leave. Careful monitoring of the law now in place can test some of the assertions about its costs and adequacy; it could provide a "usage" base against which to compute potential costs of alternative methods of financing. Nonetheless, we now offer a first rough cost estimate of an immediately feasible option, legislation that will carry the temporary disability insurance (TDI) mechanism from five states (see Chapter 4) to all states, or will apply the unemployment insurance device to wage replacement. Either method would involve a very small payroll tax levied on an employer or employee and an option for states to operate their plans—unless they prefer to leave the implementation to the federal government. Public budgets would not be burdened by costs.

In developing cost estimates we have begun with these facts: total TDI costs in the five states that now have the program, $3,224.2 million; 22 percent of the national workforce in these states; 10 to 15 percent of TDI expenditures for maternity cases. Pending updated surveys by the Commission on Leave, we estimate that complete coverage in all states would cost $2 billion annually. Following existing patterns, this could be financed completely by small employee payroll deductions (a few dollars monthly) or through employer-employee sharing. We already know, from the research of Galinsky and Bond, that the modest costs of the leaves to employers are not a serious obstacle, political rhetoric to the contrary.*

## Infant/Toddler Care

Many single mothers of under-threes and most mothers in two-parent families with infants and toddlers are already in the labor force. A child care initiative is an essential part of our initial package, not to attract parents to work but to allow them that option and to improve the quality and stability of child care for the majority of infants and toddlers who either are already in care or are likely to be in care.

Because of the interrelatedness of parental leave and child care provisions, it is difficult to put exact numbers on estimated demand and likely costs. An enhancement of FMLA of the sort outlined in Chapter 4 will decrease the numbers of infants in out-of-home care during the first three to six months of their lives. (Just as some mothers now remain at home for an unpaid twelve-week leave, others may be able to stretch it for twenty-four weeks if the first twelve weeks were paid. The policy, in fact, should eventually aim at a full-year job-protected leave, with six months paid.) Child care is more costly to the society and to the parent than is the leave option.

Clearly, there is need to plan for both upgraded and expanded child care capacity. At the very least, current substantial shortages in infant/toddler care need to be dealt with. A good beginning could be made with a soundly planned and well-implemented infant/toddler initiative in Head

---

*While urging extension of the TDI mechanism as one device for modest expansion of an income-replacing parental leave, we have not dealt with the major function of TDI in the five states that have adopted it. It is a state-mandated and administered system of sickness benefits. Elsewhere in the United States, employees are covered for sickness income by civil service laws, union contacts, employer-initiated fringe benefits, or private insurance. We have not offered a proposal herein, despite the importance of this form of income protection for children and their families, because it does not appear at all likely to have policy attention in a decade of the major health care reform. This, despite the fact that, in general, European health insurance systems do provide for sickness benefits.

Start, as already discussed. Funds have been committed but will need augmentation in the fiscal-year 1996 federal budget.

What also will be needed simulataneously is a modest increase in the federal block grant for child care, enacted in 1990, or a special, new infant/toddler grant program. The 1990 legislation (Child Care and Development Block Grant [CCDBG]), as we have seen (Chapter 6), included a small "set-aside" for early childhood education and school-age child care. Assuming equal shares for these latter two categories, the infant/toddler budget would be about $235 million over three years. This will not go very far. In future legislative appropriations or a new program, a doubling or tripling of the sum would provide a "pool" of money for needed first-stage state expansion of infant/toddler center care and family day care. Only experience, especially after improvement of family leave provisions, would establish the level of future need, but a new $500 million fund would allow planning, a good beginning, and quality-controlled phasing-in. The states would be offered support and financial help on the basis of evidence that plans have been made and a quality threshold set. Given parental preferences, it is essential that among the possibilities would be the creation of well-organized and supervised family day care "systems," either publicly operated or contracted with large private agencies. We have described the attractive Danish pattern. There is U.S. precedent as well.

## Costs

The cluster of proposals we have outlined for the first stage of action on behalf of the under-threes becomes little more than a dream unless the current level of public expenditures is reconsidered, along the lines of our earlier discussion. Under any other scenario, by merely citing the federal budgetary deficit, opponents of social programs can freeze everything. Our small children cannot afford a decade of delay. That would probably mean large numbers of poorly launched children in birth cohorts totaling forty million. Nor are we convinced, on the basis of international experience, and review of our tax and federal expenditure levels, that public expenditures for families with children must remain stagnant, to protect this country's economic health.

Following is a summary of cost estimates for our cluster of first-stage proposals:

| | |
|---|---|
| Child tax credit or child allowance | $40.0 billion* |
| Child support assurance (the high option) | $ 1.6 billion* |
| Urgent AFDC enhancements (probably an excessive total because we have made no allowance for JOBS program successes) | $10.0 billion* |

Child health prevention program (already part of     $ 0
any health reform initiative, to be paid out of program changes and cost controls and savings)

TDI Expansion to all states, to create paid maternity     $ 2.0 billion
leaves

Infant-toddler care block grant                          $ 0.5 billion

Total New Costs                                          $54.1 billion

*Covers children of *all* ages.

Is this too high or a reasonable target for new expenditures? International expenditure comparisons are difficult because of differences among
programs and budget categories. Nonetheless, for a few critical countries,
we have been able to make usable if not always precise comparisons of
current expenditures for families and children, it not being practicable to
isolate the under-threes in national budgets.[15] These comparisons cover:
*income transfers* (child conditioned cash benefits) for families with children;
*services* (including child care, foster care, and other child welfare programs,
but not elementary or secondary education); and *tax expenditures* (such as
personal exemptions for children and the child care tax credit.) These
categories also cover maternity and parental benefits linked to leaves and
advance maintance.

Translating such expenditures into proportions of the GDP (excluding
education and health and noting some variations in years covered and data
sets drawn upon), we find the following: where the U.S. is spending 1.7
percent of GDP (in 1992) on children and their families, including tax
expenditures,[16] such countries as the United Kingdom, France, Germany,
and all the Nordic countries are spending between 2.0 and 5.1 percent of
GDP, *excluding* tax expenditures, and in countries at the lower end of the
range, also excluding child care services expenditures as well.

The $54.1 billion cost total for our new proposals is roughly 1 percent
of U.S. GDP for 1992. If the U.S. could extend its effort from 1.7 to 3.0
percent of GDP to approach the Nordic countries, which have lower per
capita GDPs than we do, it would be well on the road to more generous
child policy. None of the countries cited has been damaged by this level of
expenditure; none is retreating from it, despite recent economic problems
in Europe.

Moreover, these expenditures could be phased in over four to five years,
*beginning with the under-threes,* the high priority group. Such a beginning
would bring the immediate bill of the tax credit or child allowance to $7.5
billion, the child support assurance to $300 million, and the AFDC up-

grading to $2.5 billion; the other items would be unchanged, but the bill to be paid at once would be $12.9 billion, or roughly .25 percent of GDP—not an unreasonable sum.

## The Next Stage

In the previous chapters we also introduced other components of an under-three agenda—or components of a broader family policy agenda that would have important impact on under-three policy. Although we would not expect the items that follow to achieve immediate priority status, it would be a big mistake to allow them to be lost.

### Earned Income Tax Credit (EITC)

The EITC is a nonwelfare economic boost for the working poor that was upgraded as part of the 1993 tax package. It refunds taxes to low-salary earners with dependents. In 1990, provision was made to take account of more than one child in a family. The 1993 amendments are still limited to two children. It would not be very expensive to take account of the specific numbers of children in a family. Modest upgrading of the level of refund would also be desirable. A child tax credit or allowance, a minimum wage increase, and modest EITC enhancements could be part of a package to keep every child with working parents out of poverty. Our proposed AFDC reforms could do as much for those not in the labor force.

### Housing Allowances

The country's housing policy gaps, largely created during the Reagan years, will be filled only slowly, given the cost levels involved. Some essential priorities are assigned to the homeless, including homeless families. However, housing is an essential infrastructure element in family life. The European experience dramatizes housing allowances' effectiveness in boosting the standard of living of families with children. As described in Chapter 3, housing allowances are paid to families living in standard housing, who already pay specified proportions of their incomes for it; the allowances are geared to incomes and family size.

One would hope that housing allowances will enter into consideration when the country takes on the task of revitalizing, upgrading, and expanding its housing efforts.

### A "Nonwasteable" Child Care Tax Credit

Before the enactment of the 1990 CCDBG, the Dependent Care Tax Credit (which is in large part a child care tax credit) was the largest single federal commitment to the financing of child care.[17] Since it is a financing mode worth more to those who spend more and is conditioned on payment of the federal income tax, it is essentially geared to the middle class. Those below the tax threshold do not benefit.

Here, as in many areas of family costs, it is the working poor who carry the heaviest burdens. For many years, therefore, advocates have urged (in vain) that the Dependent Care Tax Credit be refundable. A family below the threshold would collect its credit in cash, as does a family eligible for the EITC.

We have not listed this proposal among our "first major cluster" only because of the EITC. Because that very effective tax credit has become a popular device for supplementing incomes of the working poor and targets the very families that would be eligible for a refundable dependent care credit, it would appear wise to allow time to observe the implementation of the recent EITC enhancements, and the outcome of proposals for its further improvements, before acting on dependent care. Those who develop plans for an overall, integrated federal under-three initiative might consider a strategy with some elements of each. The major attraction of the Dependent Care Tax Credit component is its categorical nature, its availability only to those who must spend money for child care.

### Getting Ready for a Larger Family Support Service Initiative

Developments in our society make it very desirable that young families, single-parent families, and even some not-so-young families have access to emotional and social support services, sources of guidance and information, and emergency respite and aid. We are referring not only to the remedial and therapeutic help critical to some, but also to the "support" that is part of the normal life experience and that almost everyone needs and values. Society, in "institutionalizing" such services, whether as a governmental offering, as the service of a voluntary agency, or as a mutual aid effort, is responding to social change—the changes in and the frequent nonavailability of aid and guidance from the primary group, family, and friends.

Family support services can be very important in the lives of the under-threes, but this is not yet the time to propose a nationally defined initiative. Rather, this is a period for explorations and demonstration projects. Our report from the United States and Europe describes interesting, and sometimes research-validated developments (Chapter 7). They are sometimes anchored in child care, and other times in the health, educational, mental-health, or personal social service systems. They are sometimes targeted on high-risk groups, and sometimes on all families with very young children. While almost always called "preventive," they frequently are therapeutic and rehabilitative, too. Currently, an adequate analysis of costs is not available.

Most of the most attractive initiatives in the United States have been backed, and sometimes studied, by private philanthropic foundations. Others grew out of public child welfare, educational, medical, and mental-health funding streams. Still others were created by United Way agencies and church/synagogues—or out of self-help initiatives by people with shared problems, needs, destinies, or causes.

Federal child welfare legislation passed during 1993 ("Family Preservation and Support Services Program," an entitlement capped at $1 billion) offered funds to the states for use in expanding "family preservation" programs that provide emergency short-term guidance to families in order to avoid placement of endangered children. Another component of this legislation allows the states to deploy resources to establish expanded (but not fully defined) family support programs. We see an opportunity here.

In consultation with the states, the major large foundations, and the four to five national advocacy groups particularly active in this area, the Department of Health and Human Services (Assistant Secretary, Office of Human Development Services and/or Assistant Secretary, Planning and Evaluation) needs to develop and contract for an evaluation strategy to build on this block grant in order to clarify what might be done to raise the entire initiative several notches, for the future. Or, in the absence of a federal mechanism, this is an area in which one of the involved foundations might very well take the lead.

However successful the small projects and even the several city or county demonstrations, and however creative the personnel involved, we need now to move toward plans for more consistent support and larger coverage. None of this precludes state-level decentralization and substantial diversity in programs.

## Certainties and Uncertainties, Research, Experience, and Societal Learning

We have indicated, throughout, the "evidence" for the various suggestions and proposals. Sometimes it is very straightforward: proper prenatal care decreases low birth weight and infant mortality; the recommended course of inoculations at the right times wipes out dangerous childhood diseases. Sometimes the validation is a bit more soft: if parents and children have time to start together, their relationship will have more opportunity to thrive—and both psychological research and folk wisdom consider that desirable in the vast majority of family situations. Sometimes the case is based on comparative evidence: countries that adopt certain income transfer and tax strategies have far less child poverty than we, and child poverty is associated with—even if not always the direct *cause* of—many very undesirable child and family outcomes, which we have specified.

All policy-making involves a degree of uncertainty, but we are in a domain that has had extensive expert, political, and public scrutiny in a society where the burden of proof is on those who want government to act and to reverse a long tradition that it will not act unless a strong case is made. Despite this context, some ideas, policies, and practices have emerged on the child policy agenda. Many have U.S. precedents, exemplars, and research validations. Many have parent-consumers, political leaders, and professionals convinced but waiting for an adequate supply or needed financing. Most of what we have urged also is done in many countries and is popular with citizens and a range of political parties. Their economies have not collapsed, and their families thrive.

In short, our "case," our "argument," combines research—evaluation, international and U.S. societal learning, and consumer response. Public action is seldom better documented. And, as we have suggested, the moral argument is strong.

The question is asked: If society does what is needed to allow children to "start right," will it make a difference when they are older? What is the evidence? Our answer is that doing all these things is shown, by existing research, to pay off in educational success in the early grades, and in health and personal development as well. However, no one would claim complete knowledge of how much difference all this can guarantee in relation to problems of adolescence and adulthood in a changing world. The ultimate outcomes of nurturance, socialization, developmental, and educational experiences also relate to neighborhood experiences, educational institutions, culture, history, economic development, politics, public administration, general societal developments, and much else, at a given moment. A reasonable society should do no less than launch its children into changing communities and a world of uncertainties with the decent start that is proposed herein. Our children can be prepared and equipped even if the country cannot—and would not—guarantee and program all that follows.

We have urged both moral commitment and rational, deliberative action. The results will depend on how well it is all implemented, but also on the broader social forces listed, and more. Our suggested policies and programs need not involve more organization, control, or paternalism than Americans would be willing to consider. They are not cheap measures, but they are cheaper than the alternatives we now live with, if one considers both direct dollar costs of responding to problems, pathology, illness, and failure—and the human costs of inadequacy and neglect.

The final salvo in opposition will come from those who say that we cannot afford it all. This has been the ultimate barrier since the high deficit run-ups of the Reagan years, described by David Stockman (the then budget director) as a deliberate brake on social programs. But what can be afforded depends on choices made between private disposable income and agreed spending through governmental agencies and their agents. Some things are more efficiently done when we act as a community (insurance, for example). Some can only be done by governmental and private agencies and organizations (the development of child care resources, the building of roads, bridges, and airports). The improvement of the life-chances of our under-threes will require much from parents, but also public action, public spending, some modest decrease in personal disposable income, and probably modestly increased personal income taxes. The comparative data show us to be wealthier (in per capita GDP) than all countries cited. If we make our choices wisely, we can raise and spare the money. But we do need to make choices. Should we not get started?

# Notes

## Chapter 1

1. For documentation of the research status of many of the assertions about the developmental importance of the first three years, see National Commission on Children, *Just the Facts* (Washington, D.C.: U.S. Government Printing Office, 1993), pp. 11, 22–24; Carnegie Task Force on Meeting the Needs of Young Children, *Starting Points: Meeting the Needs of Our Youngest Children* (New York: Carnegie Corporation, 1994), pp. 6–12; Judith Musick, "Carnegie Primer on the First Three Years of Life," paper commissioned by the Carnegie Corporation Task Force on Meeting the Needs of Young Children (September 1993). For our earlier formulation of this chapter's theme, see Sheila B. Kamerman, "Starting Right: What We Owe to Children Under Three," *The American Prospect* (Winter, 1991), pp. 63–74.

2. David A. Hamburg. *Today's Children: Creating a Future for a Generation in Crisis* (New York: Times Books, 1992), p. 14.

3. *Starting Points*, p. 5.

4. Sandra L. Hofferth et al. *National Child Care Survey, 1990* (Washington, D.C.: The Urban Institute Press, 1991); Ellen Galinsky, et al. *The Study of Children in Family Child Care and Relative Care* (New York: Families and Work Institute, 1994).

5. *Cost, Quality, and Child Outcomes in Child Care Centers* (Three reports). Department of Economics, University of Colorado, Denver, 1995.

In 1991, according to the U.S. Bureau of the Census, among working parents who paid for child care, the average payment was $3,300 a year per child. See Current Population Reports, *Who's Minding the Kids?* (Washington, D.C.: U.S. Government Printing Office, 1994). The cost to government of Head Start in 1992 was $3,720 for a half-day program. Sandra L. Hofferth and Duncan Chaplin refer also to a General Accounting Office estimate of the cost of high quality child care for a preschool-aged child as $6,300 in 1990. See *Child Care: Quality versus Availability* (Washington, D.C.: The Urban Institute, 1994), p. 3.

The $8,800 figure comes from several other sources providing estimates of what good quality care would cost in 1994.

6. Institute of Medicine (IOM). *Preventing Low Birthweight* (Washington, D.C.: National Academy Press, 1985). Mentioned also in *Just the Facts*, pp. 22–24. For details of poor U.S. rankings on low birthweight, neonatal mortality, post-neonatal mortality, and infant mortality as compared with ten western industrialized countries, see Barbara Starfield, *Primary Care: Concept, Evaluation, and Policy* (New York: Oxford University Press, 1992).

7. Special analysis of U.S. Census Bureau data carried out by Susan Einbinder, at that time at the National Center for Children in Poverty and now on the faculty of the University of Southern California, School of Social Work. See also General Accounting Office (GAO), *Infants and Toddlers: Dramatic Increases in Numbers Living in Poverty* (Washington, D.C.: GAO, 1994).

8. *Just the Facts*, p. 43.

9. Ibid., p. 39.

10. Carnegie Task Force on Meeting the Needs of Young Children. *Starting Points*.

## Chapter 2

1. At the forefront of mainstream comparative welfare state literature are Peter Flora, *Growth to Limits* (Berlin: Walter de Gruyter, 1988); Peter Flora and Arnold J. Heidenheimer, eds., *The Development of Welfare States in Europe and America* (New Brunswick, N.J.: Transaction Books, 1981). Comparative social policy scholarship that incorporates a feminist perspective includes Theda Skocpol and Gretchen Ritter, "Gender and the Origins of Modern Social Policies in Britain and the United States," *Studies in American Political Development* 5, no. 1 (spring 1991): 36–93; Ann Shola Orloff, "Gender and the Social Rights of Citizenship: The Comparative Analysis of Gender Relations and Welfare States," *American Sociological Review* 58 (June 1993): 303–328; Seth Koven and Sonya Michel, "Womanly Duties; Maternalist Politics and the Origins of Welfare States in France, Germany, Great Britain, and the United States, 1880–1920." *American Historical Review* 95, no. 4 (October 1990); Susan Pedersen, *Family Dependence and the Origins of the Welfare State: Britain and France, 1914–1945* (New York: Cambridge University Press, 1993).

2. Sheila B. Kamerman. "Child and Family Policy: An International Overview," in *Children, Families and Government: Preparing for the 21st Century*, Edward Zigler et al., eds. (New York: Cambridge University Press, 1995).

3. Koven and Michel. "Womanly Duties," p. 1084.

4. Theda Skocpol. *Protecting Soldiers and Mothers: The Political Origins of Social Policy in the United States* (Cambridge: Harvard University Press, 1992).

5. Orloff. "Gender and the Social Rights," p. 308.

6. We discuss the concept of a combined income and service strategy in Sheila B. Kamerman and Alfred J. Kahn, *Child Care, Family Benefits, and Working Parents* (New York: Columbia University Press, 1981). In that book we report on a comparative child and family policy study also focused on children under age 3, carried out in the late 1970s. One major conclusion of the study was the need to pay attention to aspects of child well-being and, therefore, to use both income and service strategies.

7. The analysis of poverty of the under-threes draws on 1990 Census data and the data base of the National Center for Children in Poverty. See Susan Einbinder, *Five Million Children: A Statistical Portrait of Our Poorest Young Citizens, 1990* (New York: National Center for Children in Poverty, 1993). The special U.S. analysis from Census poverty data was prepared for us by Susan Einbinder.

8. The European under-three poverty data were analyzed by Beth Jean Heller, as part of the same research, using the Luxembourg Income Study data base.

9. The seven-country comparisons, using the Luxembourg Income Study (LIS) data base, as prepared by Beth Jean Heller, show Canada (.19), France (.11), Germany (.09), the Netherlands (.06), the United Kingdom (.25), Sweden (.09), and the United States (.27). For these international comparisons, poverty is usually defined as income below 40 percent or 50 percent of the median income for the population category. We have employed the 40-percent criterion, closest to the U.S. Census poverty line.

10. Theodora Ooms. *Families in Poverty: Patterns, Contexts, and Implications for Policy* (Washington, D.C.: The Family Impact Seminar, 1992). Also, see, Jane E. Miller and Sanders Korenman, "Poverty and Children's Nutritional Status in the United States," *American Journal of Epidemiology*, 140, no. 3 (August 1994): 233–43; Sanders Korenman, Jane E. Miller, and John E. Sjaastal, "Long-Term Poverty and Child Development in the United States: Results from the NLSY," *Child and Youth Services Review* 17, nos. 1–2 (1995): 127–135.

11. *Washington Post*, 27 March 1993.

12. Sandra and Sheldon Danziger. "Child Poverty and Public Policy: Toward a Comprehensive Anti-Poverty Strategy." *Daedalus* 122, no. 1 (winter 1993): 57–84.

13. Donald J. Hernandez. *Studies in Household and Family Formation*, U.S. Bureau of the Census, Current Population Reports, Series P-23, No.179 (Washington, D.C.: U.S. Government Printing Office, 1992).

14. Danziger and Danziger. "Child Poverty," p. 73.

15. Isabel V. Sawhill. "Young Children and Families," in *Setting National Priorities* (Washington, D.C.: The Brookings Institution, 1992).

16. Mary Jo Bane. "How Much Does Poverty Matter?" *Social Security Bulletin* 55, no. 2 (summer 1992): 69-71. See also "Household Composition and Poverty," in *Fighting Poverty: What Works and What Doesn't*. Sheldon H. Danziger and David H. Weinberg, eds. (Cambridge, Mass.: Harvard University Press, 1986).

17. Fred Wulczyn. "Status at Birth and Infant Foster Care Placement in New York City," Processed July 1992.

18. Danziger and Danziger. "Child Poverty," p. 74.

19. Lisbeth B. Schorr. *Within Our Reach* (New York: Doubleday, 1988); "What Works: Applying What We Already Know about Successful Social Policy," *The American Prospect*, no. 13 (spring 1993): 43-55.

20. Martin O'Connell. "Maternity Leave Arrangements 1960–1985", *Work and Family Patterns of American Women*, U.S. Bureau of the Census, Current Population Reports, Series P-23, No. 165 (Washington, D.C.: U.S. Government Printing Office, 1990).

21. Jonathan Gershuny. *Social Innovation and the Division of Labor* (Oxford: Oxford University Press, 1983).

22. Suzanne M. Bianchi. *America's Children: Mixed Prospects* (Washington, D.C.: Population Reference Bureau, 1990).

# Chapter 3

1. For a country-by-country review, see Social Security Administration, *Social Security Programs around the World, 1993* (Washington, D.C.: U.S. Government Printing Office, 1994). See also most recent issue of International Labour Office, *The Costs of Social Security* (Geneva: International Labour Office). For the European Community there are annual reports of developments in Wilfred Dumon, for the European Observatory of National Family Policies, *National Family Policies in EU Countries* (Brussels: Commission of the European Community). See also Jonathan Bradshaw, John Ditch, Hilary Holmes, and Peter Whiteford. *Support for Children: A Comparison of Arrangements in Fifteen Countries*, Department of Social Security, Research Report No. 21 (London: Her Majesty's Stationery Office, 1993).

2. Bradshaw et al., chap. 5.

3. Ibid., pp. 36–37.

4. Tarja Halonen. "Address by Minister Tarja Halonen at the Conference of European Family Ministers in Brussels, 19–21 May, 1987," Processed.

5. Joruko Hulkko. Analysis of data from Central Statistical Office of Finland, Statistics of Income and Property in 1987. Personal correspondence, 1992.

6. Irwin Garfinkel. *Assuring Child Support* (New York: Russell Sage Foundation, 1992).

7. Gordon H. Lester. *Child Support and Alimony: 1989,* U.S. Bureau of the Census, Current Population Reports, Series P-60, No. 173 (Washington, D.C.: U.S. Government Printing Office, 1991).

8. Although federal Child Support Enforcement officials report better collection results than the self-reports to the Census, reviewed herein, the overall picture is only moderately more favorable. See *1992 Green Book: Overview of Entitlement Programs* (Washington, D.C.: U.S. Government Printing Office, 1992), pp. 707–709.

9. Garfinkel. *Assuring Child Support*, p. 45.

10. Alfred J. Kahn and Sheila B. Kamerman, eds. *Child Support: From Debt Collection to Social Policy* (Beverly Hills. Calif.: Sage Publications, 1988).

11. Irwin Garfinkel. "Child Support Assurance," in Ibid., pp. 328–343, and *Assuring Child Support*.

12. Kahn and Kamerman. Ibid., especially Peter Dopffel, "Child Support in Europe: A Comparative View," pp. 176–224.

13. Alfred J. Kahn and Sheila B. Kamerman. *Income Transfers for Families with Children: An Eight-Country Study* (Philadelphia: Temple University Press, 1983), pp. 274–283.

14. "Social Security Programs in the United States," *Social Security Bulletin* 54, no. 9 (September 1991): 38–42.

15. *1992 Green Book*, p. 1673.

16. *1993 Green Book*, pp. 1667–1676.

17. Bradshaw et al., *Support for Children*, chap. 6.

18. Kahn and Kamerman. *Income Transfers for Families with Children*, pp. 228–242.

19. National Commission on Children. *Beyond Rhetoric: A New American Agenda for Children and Families* (Washington, D.C.: U.S. Government Printing Office, 1991), pp. 93–95, 449. See also C. Eugene Steuerle and Jason Juffras. "A $1,000 Tax Credit for Every Child: A Base of Reform for the Nation's Tax, Welfare, and Health Systems" (Washington, D.C.: The Urban Institute, April 1991).

20. Steuerle and Juffras, "A $1,000 Tax Credit for Every Child."

21. *Beyond Rhetoric*, p. 95.

22. Katharine L. Bradbury and Anthony Downs, eds. *Do Housing Allowances Work?* (Washington, D.C.: The Brookings Institution, 1981).

## Chapter 4

1. Robert Haveman and Barbara Wolfe. *Succeeding Generations: On the Effects of Investments in Children* (New York: Russell Sage Foundation, 1994).

2. Ibid.

3. Martin O'Connell. "Maternity Leave Arrangements 1960–1985," *Work and Family Patterns of American Women*, U.S. Bureau of the Census, Current Population Reports, Series P-23, No. 165 (Washington, D.C.: U.S. Government Printing Office, 1990).

4. Cheryl D. Hayes, John L. Palmer, and Martha Zaslow, eds. *Who Cares for America's Children?* (Washington, D.C.: National Research Council, National Academy Press, 1990), pp. 57–61.

5. Roberta Spalter-Roth and Heidi Hartmann. *Unnecessary Losses: Costs to Americans of the Lack of Family and Medical Leave* (Washington, D.C.: Institute for Women's Policy Research, 1990).

6. Ibid., $500 million as contrasted with $24 billion.

7. Eileen Trzcinski, "Employers' Parental Leave Policies: Does the Labor Market Provide Parental Leave?" in Janet S. Hyde and Marylin J. Esser, eds. *Parental Leave and Child Care* (Philadelphia: Temple University Press, 1991).

8. Donna R. Lenhoff and Sylvia M. Becker. "Symposium. Family and Medical Leave Legislation in the States: Toward A Comprehensive Approach," *Harvard Journal on Legislation* 26, No. 2 (summer 1989): 423.

9. Spalter-Roth (44 percent) and O'Connell (47 percent), only slightly higher than our 1981 estimate of 40 percent. See Sheila B. Kamerman, Alfred J. Kahn, and Paul W. Kingston. *Maternity Policies and Working Women* (New York: Columbia University Press, 1983). Twenty-three percent of working women are covered under the temporary disability insurance plans in effect in five states: California, Hawaii, New Jersey, New York, and Rhode Island.

10. Carnegie Task Force on Meeting the Needs of Young Children. *Starting Points: Meeting the Needs of Our Youngest Children* (New York: Carnegie Corporation, 1994), pp. xv, 46–47.

11. What follows draws on earlier research reported in Sheila B. Kamerman and Alfred J. Kahn, eds. *Child Care, Parental Leave, and the Under-3s: Policy Innovation in Europe* (Westport. Conn.: Auburn House, 1991), as well as the comparative study reported in the present volume.

12. We concur with—and draw on—the conclusions of Ellen Galinsky and James T. Bond, in their memorandum entitled "Strengthening Federal Parental Leave Policy" (New York: Family and Work Institute, 1993).

13. Ibid.

14. Ibid.

15. Ibid.

# Chapter 5

1. Susan Nall Bales. "Public Opinion and Health Care Reform for Children," in "Health Care Reform," *The Future of Children* 3, no. 2 (summer/fall 1993): 186–187.

2. National Commission on Children. *Beyond Rhetoric: A New American Agenda for Children and Families* (Washington, D.C.: U.S. Government Printing Office, 1991), p. 119.

3. *1993 Green Book: Overview of Entitlement Programs* (Washington, D.C.: U.S. Government Printing Office, 1993), pp. 1158–1165. See also *Statistical Abstract of the United States (1993–1994)* (U.S. Government Printing Office, 1994), p. 844.

4. *Beyond Rhetoric*, p. 119. See also, "U.S. Health Care for Children," *The Future of Children* 2, no. 2 (winter 1992): 11–12; and Barbara Starfield. "Child and Adolescent Health Status Measures," pp. 25–39.

5. Ibid., p. 13.

6. Andrew D. Racine, et al. "Effectiveness of Health Care Services for Pregnant Women and Infants;" Ibid., p. 44. See also Sarah S. Brown, ed. *Prenatal Care: Reaching Mothers, Reaching Infants* (Washington, D.C.: Institute of Medicine, National Academy Press, 1988), pp. 39–41; and "Advance Report of Final Natality Statistics, 1991," *Monthly Vital Statistics Report* 42, no. 3 (9 September 1993), National Center for Health Statistics.

7. Racine. "Effectiveness of Health Care Services."

8. *The New York Times*, 29 October 1993, reporting from the Center for Disease Control and Prevention, Atlanta.

9. "U.S. Health Care for Children," pp. 11–12. See also James Perrin et al. "Health Care Services for Children and Adolescents," p. 67.

10. "U.S. Health Care for Children," p. 12.

11. This is the recommended American Academy of Pediatrics standard as reported in The Report of the Carnegie Task Force on Meeting the Needs of Young Children, *Starting Points: Meeting the Needs of Our Youngest Children* (New York: Carnegie Corporation, 1994), p. 64.

12. Starfield, in "U.S. Health Care for Children," p. 33.

13. *Beyond Rhetoric*, p. 124.

14. Perrin et al., in "U.S. Health Care for Children," p. 64.

15. "U.S. Health Care for Children," p. 9.

16. Peter Budetti and Clare Feinson. "Assuring Adequate Health Care Benefits for Children and Adolescents," in "Health Care Reform," pp. 37ff, especially p. 48.

17. Ibid., p. 40.

18. Ibid.

19. Brown. *Prenatal Care*, p. 12.

20. Select Panel for the Promotion of Child Health, *Better Health for Our Children: A National Strategy*, vol. III, Analysis and Recommendations for Selected Federal Programs (Washington, D.C.: U.S. Government Printing Office, 1981), p. 1.

21. Bernard Guyer. "The Evolution and Future Role of Title V," in *Children in a Changing Health System: Assessments and Proposals for Reform*. eds. Mark J. Schlesinger and Leon Eisenberg (Baltimore: Johns Hopkins, 1990). See also Lorraine Klerman. *Alive and Well* (New York: National Center for Children in Poverty, Columbia University School of Public Health, 1991).

22. Eamon M. Magee and Margaret W. Pratt. *1935–1985: 50 Years of U.S. Federal Support to Promote the Health of Mothers, Children and Handicapped Children in America* (Vienna. Va.: Information Sciences Research Institute, 1985).

23. Marilyn Moon. "Overview: Setting the Context for Reform," in "Health Care Reform," p. 33.

24. Pamela Farley Short and Doris C. Lefkowitz. "Encouraging Preventive Services for Low-Income Children: The Effect of Expanding Medicaid." *Medical Care* 30, no. 9 (September 1992): 766–780.

25. "Health Care Reform," p. 10.

26. Ian T. Hill, Laurence Bartlett, and Molly B. Brostrain. "State Initiatives to Cover Uninsured Children," in "Health Care Reform," pp. 142–163. See also, on state initiatives and innovations, the following from the National Conference of State Legislatures, Washington, D.C.: Melissa K. Hough et al. *Maternal and Child Health Legislation: 1992* (1993); Susan C. Biemesderfer. *Healthy Babies* (1993); Martha P. King. *Healthy Kids* (1993).

27. National Commission to Prevent Infant Mortality. *One-Stop Shopping: The Road to Healthy Mothers and Children* (Washington, D.C.: Department of Health and Human Services, 1991).

28. On home health visiting associated with prenatal care, see C. Arden Miller, "Prenatal Care Outreach: An International Perspective," in Sarah S. Brown, ed.,

*Prenatal Care*, pp. 210–228. According to Miller, reporting as of the early 1980s, only the Netherlands carried out at least one prenatal home visit in all cases. Denmark and Belgium had a policy calling for such visits, which was unevenly implemented. Other countries expected prenatal visits in the instances of complicated pregnancies or to check on clinic nonattenders (p. 222).

29. Judith Ann Trolander. *Voices of Henry Street* (New York: Henry Street Settlement, 1993), p. 11.

30. "Home Visiting," Special Issue, *The Future of Children* 3, no. 3 (winter 1993).

31. In this section we have drawn freely on our jointly authored article, "Home Health Visiting in Europe," in Ibid., pp. 39–52.

32. Alfred J. Kahn and Sheila B. Kamerman. *Not for the Poor Alone* (Philadelphia: Temple University Press, 1975; and New York: Harper and Row [paperback], 1977), chap. 1.

33. *Health Visiting*, Summary of *Report I*, prepared by a committee appointed by the National Health Service of Denmark on Health Visiting and Home Nursing (Copenhagen, 1970).

34. Ibid., p. 12.

35. Ibid., p. 13.

36. For a description of this care, see M. Manciaux, C. Jestin, M. Fritz, and D. Bertrand, "Child Health Care Policy and Delivery in France," *Child Health in 1990: The United States Compared to Canada, England and Wales, France, the Netherlands, and Norway*. Supplement to *Pediatrics* 86, no. 6, part 2 (December 1990): 1037–1044.

37. U.S. General Accounting Office. "Preventive Health Care for Children: Experience from Selected Foreign Countries" (Washington, D.C.: GAO/HRD-93-62, August 1993); The Report of the Carnegie Task Force. *Starting Points*, pp. 80–83.

38. "Home Visiting," Special Issue, *The Future of Children* 3, no. 3 (winter 1993).

39. American Academy of Arts and Sciences. "Interim Report—Home Visiting Research." (Cambridge, Mass.: processed, 1993), p. 1.

## Chapter 6

1. Cheryl D. Hayes, ed. *Making Policies for Children: A Study of the Federal Process* (Washington, D.C.: National Academy Press, 1982), pp. 22–23. See also Sheila B. Kamerman and Alfred J. Kahn. *Social Services in the United States* (Philadelphia: Temple University Press, 1976), p. 83. (See chap. 1 and research references cited).

2. Cheryl D. Hayes, John L. Palmer, and Martha J. Zaslow, eds. *Who Cares for America's Children?* (Washington, D.C.: National Research Council, National Academy Press, 1990).

3. On Head Start developments, see special section, "Creating a 21st Century Head Start." *Children* 22, no. 4 (1993–1994). The report of the National Advisory

Group on Head Start was issued by the Department of Health and Human Services, 12 January 1994. See also "A Head Start on Head Start: Effective Birth to Three Strategies" (Chicago: Ounce of Prevention Fund, 1994).

4. Sandra Hofferth, April Brayfield, Sharon Deich, and Pamela Holcomb. *National Child Care Survey, 1990* (Washington, D.C.: The Urban Institute Press, 1991); Ellen E. Kisker, Sandra L. Hofferth, Deborah A. Phillips, and Elizabeth Farquhar. *A Profile of Child Care Settings: Early Education and Care in 1990* (Washington, D.C.: 1991); Barbara Willer, Sandra L. Hofferth, Ellen E. Kisker, Patrice Divine-Hawkins, Elizabeth Farquhar, and Frederic B. Glantz. *The Demand and Supply of Child Care in 1990: Findings from the National Child Care Survey 1990 and a Profile of Child Care Settings* (Washington, D.C.: National Association for the Education of Young Children, 1991).

5. Willer, et al. *The Demand and Supply of Child Care in 1990*

6. Assuming a 35-hour week and a 12-month year, this would mean an overall average of about $13,500, and less than $10,000 a year (average) for staff in for-profit centers.

7. National Commission on Children. *Beyond Rhetoric: A New American Agenda for Children and Families* (Washington, D.C.: U.S. Government Printing Office, 1991), chaps. 7, 9; Hayes, Palmer, and Zaslow, eds. *Who Cares for America's Children?*; M. Whitebook, C. Howes, and D. Phillips. *Who Cares? Child Care Teachers and the Quality of Care in America*, Report of the Child Care Staffing Study (Oakland. Calif.: Child Care Employee Project, 1989); Ellen Galinsky et al. *The Study of Children in Family Child Care and Relative Care: Highlights of Findings* (New York: Families and Work Institute, 1994); Carnegie Task Force on Meeting the Needs of Young Children, *Starting Points: Meeting the Needs of Our Youngest Children* (New York: Carnegie Corporation, 1994), pp. 14, 43–61, and related documentation.

8. For more detail and reports of field visits, see Sheila B. Kamerman and Alfred J. Kahn. *A Welcome for Every Child: Care, Education and Family Support for Infants and Toddlers in Europe*, (Arlington. Va.: Zero to Three, The National Center for Clinical Infant Programs, 1994).

9. Ibid.

10. Lynne M. Casper, Mary Hawkins, and Martin O'Connell. *Who's Minding the Kids? Child Care Arrangements: Fall 1991* (Data from the Survey of Income and Program Participation) U.S. Bureau of the Census, Current Population Reports, Series P-70, No. 36 (Washington, D.C.: U.S. Government Printing Office, 1992).

11. Willer et al. *The Demand and Supply of Child Care in 1990*.

12. Ibid.

13. Sheila B. Kamerman and Alfred J. Kahn, *Child Care, Family Benefits and Working Parents: A Study in Comparative Family Policy Analysis* (New York: Columbia University Press, 1981).

14. Kamerman and Kahn. *A Welcome for Every Child*.

15. See, for example, a working paper series from the project directed at Yale University by Sharon L. Kagan under the title "Quality 2000: Advancing Child Care and Education." There is a related pamphlet series by Sandra L. Hofferth and Duncan Chaplin, at the Urban Institute (Washington, D.C., 1994). The clinical

sophistication that exists is exemplified by several articles in the newsletter, *Zero to Three* (April/May 1994), from the National Center for Clinical Infant Programs, Washington, D.C. On European approaches to quality, see Jennifer Bush and Deborah Phillips. "Expanding the Lens on Child Care: International Approaches to Defining Quality" (1994, Part of the Yale "Working Paper" Series).

16. Alfred J. Kahn and Sheila B. Kamerman. *Child Care: Facing the Hard Choices* (Dover, Mass.: Auburn House, 1987), pp. 224–229.

17. Edward Zigler and Sally J. Styfco. "An Earlier Head Start: Planning an Intervention Program for Economically Disadvantaged Families and Children Ages Zero to Three," *Zero to Three* 14, no. 1 (October/November 1993).

## Chapter 7

1. National Commission on Children. *Beyond Rhetoric: A New American Agenda for Children and Families* (Washington, D.C.: U.S. Government Printing Office, 1991). See also Carnegie Task Force on Meeting the Needs of Young Children. *Starting Points: Meeting the Needs of Our Youngest Children* (New York: Carnegie Corporation, 1994).

2. Home visiting services, as one form of family support service, are delivered under an equally diverse range of auspices. Powell reports the results of a 1988 survey of four thousand home visiting programs carried out by Roberts and Wasik: 39 percent were under education auspices; 36 percent under health auspices; 23 percent under social services auspices; and 2 percent under Head Start. Douglas R. Powell. "Inside Home Visiting Programs," in "Home Visiting." Special Issue, *The Future of Children* 3, no. 3 (winter 1993): 25.

3. The first effort at national recognition of these developments occurred in 1983, with a conference held at Yale University under the auspices of the Bush Center. See E. Zigler, H. Weiss, and S.L. Kagan. *Programs to Strengthen Families* (New Haven, Conn.: Bush Center in Child Development and Social Policy, 1983). See also E. Zigler and H. Weiss. "Family Support Systems: An Ecological Approach to Child Development," in *Children, Youth, and Families: The Action-Research Relationship.* ed. R. Rapoport (Cambridge, Mass.: Cambridge University Press, 1985).

4. Sharon L. Kagan and Alexandra Shelley. "The Promise and Problems of Family Support Programs," in *America's Family Support Programs.* eds. Sharon L. Kagan et al. (New Haven, Conn.: Yale University Press, 1987). For Powell, see note 2.

5. Heather B. Weiss and Francine H. Jacobs, eds. *Evaluating Family Programs.* (New York: Aldine De Gruyter, 1988). See also David L. Olds and Harriet Kitzman, "Review of Research on Home Visiting for Pregnant Women and Parents of Young Children," in "Home Visiting." Special Issue, *The Future of Children* 3, no. 3 (winter 1993). Also, *Ibid.*: 6.

6. *Beyond Rhetoric*, p. 73; *Starting Points*, pp. 85–104.

7. Program detail from brochures of the Center for Mother-Child Home Program, State University of New York at Stony Brook. Research summary and

documentation in Phyllis Levenstein. "Mother-Child Home Program, Research Results," from the Center. Processed.

8. David L. Olds and Harriet Kitzman. "Review of Research on Home Visiting," pp. 53–92.

9. Full citations for the Elmira study in Ibid.

10. Note the Maison Verte movement in France, for example. Maison Verte. *Dix Ans Après, Quel Avenir?* (Paris: Fondation de France, 1991).

11. Tullia Musatti. *La Giornata del Mio Bambino* (Bologna, Italy: Il Mulino, 1992).

12. Luigi Anolli and Susanna Mantovani. *Tempo per la Famiglie*. Reports prepared for Bernard Van Leer Foundation (Milan: Tempo per la Famiglie). Processed, undated.

13. Alfred J. Kahn and Sheila B. Kamerman. *Child Care: Facing the Hard Choices* (Dover, Mass.: Auburn House, 1987), p. 54.

14. For program descriptions, see Sheila B. Kamerman and Alfred J. Kahn. *A Welcome for Every Child: Care, Education and Family Support for Infants and Toddlers in Europe* (Arlington, Va.: Zero to Three, The National Center for Clinical Infant Programs, 1994).

15. C. Warren. "Family Centre Survey." *Family Centre Network Newsletter*, no. 2 (1989), pp. 7–10. See also "Toward a Family Centre Movement: Reconciling Day Care, Child Protection, and Community Work." *Child Abuse Review* 1, no. 3 (1986).

16. Warren. "Family Centre Survey." p. 67.

17. Edward Zigler and Sally J. Styfco. "An Earlier Head Start: Planning an Intervention Program for Economically Disadvantaged Families and Children Ages Zero to Three," *Zero To Three*, 14, no. 1 (October/November 1993): 25.

## Chapter 8

1. National Commission on Children. *Beyond Rhetoric: A New American Agenda for Children and Families* (Washington, D.C.: U.S. Government Printing Office, 1991).

2. Carnegie Task Force on Meeting the Needs of Young Children. *Starting Points: Meeting the Needs of Our Youngest Children* (New York: Carnegie Corporation, 1994). See also David A. Hamburg, *Today's Children* (New York: Times Books, 1992).

3. *OECD in Figures*, 1991, 1992, 1993, 1994 editions, Expenditures and Taxation Tables (Paris: OECD); Jonathan Bradshaw, John Ditch, Hilary Holmes, and Peter Whiteford, *Support for Children: A Comparison of Arrangements in Fifteen Countries*, Department of Social Security, Research Report No. 21 (London: Her Majesty's Stationery Office, 1993); Sheila B. Kamerman and Alfred J. Kahn. "Government Expenditures for Children and Their Families in Advanced Industrialized Countries, 1960–1985," *Innocenti Occasional Papers*, Economic Policy Series Number 20 (Spedale Degli Innocenti, Florence, Italy, September 1991); Peter Saunders. "Recent Trends in the Size and Growth of Government in the OECD Coun-

tries," discussion paper, Social Policy Research Centre (Australia: University of New South Wales, 1992).

4. Dr. Marsden Wagner, Testimony Before the U.S. Commission to Prevent Infant Mortality, 1 February 1988. Processed.

5. Sheila B. Kamerman and Alfred J. Kahn. "Home Health Visiting in Europe," "Home Visiting." Special Issue, *The Future of Children*. 3, no. 3 (winter 1993).

6. This concept of health care as including all social policy, or at least a very wide range of social policies, is stressed repeatedly by most European experts; they reject the concept of a narrow medicalized definition of health care. For some illustrations of this position, see, for example, Michel Manciaux et al., "Child Health Care Policy and Delivery in France"; Shirley Goodwin, "Child Health Services in England and Wales: An Overview," in American Academy of Pediatrics, *Child Health in 1990: The United States Compared to Canada, England and Wales, France, the Netherlands, and Norway*. Supplement to *Pediatrics* 86, no. 6 (December 1990); Marsden Wagner, WHO. "Cross-National Comparisons of Child Health: The U.S. Dilemma"; and Hans Verbrugge, M.D., D.P.H, "Youth Health Care in the Netherlands," in U.S. House Of Representatives, Select Committee on Children, Youth, and Families, *Hearing on Child Health: Lessons from Developed Nations* (Washington, D.C.: U.S. Government Printing Office, 1990). Personal communications in Finland and Sweden. See also Bret C. Williams and Arden Miller, *Preventive Health Care for Young Children: Findings from a Ten-Country Study and Directions for U.S. Policy* (Arlington, Va.: National Center for Clinical Infant Programs, 1991).

7. Michel Manciaux et al. "Child Health Care Policy and Delivery in France," p. 1039.

8. Ibid., p. 1042.

9. Shirley Goodwin. "Child Health Services in England and Wales: An Overview."

10. Sheila A. Pires, ed. *International Social Welfare Systems: Report of a Workshop* (Washington, D.C.: National Academy Press, 1993).

11. *Beyond Rhetoric*.

12. C. Eugene Steuerle and Jason Juffras. "A $1,000 Tax Credit for Every Child: A Base of Reform for the Nation's Tax, Welfare, and Health Systems" (Washington, D.C.: The Urban Institute, April 1991).

13. Daniel R. Meyer et al. "The Effects of Replacing Income Tax Deductions for Children with Children's Allowances: A Microsimulation." *Journal of Family Issues* 12, no. 4 (December 1991), pp. 467–91.

14. Irwin Garfinkel. *Assuring Child Support* (New York: Russell Sage Foundation, 1992), p. 114, and forthcoming report of simulation. See also Elaine Sorensen, "What Would A Child Support Guarantee Cost?" *Policy and Research Report*, 24, no. 1 (winter/spring 1994): 19.

15. Child care expenditures data are not fully available except in Scandanavia and tax expenditures are unevenly reported, if at all. Social service costs are often not provided and countries are inconsistent with regard to child-conditioned social security payments (not here included). Nonetheless, we have managed a relatively

consistent standard and the range of possible error will not negate our main argument since we have compared European results with U.S. GDP totals with and without tax expenditures and Medicaid costs.

16. Irwin Garfinkel. "Economic Security for Children," in Jennifer Hochschild, Sara McLanahan, and Irwin Garfinkel, eds. *Social Policies for Children* (Washington, D.C.: The Brookings Institution, 1995); or, National Commission on Children, *Just the Facts* (Washington, D.C.: U.S. Government Printing Office, 1991): 167–170.

17. Alfred J. Kahn and Sheila B. Kamerman. *Child Care: Facing the Hard Choices* (Dover, Mass: Auburn House, 1987), chap. 7, p. 19.

# Appendixes

In discussing program costs, fees, and salaries throughout the text, we have applied OECD exchange rates for the applicable years. These direct currency exchanges do not, however, suggest a currency's true purchasing power in its own country. The purchasing power parity (PPP) rate, which we have *not* applied, comes closer to that. The reader will note the ratios between exchange and PPP rates.

**Appendix A.** Exchange Rates and Purchasing Power Parities (PPP) per U.S. Dollars ($1), as Reported by OECD, 1991–1992

| Country | 1991 | | 1992 | |
|---|---|---|---|---|
| | Exchange, per $1 | PPP per $1 | Exchange, per $1 | PPP per $1 |
| Denmark | 6.396 (= $ .156) | 9.17 (= $ .109) | 6.038 (= $ .166) | 9.94 (= $ .101) |
| France | 5.642 (= $ .177) | 6.52 (= $ .154) | 5.294 (= $ .189) | 6.55 (= $ .153) |
| Finland | 4.044 (= $ .247) | 6.30 (= $ .159) | 4.479 (= $ .223) | 6.40 (= $ .156) |
| Germany | 1.666 (= $ .600) | 2.09 (= $ .478) | 1.562 (= $ .640) | 2.11 (= $ .474) |
| Italy | 1240.610 (= $ .0008) | 1462.00 (= $ .0006) | 1232.41 (= $ .0008) | 1485.00 (= $ .0007) |
| United Kingdom | 0.557 (= $1.700) | 0.535 (= $1.58) | 0.570 (= $1.750) | 0.629 (= $1.59) |

*Source:* OECD.

**Appendix B.** European Currency Unit (ECU) Value in U.S. Dollars, 1991–1993

| | |
|------|---------|
| 1991 | 1.23916 |
| 1992 | 1.29810 |
| 1993 | 1.17100 |

*Source:* OECD.

# Index